3005

D1440920

IN PURSUIT
OF JUSTICE

IN PURSUIT
OF JUSTICE

REFLECTIONS OF A
STATE SUPREME COURT
JUSTICE

JOSEPH R. GRODIN

With a Foreword by
Justice William J. Brennan, Jr.

University of California Press
Berkeley · Los Angeles · London

University of California Press
Berkeley and Los Angeles, California

University of California Press, Ltd.
London, England

© 1989 by
The Regents of the University of California

Library of Congress Cataloging-in-Publication Data

Grodin, Joseph R.
   In pursuit of justice : reflections of a State Supreme
Court Justice / Joseph R. Grodin ; with a foreword by
Justice William J. Brennan, Jr.
      p.   cm.
   Bibliography: p.
   Includes index.
   ISBN 0-520-06654-5 (alk. paper)
   1. Grodin, Joseph R.   2. Judges—California—Biography.
3. Justice, Administration of—California—History.
I. Title.
RF373.G75A3   1989
347.73'2634—dc19   88-38926
[347.3073534]   CIP

Printed in the United States of America
1   2   3   4   5   6   7   8   9

To my wife, Janet

Justice, justice shalt thou pursue.

Deuteronomy 16:20

Contents

Foreword

Justice William J. Brennan, Jr.

Many Americans mistakenly believe that justice is dispensed primarily by the United States Supreme Court, or at least by the federal judiciary. This splendid book exposes the fallacy of that belief. The fact is that under our complex structure of federal and state governments, state courts have the duty of rendering the final decision in the overwhelming majority of the controversies in this country that end up as cases in court. A bare handful of millions of state court decisions are reviewed in the United States Supreme Court or indeed in any federal court. It is true, of course, that the Supreme Court of the United States has the final word in resolving whether state actions—be they executive, legislative, or judicial— violate the federal constitution; that is one of the essential tasks discharged by the Court. As Justice Holmes said, "I do not think the United States would come to an end if we lost our power to declare an Act of Congress void. I do think the Union would be imperiled if we could not make that declaration as to the laws of the several states."[1] And actually many federal constitutional decisions owe much to previous state court consideration of the questions decided. State courts have often been notably perceptive and forthright and have led the way for federal judges. From my own experience in writing opinions in such areas as reapportionment, obscenity, the First Amendment guarantees of freedom of religion, the rights of criminal suspects, and the application to the states of

1. Oliver Wendell Holmes, *Speeches* 102 (1934).

the other guarantees of the Bill of Rights, I know how much federal judges owe to trailblazing state court opinions in these areas.

It is the states, not the federal government, that create the vast majority of the laws and rules by which we live. State powers, James Madison said, "extend to all the objects which, in the ordinary course of affairs, concern the lives, liberties, and properties of the people, and the internal order, improvement, and prosperity of the State."[2] And it is the state courts, not the federal courts, that have the primary responsibility for the enforcement and application of those laws and rules. As John Marshall said, "The judicial department comes home in its effects to every man's fireside, it passes upon his property, his reputation, his life, his all."[3] Federal court responsibility, especially that of the United States Supreme Court, is limited to overseeing that enforcement to assure that the laws and rules, and their application, do not violate any restraining provisions of the federal constitution or laws applicable to such actions. Moreover, since the "obligation rests upon the state courts, equally with the courts of the Union . . . to *guard*, enforce and protect every right granted or secured by the Constitution of the United States,"[4] there may also be Supreme Court review of high state court decisions of federal law.

In this engaging book, Justice Grodin has given us a vivid account of his experience as a court of appeals judge, including his service as presiding judge, and as a justice of the California Supreme Court. One cannot read it without knowing how true it is that distributing judicial justice in this country is primarily the achievement of the courts of the states. Relatively few nonlawyers know how appellate courts work or what their crucial role is in the shaping of law. In these regards, Justice Grodin has crafted a badly needed educational tool, one that deserves the broadest possible audience. The publication of the book is particularly opportune because it comes at the time of a major development in constitutional jurisprudence: *state* constitutions may be becoming the primary defenders of liberty. A brief discussion of this phenomenon may be appropriate.

2. *The Federalist*, no. 45.
3. *Marbury v. Madison* 1 Cranch 137 (1803).
4. *Robb v. Connolly* 111 U.S. 624, 637.

The modern problems of the consistency of state action with the Constitution are of a different order from those the Supreme Court grappled with even thirty years ago. Now implicated more frequently are the various constitutional guarantees designed to protect individual freedom from repressive governmental action. I don't think there can be any challenge to the proposition that the ultimate protection of individual freedom is found in court enforcement of these constitutional guarantees. This principle is strikingly illustrated by the reapportionment cases. Freedom of the citizens of a state to experiment with their own economic and social programs is hardly meaningful if the political processes by which such programs must be achieved are controlled by only *some* of the people. The ideal is government of *all* the people, by *all* the people, and for *all* the people. Decisions in the reapportionment cases have enforced this ideal, and the result has been, not the return of discredited judicial intrusion into the field of political judgment, but a more effective operation of the processes by which political judgments are reached.

In the same area of responsibility falls the series of decisions extending guarantees of the first eight amendments to the states. The Bill of Rights is the primary source of expressed information as to what is meant by constitutional liberty. Its safeguards secure the climate the law of freedom needs in order to exist. It is true that those amendments were added to the Constitution to operate solely against federal power.[5] But the Fourteenth Amendment was added in 1868 in response to a demand for national protection against abuses of state power. A series of decisions over the last twenty-five years has held that many rights were applied to the states by that amendment. Indeed, it is fair to say that from 1962 to 1969 the very face of the law changed. Those years witnessed the extension to the states of nine of the specifics of the Bill of Rights, decisions that have had a profound impact on American life and have required the deep involvement of state courts in the application of federal law.[6]

A truly thrilling development has followed in the wake of these decisions. More and more state courts are construing state consti-

5. *Barrow v. Baltimore* 32 U.S. 243, 247 (1833).
6. *Hurtadov v. California* 110 U.S. 516, 535 (1884).

tutional counterparts of provisions of the Bill of Rights as guaranteeing citizens of their states greater protection than the federal provisions, even though the two may be identically phrased. The California Supreme Court has been a leader in this trend. Every believer in federalism must salute this development. Unfortunately, federalism has taken on a new meaning of late. In its name, many door-closing decisions have been rendered by the United States Supreme Court.[7] Under the banner of vague, undefined notions of equity, comity, and federalism, the Court has condoned both isolated[8] and systematic[9] violations of civil liberties. Such decisions hardly bespeak a true concern for equity; nor do they properly understand the nature of our federalism. Adopting the premise that state courts can be trusted to safeguard individual rights[10] and therefore that the task should be left to them, the Supreme Court has curtailed the protective role of the federal judiciary. But in so doing, it has forgotten that one of the strengths of our federal system is that it provides a double source of protection for the rights of citizens. Federalism is not served when the federal half of that protection is crippled.

The very premise of the cases that foreclose federal remedies constitutes a clear call to state courts to step into the breach. With the federal locus of our double protection weakened, our liberties may suffer irretrievably if the state courts are not quick to take on the challenge the United States Supreme Court has laid down. With federal scrutiny diminished, state courts must respond by increasing their own scrutiny under the state constitutions. Through the state courts, then, we can produce an even stronger system of American justice geared toward protecting individual rights. A recent study discovered more than 450 cases in which state supreme courts interpreted the guarantees of state constitutions as going beyond federal guarantees.

Thus, the significance of the role of state courts in dispensing

---

7. See *Stone v. Powell* 428, 465 (1976); *Francis v. Henderson* 425 U.S. 536 (1976); and *Hicks v. Miranda* 422 U.S. 332 (1975).

8. See *Paul v. Davis* 424 U.S. 693 (1976).

9. See *Rizzo v. Goode* 423 U.S. 362 (1976), and *O'Shea v. Littleton* 414 U.S. 488 (1974).

10. See *Stone v. Powell* 428 U.S. 465, 493–494 n.35; *Doran v. Salem Inn* 422 U.S. 922–930 (1975).

justice becomes greater each day. Without detracting in the slightest from the work of the federal courts, it is fair to say that the decisions that affect people's day-to-day lives most fundamentally are
increasingly made by state courts. One has only to read Justice
Grodin's book to learn how and why this is so. For he has penned a
work that may be enjoyed and understood by all. This is not to say
that it will not also be important to lawyers; quite the contrary. This
is a book of personal experience, providing a rare glimpse of the
inner workings of a first-rate judicial mind. In sum, this illuminat-
ing book will be useful to the bench, the bar, and the public. We
must be grateful to Justice Grodin for writing it. He shows us, indeed, that "the soul of a government of laws is the judicial function, and that function can only exist if adjudication is understood
by our people generally to be—as it is—the essentially disinterested, rational, and deliberate element in our democracy."[11]

11. Address by Arthur E. Sutherland, Saint Paul, Minnesota, June 17, 1964.

Preface

For seven years I had the privilege of serving as an appellate justice in what is generally regarded as one of the best state judicial systems in our land. My tenure on the California Supreme Court came to an end in January 1987 as a result of an election in which a majority of California voters decided that I, along with my colleagues Chief Justice Rose Bird and Associate Justice Cruz Reynoso, should do something else. I have since returned to what I was doing before I donned the robes—teaching, writing, lecturing, arbitrating, and a modicum of backpacking.

They were not easy years—the last four, on the Supreme Court, were especially stressful—but they were wonderful, stimulating, and rewarding years, and I would not trade them for any other experience I know. If in 1979 anyone had asked me to serve two years as an associate justice of the California Court of Appeal, then a year as presiding justice on that court, followed by four years as an associate justice of the California Supreme Court, on the condition that I would then return to my former activities, I would have jumped at the chance. I would do so again. I have no regrets.

I learned a great deal during that seven-year period about judges and judging, about courts and society, certainly more than my previous seventeen years of law practice and seven years of law teaching had taught me. In part that education was a matter of broader exposure to the process—I had been something of a specialist before I went on the bench—but in larger part it was a matter of perspective. One's view of the legal system, its operation, and its relationship to the larger society cannot help but change depending on where one stands—or sits.

Although the experience was not one I would like to repeat, being a candidate in a statewide judicial election had its pedagogical rewards as well. Traveling about the state, meeting individuals and talking with various community groups, I learned something of how ordinary citizens view courts and judges. Beyond that, the process of campaigning constantly brought me into situations in which I was forced to rethink and reevaluate my views regarding the relationship of the judicial process to the democratic process, of courts to the other branches of government, and of judges to the electorate.

This book is based on those experiences and my subsequent reflections on them. It is intended to fill what I perceive as a gap in our literature about the law. The bicentennial celebration and the Senate Judiciary Committee hearings on the nomination of Robert Bork to the United States Supreme Court have spawned much useful commentary on the federal judicial system and on the role of federal courts in reviewing claims asserted under the Constitution of the United States. These institutions and their functions are certainly of the greatest importance, but so are the judicial systems of the various states. Looking to state constitutions and state law, state courts routinely decide cases—marital property and custody cases, criminal cases, environmental cases, liability cases, consumer protection cases, cases of all dimensions and varieties—that have at least as great an impact, and often a greater one, on the life of the average citizen. Yet commentary on their roles—especially by judges and lawyers—is relatively scarce. State court judges have at times written about their work, but mainly in the legal journals and for a legal audience. And while most states depart radically from the federal model of lifetime judicial appointments by subjecting judges to popular elections, there has been little public dialogue in recent years as to the purposes judicial elections are supposed to serve, the criteria appropriate to such elections, or their impact on perception and performance of the judicial function.

This, then, is a book written from the viewpoint of a former judge about state courts, specifically about state appellate courts—what they do, how they do it, their relationship to the other institutions of government, and the implications of all that for the manner in which we select, and decide whether to retain, state appellate judges. Part One (chapters 1 through 4) describes how lawyers get to be appointed judges and explains the structure and mode of operation of the state appellate system—the relationship among the various levels, the functions of appellate review, the diversity of the caseload, how judges perceive the arguments of counsel, how they write opinions, how they relate to one another, how a court with selective jurisdiction chooses the cases it wants to hear, and so forth. These chapters are partly autobiographical. I describe my own appointment and elevation through the system—not because I consider my personal history on the bench to be particularly noteworthy but because it illustrates experiences I believe to be common to most judges.

In Part Two (chapters 5 through 8) I examine more closely certain responsibilities of state courts that are in some significant degree distinctive to the state system. I begin with a look at the common law, almost exclusively the province of state courts, and at the relationship between that ancient process of judicial lawmaking and the modern legislature. I consider the criminal law system, predominantly state-oriented, and the tension that often exists in that system between public expectations and what judges deem to be their legal obligations. I examine the special problems that courts face when constitutional or statutory changes are made through the process of direct democracy—the initiative and referendum. Finally, I focus on the role of state courts in relation to state constitutions, and the broader protection they sometimes provide for individual rights and liberties.

In Part Three (chapters 9 and 10) I take a broader and somewhat more theoretical look at the judicial process, with particular emphasis on the state level, and a closer look at how we select, and decide whether to retain, state court judges. In chapter 9 I address the question that has plagued legal philosophers for centuries— whether judges make law (as opposed to simply finding and applying it), and if so, in accordance with what procedures and criteria. On the premise that the answer will vary depending on the judicial task being performed, I view the question separately in the contexts of common law, statutory interpretation, and constitutional adjudication. Finally, in chapter 10 I examine the phenomenon that in a sense gave rise to this book—the judicial election. As a means of selecting appellate judges or of deciding whether they should be retained in office, the judicial election is peculiar to the American scene and to state courts. I express my doubts whether it is on balance a desirable method. But assuming we are to continue having judicial elections, one wonders on the basis of what criteria an intelligent voter is to decide how to cast his or her ballot; in chapter 10 I address that question as well.

Neither question can be answered without an understanding of what we expect state appellate judges to do, and to that end Part Three draws on the observations made, and conclusions reached, in previous parts. In addition, however, both questions call for an awareness of the realities of a modern judicial election campaign— the fund-raising, the television spots, the inevitable distortions and oversimplification of issues, and the very serious tensions that such an election generates between campaign efficacy and judicial propriety, between public relations and judicial integrity, between what is pleasing to the public and what is essential to the judicial function, between what we like to call "accountability" and the rule of law. For that sort of information in Part Three I rely heavily, and unashamedly, on my own experiences in the California state judicial election of 1986. Some aspects of that election may have been unique, but that it taught important lessons of general application I have not the slightest doubt.

I have attempted throughout to translate technical legal and theoretical terminology into words that the intelligent reader who is not a lawyer can understand. I have also attempted to be as objective as possible, though I realize that my dual status as participant and observer, particularly as regards the 1986 election, may well color my outlook. I leave the necessary discount for bias to the reader.

Acknowledgments

I am indebted to a good many people who, in one way or another, have helped make this book possible. They include my friends Phil Selznick, Jerome Skolnik, and Sheldon Messenger of the Center for the Study of Law and Society, the University of California, Berkeley, who provided a haven for me to think and work during my first few months off the court, and numerous friends and colleagues who were kind enough to read portions of the manuscript and provide both advice and encouragement. These include my colleague Calvin Massey at the University of California, Hastings College of Law; Sanford Kadish and Melvin Eisenberg at the University of California, Berkeley, School of Law; Victoria Gibson; and Hal Cohen, Jane Brady, Rick Seitz, Jake Dear, and Beth Jay, all staff attorneys at the California Supreme Court.

PART ONE

STRUCTURE

1

On Becoming a Judge

People, especially lawyers, frequently ask me how one gets to be a judge. That can be an easy or difficult question to answer, depending on what it is that the questioner wants to know.

The mechanics, for any one state, are easy enough to describe. There is, however, considerable variation among states, and even among different courts within the same state. Roughly, there are four models: popular election, selection by the legislature, selection by other judges, and selection by the governor.

On paper, popular election is the most common mode; the constitutions of forty-three states provide for election of at least some judges, forty of them for most or all judges. In the majority of these states, however, vacancies are filled initially by the governor, and though the appointee must appear on the ballot at election time, there will often be no opposition. Running against an incumbent is one way to become a judge, but relatively few judges acquire their robes in that manner.

Selection of judges by the legislature is rare, now confined to South Carolina, Virginia, and Rhode Island. Selection by other judges is even rarer; it is used to fill temporary judicial vacancies in Illinois and Louisiana, and in a few states to fill minor positions such as magistracies.

In most states, and for most judges, the path to judicial office is through the governor's door. More than half the states now have a system by which the governor's discretion is limited to candidates who are nominated by some form of commission; and in those states that do not have such a system the governor's appointment must be confirmed by some body—usually a commission or a branch of the state legislature—but it is still the governor who does the appointing.

The California system is mixed. A lawyer may become a trial court judge either by running for office in a popular election or by gubernatorial appointment, but to serve on the Court of Appeal or the Supreme Court appointment by the governor is the only way. The governor must submit the names of prospective appointees to the state bar for its evaluation, and the appointment must be confirmed by the Commission on Judicial Appointments, but otherwise (subject to eligibility requirements such as at least ten years in the state bar) there is no legal limitation on the governor's choice. Once appointed, a judge must stand for a "retention" vote at the next gubernatorial election, but that story I defer to a later chapter.

Those who ask me how one becomes a judge usually have something other than these legalities in mind. They know it is the governor who does the appointing in a state like California; they want to know how he or she does it, or, if they are lawyers hankering after the robes, how to get him or her to do it, and that is a much more difficult question.

Honesty compels me to say that appointment is not simply a matter of merit. I recognize there were many lawyers, including many fine trial court judges, whose academic and professional records were at least as good as mine, and I am sure they would have performed at least as well on the appellate court.

Nor, in my case, was it a matter of being particularly friendly with or supportive of the governor. My acquaintance with Governor Jerry Brown was in fact quite thin when he appointed me to the Court of Appeal. Our paths had crossed during Eugene McCarthy's campaign for the presidency in 1968, in which we were both active, but our contacts then were minimal. I had not been particularly active in mainstream Democratic politics. I supported his candidacy for the governorship in 1974, but not in any way that he or his advisers are likely to have noticed; I think I contributed a total of two hundred dollars to his campaign.

A year later, while I was teaching at Hastings Law School, the governor appointed me to a one-year term on the then newly cre-

ated Agricultural Labor Relations Board. I did not seek the appointment, and I did not know it was coming. Apparently, it resulted
from the urging of advisers who told the governor he needed
someone with a labor law background on the agency. Nor did I
meet with the governor prior to the appointment. He tracked me
down when I was backpacking with my wife Janet in British Columbia. I like to say that a Royal Canadian Mountie came riding up
to our campsite in full regalia to fetch me for a helicopter ride to
Sacramento, but it was not quite so: the offer and acceptance both
took place by telephone.

During my brief tenure on the board, from August 1975 to
March 1976 (it was actually cut short by a budget crisis) I can recall
only three meetings with the governor. The first occurred in his
office when I arrived in Sacramento to report for duty. As I entered,
he was seated at a low table with a coffee cup in front of him. He
asked me if I wanted coffee, and when I answered yes, he pushed
the cup toward me and said, "Here, take mine." The gesture was
typical of the informal and direct style that characterized him and
his administration. The other two meetings, held to discuss administrative matters, were affable, but as I recall, others did most of the
talking, and I cannot say that the governor and I became fast friends.
After I left Sacramento, the governor tried to get me to return as
general counsel to the agency; but I knew that position to be a political punching bag, and having had my fill of the capital city, I
declined.

What, then, accounted for the lightning that eventually struck?
My best guess—and I think it a good one—is that the governor and
I had a mutual friend.

I first met Mathew Tobriner in 1951 when I was a senior at the
University of California, Berkeley. I was trying to decide whether
to go to graduate school in political economy, as I had planned
(I had in fact already enrolled to do graduate work at Harvard), or
to go instead to law school, as some of my instructors at Berkeley
were advising. Like most idealistic young people of that period
I was intrigued with the labor movement, and a family friend
suggested that I speak with Tobriner, who was at that time a well-
known and highly respected labor lawyer. I did so; we took an instant liking to one another, and thereby began one of the most re-

warding relationships of my life. He was for me a friend, a mentor, and (my father having died when I was 14) a substitute father as well.

Mat (as I came gradually to call him) was instrumental in persuading me to study law and to enter the field of labor law. At his urging I switched my enrollment from Harvard Graduate School to Yale Law School (I had heard it was a lot like a graduate school in political science, anyway) and I never regretted that decision for a minute. I worked in his law firm—then known as Tobriner & Lazarus—during the summers after my first and second years of law school, and during my third year I received a Fulbright grant to study at the London School of Economics. There, under the supervision of a magnificent scholar by the name of Otto Kahn-Freund, I wrote a dissertation that compared the rapidly developing British and American law relating to the governance of labor unions, and ended up with a doctorate in labor law and labor relations.

Janet and I returned to California in the winter of 1955, and I went to see Mat in the expectation that he would offer me a job. I was intent on a career teaching law, but I wanted to practice labor law for a few years first, and Mat's firm was certainly the best place to do that. At the outset he told me that though he would really like to have me in the firm, they had just hired another lawyer, and it did not seem possible to take me on. So, I found a job with another labor law firm and called Mat to tell him the news, expecting him to be pleased. Instead, he seemed irritated; "You can't do that," he said, confiding that the other firm was his principal competitor. I said I knew that but that my wife was pregnant, and in all probability the baby would need to be fed and clothed. Mat said he would talk to his partners. He called me back that night and offered me a job at three hundred dollars a month. After the other firm graciously relieved me of my commitment, I accepted, and I embarked on a career as a lawyer, which lasted a good deal longer than I had planned.

I worked directly with Mat, doing research and writing memos for him, participating in meetings with clients, and helping to advise clients and plan litigation strategy. He was meticulous, always insisting that he read the cases himself, and creative, constantly in search of new ways to combine old principles. Above all, he was a lawyer whose judgment was sound, because it was based on the solid foundation of a mature, centered man. He was dedicated to his clients, and they to him. It was in some ways an odd alliance—this thoughtful, intellectual, gentle man and those Teamster business agents, rough and tough and worldly wise—but Mat believed fervently in their cause, and they knew it. He was not an ideologue—far from it. He knew the limitations of the labor movement, and though unions on the West Coast were for the most part free of the corruption that characterized unions elsewhere, he was keenly aware of the tendency toward bureaucracy and complacency that infects organizations when they emerge from antiestablishment status to become part of the establishment themselves. He felt strongly about the rights of workers to fair treatment within unions—it was he who suggested my dissertation topic when I went to England—and he was willing to stand up for those rights even when that offended union leadership. I remember one occasion when he tried to explain to David Dubinsky, then president of the International Ladies' Garment Workers Union, why under developing California law the union would have to give dissident members notice and a hearing before it could expel them. Dubinsky, who regarded his union as a sort of fiefdom over which he ruled—benevolently but absolutely—did not take kindly to the advice; but he did not leave the office either. Mat believed in unions as a force for the betterment of working conditions but also as a counterbalance to the power of industry and government.

In 1959, four years after I came to the firm, Mat was appointed by the newly elected governor, Edmund G. ("Pat") Brown—Jerry Brown's father—to the California Court of Appeal. That appointment came as no surprise. Mat and Pat Brown had been friends since boyhood, and they had worked together within the Democratic party in San Francisco ever since the early Franklin Roosevelt days when Mat convinced Pat—in the men's room of their office building, the story goes—to switch from the Republicans.

Shortly thereafter Pat Brown appointed the other half of Tobriner & Lazarus, Leland Lazarus, to the trial bench, leaving the firm without a name, and leaving me, at age twenty-nine, a de facto partner in a successful and highly regarded labor law firm, the largest west of the Mississippi. I enjoyed the practice; it provided interesting clients, constant intellectual stimulation, and an opportunity to make genuine contributions to the welfare of working people. I did not believe that the goddess of justice was always on my clients' side—there were occasions when I thought I saw her hovering over my opponents' shoulders—but she was there enough to keep my conscience clear. In addition, the practice and my understanding partners gave me enough space to do *pro bono* work in civil rights and civil liberties causes for organizations such as the American Civil Liberties Union and the National Association for the Advancement of Colored People—an activity I found richly rewarding. Assuaging my academic impulses with part-time teaching and some writing, I deferred my plans for a teaching career and wound up staying with the firm for seventeen years. In 1971, having reached in the practice what I considered to be a point of diminishing returns, I took a year's leave of absence to teach constitutional law, administrative law, and labor law at the University of Oregon Law School; I found that I liked it a great deal, and the next year I accepted a full-time teaching position at Hastings Law School in San Francisco. Except for a leave of absence to teach at Stanford Law School and to serve on the Agricultural Labor Relations Board, that is where I stayed until 1979, when I went onto the bench.

Meanwhile, Mat's judicial career had taken off. After two years on the Court of Appeal, Pat Brown had appointed Mat to the California Supreme Court, and there he quickly established a reputation as one of the outstanding state court judges in the country. To summarize his contributions briefly is difficult—in 1977 an entire issue of the *Hastings Law Journal* was devoted to his work—but there are a number of opinions for which he is particularly well known. These include cases holding that a mother who suffers emotional trauma from witnessing an accident involving her child may sue the person who negligently caused the accident for her emotional distress (*Dillon v. Legg*); that a psychotherapist who becomes aware that his or her patient poses a risk of physical harm to another person has a duty to warn that person or the police (*Tarasoff v. Board of Regents*); and that a tenant may withhold rent from a landlord who fails to maintain the premises in a habitable condition (*Green v. Superior Court*). He was also the author of opinions establishing or expanding constitutional rights for welfare recipients and for practitioners of unconventional life-styles, and he broke new ground in protecting consumers against boilerplate contracts that purported to limit or waive their reasonable expectations in the transaction or relationship. Many of Mat's opinions appeared in law school casebooks. During the first year our daughter Sharon was in law school, she wrote us that she was astonished that Mat, whom she knew as a family friend, was "such a famous judge."

From the time that he left the law firm in 1959 until about six months before his death in 1982, Mat and I had lunch together once a week, without fail, unless one of us was out of town. The ritual was important to both of us, and we took care to arrange our schedules so that they would not interfere. We would go to some place where Mat could order what was for him the staple of our weekly luncheon—an "all-around chocolate soda." And we would talk—about our personal lives, about books or movies, about vacation places, about the law. Usually Mat had a legal problem that was bothering him. There is a canon of judicial ethics that prohibits a judge from discussing a case with anyone outside the court, but it does not require a judge to become a hermit. At some level almost anything intelligent people would want to talk about could have a bearing on how a case should be decided. Most judges I know interpret the canon in a practical way that does not preclude general or philosophical dialogue simply because it may be relevant to a legal issue, and most of my dialogues with Mat were of that character.

Mat maintained he benefited from our weekly discussions. I hope that is so, because for me they were extraordinary, and in many ways. One product of our conversations was a law review article in which in broad terms we traced the development of legal principles that protect individuals against arbitrary action by private centers of power—an idea at the core of Mat's thinking about the law.

In his famous essay "The Hedgehog and the Fox" Isaiah Berlin distinguished thinkers according to two ways of looking at the world: those who know several truths (the foxes) and those who know one big truth (the hedgehogs). I said once, in a speech about Mat, that he was an aspiring hedgehog, forever seeking the one big truth but far too modest ever to assert, or even think, that he had found it. He did admit, however, to knowing several very important truths, and one of these was that the purpose of the law is to serve the interests and needs of individual human beings. How to protect the welfare, freedom, privacy, and integrity of the individual in a society without jeopardizing the institutions necessary for its collective existence was for him the central challenge both when he was a lawyer representing unions and when he became a judge. He was a legal scholar capable of seeing the patterns in the law and of depicting them in terms of legal theory, but he was also a wise man and an artist who never permitted the patterns and the theory to obscure his vision of what was essential.

Jerry Brown, as it happens, also had a close relationship with Mat Tobriner. They knew one another through Mat's friendship with Jerry's father Pat while Jerry was growing up. After Jerry graduated from Yale Law School, he went to work as one of Mat's law clerks at the California Supreme Court. It is said that Jerry tended to shy away from friends of his father; but his relationship to Mat was personal and direct, and so even after he left the court Jerry continued to seek Mat's advice on a variety of matters, including his own political future. After Jerry was elected secretary of state—largely because of name recognition—I know that Mat advised him to run for the governorship. It seemed a long shot—Jerry was young and had developed no political base—but Mat was convinced that he had the personality and creativity of thought suitable to the times. And Mat was right. Jerry became governor in January 1975.

When Governor Brown appointed me to the Agricultural Labor Relations Board later that year, I doubt that Mat had much to do with it. But when I left the board eight months later—the agency having temporarily ceased to operate for lack of funds—Tobriner began an indefatigable campaign to have the governor appoint me to the Court of Appeal. I had not seriously considered a judicial appointment before then, and I was not sure at first that I wanted one; but once I began talking about the idea, my enthusiasm grew. Mat, who always had a way of making people feel good about themselves, insisted that I had the perfect qualifications for the bench and that the state would be lucky to have me. I know that he carried that message to the governor more than once—I fear more often than the governor cared to hear it. Eventually, he succeeded.

Governor Brown submitted my name (along with others—there were several vacancies on the Court of Appeal) to the state bar. It conducted its usual survey, which consists of sending out hundreds of questionnaires to judges and lawyers asking for their confidential appraisal of the candidate under various headings—knowledge of the law, judicial temperament, and so forth. In addition, the bar interviews a number of people, including the candidate, and reports to the governor its findings—whether it considers the candidate "exceptionally well qualified," "well qualified," simply "qualified," or "unqualified." I learned later that I had received the highest rating.

Janet and I were on an eight-day raft trip down the Colorado River when the governor finally decided on my appointment. As we were checking into a motel at the Grand Canyon after our trip, the desk clerk said that I had a message from "a Jerry Brown" in Sacramento and that if I could not reach him, I was to call "a Tony Kline." Anthony Kline, now himself a justice on the Court of Appeal, was at that time legal affairs secretary to the governor. I placed a call to the governor and reached him in Los Angeles. Though I had heard rumors of my pending appointment, it was still a thrill when the governor made the offer. I thanked him and accepted with enthusiasm. Then I went downstairs and bought a small bottle of scotch, drank it with my wife in celebration, and went to bed.

There is a sequel to the story. The next morning Janet and I checked out and resumed our planned trip to the nearby Hopi reservation. Meanwhile, Tony Kline was not aware that I had spoken with the governor, and he was anxious to have my consent before he released the appointment that day to the press. So he called my home and explained to our younger daughter Lisa why he was calling. Lisa, who was seventeen at the time, replied that she did not know where I was but she was sure that I would accept, and Tony took her word for it. So in a way, my appointment was the product of Tobriner's nomination and my daughter's acceptance.

There was one more river to cross; my appointment had to be confirmed by the Commission on Judicial Appointments. In California, the commission consists of three persons: the chief justice of the Supreme Court, the senior justice of the Court of Appeal district to which the appointment is being made (or, in the case of a Supreme Court appointment, the senior justice of the Court of Appeal statewide), and the attorney general. This arrangement, which was part of a 1934 amendment to the state constitution, was an attempt to provide a reassuring review of the governor's choice by persons within the justice system presumably familiar with the requisite qualifications. The goal is admirable, but the system is strange. In Supreme Court appointments it is awkward for the chief justice to be passing on someone who may become a colleague, and in all appointments it is awkward for the attorney general to be passing on candidates who may decide cases in which he is an advocate. Many commentators have suggested that the commission would be more useful, and more credible, if its membership were altered and expanded, and I agree.

Since its inception in 1934, and up to the time it considered my appointment, the commission had formally rejected only one candidate. That was Max Radin, a professor at the University of California Law School whom Governor Culbert Olson sought to appoint to the Supreme Court in 1939. Radin had something of a left-wing reputation, but according to Bernie Witkin, who was a law clerk to Chief Justice Phil Gibson at the time, the principal impetus for rejecting him came from among employers who were fearful that he would cast a decisive vote the "wrong" way in important cases involving labor law then pending before the court. The commission that sat on his appointment consisted of Chief Justice Gibson, Justice John T. Nourse of the Court of Appeal, and the attorney general, whose name was Earl Warren and whose political career owed a great deal to the support of the conservative publisher of the *Oakland Tribune,* William Knowland. Gibson voted to confirm Radin, but he was outvoted by the other two. It was not Earl Warren's finest hour.

Whatever the motivation of Radin's opponents, subsequent events must have proved frustrating to them. The labor cases (in which Mat Tobriner was the principal attorney) were decided in favor of the union position by a four-to-three majority that included a justice appointed as a temporary replacement by Chief Justice Gibson. Meanwhile, Governor Olson appointed Roger Traynor, a law school colleague of Radin's, to the vacancy, and Traynor went on to achieve a reputation as one of the truly great state court judges in the land, partly through opinions that would not at all have pleased the conservative community whose opposition to Radin made Traynor's appointment possible. Perhaps Earl Warren knew what he was doing after all.

The commission that passed on my nomination to the Court of Appeal in 1979 consisted of Chief Justice Rose Bird, First District Presiding Justice Thomas Caldecott, and Attorney General (later Governor) George Deukmejian. Neither Bird nor Caldecott had ever voted to reject an appointment, and it did not seem likely that either would do so in my case; but the attorney general's vote was less predictable. He had voted not to confirm some of Jerry Brown's earlier appellate appointments, and a group that called itself the Committee on Law and Order was opposing my appointment on grounds that Deukmejian might have found attractive. That group had written a letter to the commission setting forth various events in my career: I had been lawyer in a suit against the sheriff of Alameda County (it was a class action on behalf of persons arrested in a mass demonstration whom we alleged, and the federal district court agreed, were being mistreated after their arrest); and I had traveled to Mississippi with some civil rights lawyers in 1965 to do legal work in connection with voting rights. Whereas I regarded these and other legal activities in which I had engaged as proud moments in my legal career, the Law and Order folk viewed them as evidence of left-leaning tendencies that should disqualify me as a person of judicial temperament.

At the time of Max Radin's appointment the commission met in private and simply announced its decision. In more recent years it had been meeting in public, with various "witnesses" speaking for and (occasionally) against confirmation and with the candidate present to make a statement and respond to questions. Mat Tobriner appeared on my behalf, along with a management attorney, Bill Diedrich, who knew me from labor and arbitration practice, and a representative of the state bar, who reported the results of their investigation. The only opposition was from a representative of the Committee on Law and Order, who read for the record the letter of grievances that the organization had previously submitted.

The attorney general focused on my qualifications and voted to confirm. We met afterward in the chief justice's chambers, and he congratulated me on my appointment. My mother, who was then in her late eighties, met him and told me she thought he was a fine man.

Justice Tobriner administered the oath of office to me on July 20 in the elegant San Francisco courtroom that serves both the Supreme Court and the Court of Appeal. The date was my wife's and my wedding anniversary, so the occasion had added meaning. Most of our friends and relatives were there, including our daughter Lisa who, being partly responsible for the event, helped me on with my robe. Tobriner spoke, as did my new colleagues, all of them so graciously and with such extravagant praise as to lead one to believe that nothing stood between me and instant acclaim as a first-rate jurist but the time it would take for me to write my first opinion. They exaggerated.

2

The Court of Appeal

California, like most populous states, has a three-tier judicial system. At the bottom are the trial courts; here juries are impaneled, witnesses testify, evidence is presented, and judgments are entered. Next is the intermediate appellate court (Court of Appeal) to which any litigant dissatisfied with the judgment in the trial court can take his or her case. At the top is the Supreme Court, which has the last word on matters of state law; it typically exercises selective jurisdiction, hearing only those cases it considers important enough to warrant its attention. Some states use different nomenclature—New York insists on calling its trial courts "supreme courts" and its highest court the "court of appeal"—but the structure is essentially the same.

There are variations on the three-tier theme. In California, for example, trial court jurisdiction is divided between the municipal court and the superior court, the municipal court being limited to civil cases involving smaller dollar amounts, misdemeanor criminal cases, and other "less significant" cases. Within the municipal court is a small-claims department—like Judge Wapner's court of television fame—which hears disputes involving very small amounts and without benefit (or detriment) of lawyers and juries. A defendant who is unhappy with the decision there may insist on a full trial in the municipal court. Moreover, someone who loses in the municipal court may appeal to an *appellate department* of the superior court, consisting of superior court judges who are assigned temporarily to that department. These procedures can be viewed as additional appellate layers. Some states with small populations, however, have only two tiers; all appeals go from the trial court to the Supreme Court. And to make matters more complicated, some states have separate appellate tribunals for criminal and civil cases. In this chapter I will ignore these variations and focus on the intermediate and final levels of the three-tier system, which is where my own judicial experience lies.

Because the intermediate appellate court, unlike the Supreme Court, does not get to select the cases it hears, its volume of cases is enormous. In California there are more than sixteen thousand contested matters in the Court of Appeal each year. Obviously that is far too many cases for a single panel of judges to hear and decide, so the work load is divided among several panels of justices throughout the state. (The word *justice*, by the way, is used in most states to refer to all judges who sit on an appellate tribunal, whether intermediate or final. In other states, as in the federal system, only judges of the highest court are justices. Don't ask me why.) The state is divided into six appellate districts, one for each of the major metropolitan areas: San Francisco, Sacramento, San Jose, Fresno, Los Angeles and San Bernardino-San Diego. Within each appellate district there are one or more *divisions*, each consisting of three or more justices. All cases are decided by panels by three justices. As appeals are filed in the clerk's office, they are assigned in rotation among divisions, and among judges within divisions.

My appointment was to Division One of District One in San Francisco. It is the oldest division of the California Court of Appeal, and it has a special history. Mat Tobriner served on that division, as did many other distinguished justices who were later appointed to the California Supreme Court, including Raymond Sullivan and Raymond Peters. When Justice Peters came to Division One in 1939 as presiding justice, there was apparently a tradition of consensus; when he was about to file his first dissenting opinion, he was told by his colleagues that instead he should simply allow the opinion to be filed in the names of the other two justices, without dissent. Peters thought that was a foolish tradition and refused to conform to it. His refusal created a certain amount of friction. Then one Friday Peters invited his colleagues out for lunch. They dissolved their differences in martinis, or so the story goes, and they were not seen until the following Monday. The episode started another tradition for Division One—a weekly

Friday lunch to which all present and former justices of the division are invited. The lunch is no longer as long, nor as alcoholic, but it is collegial nonetheless.

It was at a Friday lunch that I first got to know my new colleagues, though I had met them each before. There was the presiding justice, John Racanelli, a wise and marvelous human being; William Newsom, a witty and erudite man of many talents; and Norman Elkington, an experienced prosecutor and trial judge whose longevity on the court was matched only by his extraordinary energy. Elkington was the keeper of the division's oral tradition, the source of its history. Racanelli and Newsom were appointees of Jerry Brown, Elkington of Pat Brown. All three became my close friends.

Justice Racanelli assigned me my first cases—four of them, to be argued on the next court calendar. In each of the cases a law clerk had already written a memorandum setting forth the issues and the contentions of the parties. It was my job to read the lawyers' briefs, containing their arguments and citations of authority, and to be prepared to explain my views to a conference of the court scheduled to take place prior to oral argument. If my views won the approval of at least one of my colleagues, then the case would be "mine"—that is, I would get to write the opinion; otherwise, the case would be assigned to someone else.

I remember one of the four cases. A woman had died and left a will that contained a number of bequests. The will was in proper form, and there were three witnesses, but two of them—Ms. Nielsen and Ms. Gower—were also beneficiaries, and the Probate Code provided that a gift to a subscribing witness is void unless there are two other "disinterested" subscribing witnesses. Nielsen, who stood to inherit only one hundred dollars, tried to save the situation by "disclaiming" her interest, on the theory that she would thus become "disinterested" and then Gower, at least, could inherit.

The question before our court, then, was whether the term *disinterested* as used in the Probate Code refers to the time that the will was executed (in which case both gifts were invalid) or to the time that the will was probated (in which case the subsequent disclaimer would be valid). From an examination of the history of the law relating to wills and succession dating back to an act of Parliament in

1752, I became convinced that the statute should be interpreted to refer to the time that the will was executed. The purpose of the statute was to protect the testator from fraud or undue influence of an interested party at the time he or she executes a will, so a subsequent disclaimer of interest wouldn't do the trick. The tradition in California had been to hold testators strictly to the formal requirements for wills, and on that basis my colleagues agreed with me that the will was not valid.

Although I thought the decision was "correct" in terms of the original purposes of the statute, and although a law professor who specialized in the law of wills told me he thought it was a fine decision, I was troubled by it. In fact, my opinion acknowledged that our own policy preferences inclined us toward a different answer. There was no evidence that either of the beneficiaries had engaged in fraud or any other misconduct, and most academic commentators argued that there was no need for a prophylactic rule such as the California statute seemed to prescribe. Many states had adopted a model probate code that dispensed with the rule, and our opinion called on the California legislature to consider such a change. I was pleased when two years later the legislature amended the law.

In addition to the cases assigned to me, I was of course expected to prepare for conference and oral argument on the remainder of the cases on the docket. The court held oral argument once a month, and the practice at that time was to assign a minimum of four cases to each justice, for a total of twelve cases per panel. Since then, the number has increased considerably.

I would prepare by reading the memorandum that circulated with each case and then looking at the briefs. I can't say that I read every brief in every case, but I made it a practice to read at least the brief of the party who stood to lose by the recommendation of the justice assigned to the case so as to make sure that the memorandum and recommendation did not overlook or undervalue arguments I considered to have merit. In addition, if the memorandum or the briefs reflected disagreement about what the record showed, I would examine the relevant portions of the record as well.

I want to emphasize here a point concerning the nature of appellate review that readers who are not lawyers may not fully appreciate. Courtroom drama is always captivating on television, and from my personal observation there is not a single hour between six and ten P.M. on weekdays that does not contain at least one courtroom scene. But what we see on television is the trial court, with impassioned lawyers cross-examining the witness or addressing the jury. We never see appellate courts, and for very good reason. From the standpoint of drama (as distinguished from social significance or intellectual stimulation) what goes on in an appellate court is for the most part intensely boring. To be more precise, whatever drama an appellate argument may offer cannot be readily captured on a half-hour television show.

The same is true of television news coverage. There has been considerable controversy throughout the land concerning whether television cameras should be allowed in the courtroom. When I came to the Court of Appeal, it had been decided to admit cameras on special request. During the time I was there I can recall only two such requests, and though both were granted, what made it on the air was a total of thirty seconds of each case, showing the court parading in to the courtroom and a few seconds of a lawyer's argument.

The lack of media interest in the appellate courtroom follows from the nature of appellate review. An appellate court does not retry the case. It does not sit with a jury, it does not hear witnesses, and as a general rule it does not receive evidence. It reviews the case on the basis of the record that was made in the trial court and the evidence that was presented there. That record consists of three parts: the clerk's transcript (the various briefs, memoranda, and declarations that were filed in the trial court), the reporter's transcript (a transcription of what was said in the courtroom by witnesses and others), and whatever exhibits the trial court received.

When an appellate court "hears" a case, that means it hears from the lawyers. The parties in the case—the criminal defendant, or the civil litigants who stand to gain or lose from the outcome—are usually not even present, but if they are, they are not heard from. There is very little in that sterile atmosphere for a television camera to focus in on.

How, then, does an appellate court decide whether the trial court was right or wrong? The answer is that so far as the *facts* of the case are concerned—whether the defendant made a particular promise, or acted negligently, or stole money—it doesn't. Whatever facts the "trier of fact" (either the trial judge or, in a jury trial, the jury) found to be true the appellate court accepts as true so long as the finding is supported by *substantial evidence.* (In some states the test is phrased differently, but it amounts to pretty much the same thing.) This holds not only for *express* findings, such as a judge might be called on to make in a case tried without a jury; it holds also for *implied* findings, such as those implicit in a jury verdict of guilty. And substantial evidence does not mean the preponderance of the evidence, or evidence sufficient to persuade the appellate justices that the finding was correct. Different people will often reach different conclusions on the same evidence; besides, the appellate justices do not have the opportunity to observe the demeanor of the witnesses while they are testifying. Substantial evidence means such evidence as might lead a reasonable trier of fact to the finding that was reached, whether or not it would lead the appellate justices to that finding. I can recall many occasions when, reading through the record, I thought to myself that I would not have done what the jury did; but that is not the test. Lawyers on occasion will ignore these principles and argue to the appellate court as if they were arguing to a jury, but the fact is that for an appellate court to reverse the judgment of a trial court on factual grounds is extremely rare.

What is considered on appeal are *legal* issues—whether the trial court followed appropriate legal procedures in trying the case and whether it applied correct legal principles in deciding the case or instructing the jury. The probate case I mentioned earlier is an example. At the time it was decided it was a case of *first impression,* meaning that no appellate court in California had previously addressed the issue. The trial court had decided the case on the basis of what we considered to be an incorrect interpretation of the applicable statute, and so we reversed the decision.

Not all legal errors require reversal, however. If they did, there would be very few trial court judgments left standing since in the course of a long and complicated trial it is inevitable that some mistakes will be made along the way. An appellate court will affirm a judgment even when it finds error in some aspect of the trial court's procedure or opinion if it considers that the error was not of sufficient significance to have affected the outcome. This is the principle of *harmless error.* In California the test is whether it is "probable" that there would have been a different result if the error had not occurred. Assessing probability in that context is a very tricky business and does enmesh the appellate court unavoidably in the evidentiary portion of the record. I shall have more to say about that in the chapter on criminal cases.

Apart from the sheer volume of the work, what struck me most on becoming an appellate judge was the enormous diversity of cases I was expected to decide. There are some specialized courts in the federal system (bankruptcy and tax courts, for example) and in some state systems (probate courts, domestic courts); and of course we have specialized administrative agencies performing some judicial-like functions, but these are at the trial level. The general rule in our common-law tradition—one almost universally observed at the appellate level—is that each court, and consequently each judge regardless of his or her background, is expected to decide every kind of case that comes along. At the level of the intermediate appellate court that means deciding any case that a disgruntled litigant with enough money to pay the filing fee wants to appeal.

Throughout my professional career I had been pretty much a specialist, concentrating in labor law and related matters; but over a period of twenty years even a specialist is likely to be exposed to a fairly broad agenda. Representing labor unions and their members, as well as engaging in a variety of "extracurricular" legal activities such as civil rights and civil liberties litigation, gave me what I thought was a rather broad exposure to legal issues. But when I was brought face to face with the extraordinary variety of disputes people can and do bring into court in our legal system, I realized how limited my experience actually was.

I was aware, of course, that about half of the appellate court's workload would be in the area of criminal law and criminal procedure, where I had very little exposure. But there were many other cases—custody disputes, commercial disputes, and so forth—in which I was forced to learn the law starting from a condition of nearly blissful ignorance.

The tradition that judges are expected to be generalists has a corollary, which is that judges who have had specialized experience can't rely on their colleagues to defer to them in their area of expertise. I learned that lesson the hard way. One of the first cases that came to our court after my appointment was not simply a labor case but one arising out of the public sector, which had been my academic specialty for several years. Moreover, the issue, arbitrability, was one on which I regarded myself as an expert; as a law professor I had recently written and published a detailed work on the subject based on a study of all appellate decisions in the country. If there was anything I knew well, I thought, this was it.

It was the practice in our division for the presiding justice to assign cases randomly, and by the luck of the draw I was assigned that case. Although I had a law clerk, I felt this was a case in which I could and should do the memorandum myself—and I did, with what I thought to be suitably modest reference to my own work. After oral argument my two colleagues on the case—Justice Elkington and Justice Newsom—expressed some reservation about my conclusion but suggested I write a proposed opinion so they could have a chance to study it. I then gave the case all I had, producing an opinion that I knew to be unduly lengthy but I thought entirely persuasive.

As was the custom in Division One, the opinion circulated first to the senior judge, who was Justice Elkington. In what seemed to me an inordinately short time (Justice Elkington, though pushing eighty, worked harder and faster than any judge of my experience) there appeared on my desk a pithy dissent, adopting the position of a New York court in a case I felt bound to mention (the litigants had not done so) but the reasoning of which I had done my best to discredit. I modified my opinion to respond briefly to the dissent, Justice Elkington approved his dissenting opinion in the light of my modification, and the two opinions then went to Justice Newsom. I was counting on Newsom for my second vote, but he found himself persuaded by Elkington's views and signed the dissent instead. Justice Elkington, who was presiding justice in the case, reassigned the case to himself for a majority opinion, and my magnum opus, containing what I thought to be great wisdom born of specialized experience, found its way into the law books as an overlong dissent. It was for me a lesson in humility—particularly after the Supreme Court refused to hear the case.

Despite my frustration in that case—and in one or two others—I would not want to change the generalist tradition. Certainly there is value in specialization; a judge who has an intensive background in labor relations, medicine, or business can bring to bear not only a more focused knowledge of applicable law but also a certain expertise in the subject matter. He or she may, for example, have a more enlightened understanding of employer and worker perspectives on particular kinds of grievances, or may be better able to evaluate technical medical or economic data. But that value is in my judgment more than counterbalanced by the virtues of breadth and diversity.

Law professors like to talk about the seamless web of the law, and there is merit in the metaphor. In our system legal principles are interwoven from one context to another by a process of reasoning that is analogical. What constitutes due process of law, for example, or bad faith, or negligence, cannot be defined for one legal context without affecting others. In the same vein, growth in the law—the evolution of legal principles that characterizes the common-law process—depends to a considerable extent on applying analogies, and accompanying legal principles, from one area to another.

In a famous case, *James v. Marinship Corporation*, the California Supreme Court was confronted with the spectacle of a Boilermakers Union that practiced discrimination against black workers by relegating them to membership in a separate "auxiliary" union to which they were required to pay dues as a condition of their employment. This second-class membership satisfied the requirement imposed by the union's collective bargaining agreement that employees be union members, but it did not allow the black workers a voice or vote in the affairs of the all-white local that actually conducted the bargaining and handled grievances.

The year was 1944, long before the development of modern civil rights principles, and there did not appear to be any statute which made the union's conduct illegal. The California Supreme Court, in an opinion by Chief Justice Gibson, nevertheless held that the black workers were entitled to legal relief. In reaching that conclusion, the court looked to some very old principles that regulated public utilities prior to statutory regulation. According to these principles, a business that "held itself out" to the public as performing particular services, and particularly one that had a monopoly of those services, was obliged to serve all members of the public impartially and without discrimination. The court found that a union, particularly one that had a closed-shop agreement with an employer, was like a public utility in that traditional sense and should be subject to similar constraints. It could not hold itself out as bargaining representative, enter into a contract requiring membership as a condition of employment, and at the same time exclude workers from meaningful participation in union governance.

Chief Justice Gibson was not a labor specialist, and if he had been, the analogy might not have occurred to him. Arthur Koestler, in *The Act of Creation*, defined the essence of creativity as the ability to recognize relationships between contexts that at first glance appear disparate. Though he was not talking about the law, I think the definition applies.

There is a deeper, and in my opinion even more persuasive, argument against specialization in the courts. In our democratic society we expect judges to bring to bear, when deciding difficult cases, not simply a technical knowledge of the legal authorities applicable to a particular issue, or a knowledge of the subject matter, but also a broad awareness of our society, its history, its institutions, and its values. Knowledge of particular subject matter can be acquired, and experts can be called on to testify and evaluate, but no expertise can substitute for the broad vision that we expect judges to have. In some legal systems judges are regarded as bureaucrats—part of the administrative apparatus of the state—and in that model specialization fits. In our system we build expertise into some of our administrative agencies—specialized labor boards, medical boards, environmental commissions, and the like. But when it comes to reviewing the work of those agencies, I think we are wise in assigning that task to the generalists.

One by-product of the generalist principle—and a highly desirable one, in my view—is that it is likely to bring together on an appellate tribunal a diversity of backgrounds and outlooks. This diversity helps assure a breadth of vision; it avoids the risk of single-mindedness and provides a kind of ferment to the collegial process. Of my three colleagues in Division One, for example, two—Justices Racanelli and Newsom—came to the judiciary after a general legal practice whereas the third, Justice Elkington, had an extensive background in criminal law as an assistant district attorney and assistant attorney general. All three had served on the trial bench before appointment to the Court of Appeal, an experience that is an invaluable asset to an appellate court but, I like to think, not a necessity for each member of the court. Indeed, some of the most highly respected appellate judges in California (Gibson, Traynor, Tobriner, Peters) and in the federal system (Frankfurter,

Brandeis, Warren) never served as trial court judges, just as none of my colleagues in the First Division had the experience in academic and administrative agencies that was part of my background.

In the collegial process—in the course of deciding a case—experience is shared. In conference a judge will refer to cases he or she handled as a trial judge or a lawyer, or to knowledge of particular areas of law, or simply to perceptions of the world—political realities, human relationships, the legislative process, or any expertise that a person active in public affairs is bound to acquire. Over time one gets to know one's colleagues intimately and to have a feel for what they can contribute to one's own thinking.

Of course, diversity on a court is likely to produce strong differences of opinion, so that a person reading what appears to be an angry dissent may wonder whether the judge who wrote it will ever again speak to his colleagues. The truth is that while the feeling of anger that produces such a dissent is perfectly genuine, it does not persist as personal anger. I cannot recall a single instance in which these sorts of differences led to any animosity among us, and on occasion they would result in a judge being persuaded to modify his views. On the Division One court, and on other courts on which I have served, differences were mediated by a strong underlay of mutual respect.

Of the many cases I worked on in Division One there are a few I will remember not so much for the legal principles they involved as for the human problems they presented. The most heart-wrenching was the case of Brenda Payton. She was a thirty-five-year-old black woman who suffered from a permanent and irreversible loss of kidney function. To stay alive, she had to submit two or three times a week to kidney dialysis, a process in which the patient's circulatory system is connected to a machine through which the blood is passed. On top of that she had been addicted for over fifteen years to heroin and barbiturates, she was an alcoholic, she was overweight, and (not surprisingly) she suffered from emotional difficulties. Unable to care for her children, she lived alone in a low-income housing project in West Oakland, subsisting on $356 a month from Social Security. She had no family support; one brother was in prison, another a mental patient. She was at the bottom of the heap.

Despite these difficulties, Payton appeared from the record to be

a marvelously sympathetic and articulate individual who in her lu-
cid moments possessed a great sense of dignity and was intent on
preserving her independence and her integrity as a human being.
She resisted any attempt to impose a guardian for her, and Alameda County had apparently decided there were no legal grounds
for doing so. At times, however, her behavior made it extremely
difficult for anyone to care for her.

That is what Dr. John C. Weaver discovered. Dr. Weaver, who
operated an outpatient dialysis clinic at an Oakland hospital, began
treating Payton in 1975. A close bond developed between them,
but over a period of three years Payton became so uncooperative
that Dr. Weaver decided he could treat her no longer. She refused
to adhere to any diet, gaining as much as thirty-five pounds between dialysis treatments; she continued to buy barbiturates from
pushers at least twice a week; she quit a program of counseling that
Dr. Weaver had arranged. But worst of all for Dr. Weaver, and for
his other patients who underwent dialysis with her, she made the
dialysis sessions into a nightmare. She would frequently appear for
treatment late or at unscheduled times, drugged or drunk; she
would use profane and vulgar language; and she sometimes engaged in disruptive behavior such as bothering other patients, curs-
ing staff members, exposing her genitals, screaming and demand-
ing that the dialysis be turned off, and pulling the dialysis needle
from the connecting shunt in her leg, causing blood to spurt.

Dr. Weaver sent Payton a letter in late 1978 referring to these
matters and stating he would no longer treat her, but nevertheless
he did continue to treat her for another five months. In April 1979
he sent her a second letter dismissing her as a patient, and this led
to a lawsuit that was settled temporarily through an agreement by
Dr. Weaver to continue treatment if Payton complied with certain
conditions, including submission to counseling. But Payton kept
none of the conditions, and though Dr. Weaver continued to treat
her for nearly a year more, he finally gave up altogether.

Payton then went back to court, contending that Dr. Weaver
owed her an obligation of continued treatment, and contending
also that various hospitals in the area had violated their obligations
by refusing to admit her as a regular outpatient in their dialysis
units. The trial court, after a lengthy hearing, found that Payton
had displayed "gross noncooperation" with her treating physician

and hospital, that her behavior was "knowing and intentional," and that neither Dr. Weaver nor the hospitals had any further obligation to her other than to provide her with medical care on an emergency basis. Payton appealed, and the trial court ordered Dr. Weaver and the hospital to continue to provide her with regular dialysis while the appeal was pending.

I began the opinion for our court saying "Occasionally a case will challenge the ability of the law, and society, to cope effectively and sensitively with fundamental problems of human existence." And it remains true: there are limits to what courts can do. The trial court found that Dr. Weaver had "the patience of Job." Clearly he had behaved according to the highest standards of the medical profession. He had reasonable cause to discontinue treatment under the circumstances; he had given reasonable notice, and for a court to order him to treat Payton in perpetuity smacked of involuntary servitude. In any event, there was no legal basis for such an order. And though the hospitals had an obligation as recipients of federal funds to provide emergency service, there was no evidence that they had failed to do so. It is not usually the function of a court to give advice to lawyers, but we grappled in our opinion with various theories on which some relief might be sought, including the public-utility theory suggested by *James v. Marinship Corporation;* we also discussed various possibilities of guardianship or conservatorship that had not been advanced by the litigants but that might be considered in further proceedings. In the end, however, on the basis of the case as it was presented to us, we found nothing more we could do for Payton. I have no doubt that her attorney did everything that could possibly be done for her. But not long after our opinion, she died.

Not all my cases had tragic endings. Many left me with a feeling of accomplishment, and one of these was *Pugh v. See's Candies.* The case involved an employee, Wayne Pugh, who was fired by his employer, See's Candies, after thirty-two years of employment. According to Pugh, he had worked his way up the corporate ladder from dishwasher to vice president in charge of candy production and a member of the board of directors. He had received commendations for his work and loyalty to the firm: his work had never been criticized, and he was assured by the company president that if he was loyal to See's, his future would be "secure" (it was the company's practice not to terminate administrative personnel except for good cause). Pugh contended, he was fired abruptly and without cause; when he inquired as to the reason, he was told he should "look deep within [him]self" to find the answer. Pugh says he looked, found nothing of relevance, and filed a lawsuit.

These, at any rate, were Pugh's allegations, and at trial he presented evidence in support, but at the end of his presentation See's moved for what is called a *directed verdict,* and the motion was granted. This meant that in the trial judge's opinion, even if the jury believed everything that Pugh and his witnesses said, Pugh was not entitled to any relief under applicable legal principles. The case was over, without See's having to present any contrary evidence or explanation. Pugh appealed, and so the question before our court was whether the trial judge's ruling was correct.

That question was purely a matter of law. We were not concerned with whether Pugh had told the truth in his testimony; that would be a question for the jury if the case were to proceed. Nor were we concerned with whether Pugh's employer might have had a good explanation for firing Pugh; See's would have ample opportunity to present its case if we were to decide the appeal in Pugh's favor. The question was whether Pugh would be entitled to relief *if* the jury believed him and *if* his employer were unable to present an adequate defense.

At the time we decided the *Pugh* case, the law governing employment tenure was in a state of transition. In fact, it still is. In most Western democracies employees are guaranteed some job security through statutes that prohibit arbitrary dismissal. Indeed, there is a convention of the International Labor Organization (an agency of the United Nations) covering the subject. A convention is similar to a treaty, binding on the countries that ratify it. Convention 158, which has been ratified by nearly every industrialized country in the world, provides that workers are not to be terminated without a "valid reason" and that a worker who wishes to contest the reason for his or her termination should be permitted to do so before an impartial body such as a court, an administrative agency, or an arbitrator.

The United States, however, is not a party to that convention. In this country the general rule (outside of civil service) has been that the employment relationship is "at will," which is taken to mean that it can be terminated by either party at any time for any reason.

In recent decades, the at-will doctrine has been eroding on several fronts. The erosion began during World War II with the growth of arbitration provisions in collective bargaining agreements, and insistence through arbitration that workers be dismissed only for "good cause." Then came Title VII of the Civil Rights Act of 1964 prohibiting discrimination on the basis of race, sex, religion, or national origin. Litigation under Title VII required employers to come forward with explanations of their employment decisions, including dismissal, whenever the plaintiff made out a *prima facie* case of discrimination; that burden subjected previously "private" employment practices to considerable public scrutiny by administrative agencies and the courts. Moreover, doctrine developed under Title VII included the principle that if an employment practice (such as an examination or a requirement based on height or physical ability) operates as an obstacle to women or minority groups in hiring or promotion, then the employer has the burden of demonstrating that the practice is "job related," i.e., significantly related to job performance; this principle holds true even if the employment practice under challenge is neutral on its face and not discriminatorily motivated. The practical effect of this principle was to call into question the validity of a wide range of employment practices that had previously been taken for granted and to introduce even into the nonunion workplace some legally supported notion of fairness.

The impact of Title VII was amplified by a variety of other statutes, both federal and state, establishing further limitations on employer autonomy: statutes prohibiting discrimination against handicapped persons and requiring "reasonable accommodation" to their needs; statutes prohibiting discrimination on the basis of age or marital status; statutes regulating safety in the workplace; statutes regulating pension and medical-care plans. This range of regulation cut deeply into the notion that the nonunion employer was sole master of his own domain.

The at-will principle was not dead; except as limited by statute, it was still taken to be the general rule. But the atmosphere of social expectations had changed, and it was predictable that sooner or later courts would respond.

The first response came with decisions imposing limitations on dismissals made for reasons that offend public policy. Actually, the first public-policy limitation case came quite early; it was from California in 1959, and it involved a labor union as employer. A Teamsters union local in Santa Barbara fired its business agent, a man named Petermann, for refusing to testify untruthfully before a legislative committee in Sacramento. The court in that case held that the dismissal was unlawful because it was contrary to the public policy that encouraged citizens to participate in the affairs of government and give truthful testimony under legislative inquiry. A number of state courts have built on the *Petermann* principle, invalidating dismissals for such activity as reporting violations of law to government agencies, filing worker compensation claims, or attending to jury duty. In California the leading opinion is one by Justice Tobriner (*Tameny v. Atlantic Richfield*) holding that an employee may not be dismissed for refusing to participate in criminal conduct.

The *Pugh* case did not appear to fall within the public-policy exception to the at-will principle, but there was another category of exception that did at least potentially apply. As a matter of law it had always been clear that a worker could have a right to job tenure on the basis of a contract for a specified term, or for an indefinite term with the worker subject to dismissal only for specified reasons. Pugh did not have a *written contract* of any kind, nor did he claim an *express oral contract* of any such specificity; but he did contend that his history and the nature of his relationship with See's gave rise to an *implied contractual commitment* by See's not to fire him without cause.

That a contract, whether written or oral, may contain certain terms by *implication* is not a new concept in the law. Every first-year law student learns how a fellow named Wood, who undertook to be the exclusive distributor of perfume manufactured by Lady Duff-Gordon, was deemed by the court to have an implied obligation not to sit on his duff but to put forth his best effort to sell the lady's product. In modern times courts have found room for implied obligations in the relationship between landlords and tenants, between sellers and buyers, between unions and members, and between live-in lovers. In *Marvin v. Marvin* the California Supreme Court held that under certain circumstances the relationship of a couple living together could give rise to an implied promise of support. There are now statutes that require that union members be accorded a fair hearing before they are disciplined by a union tribunal, but even before those statutes courts were holding, as a matter of common law, that a right to a fair hearing was implicit in the nature of the relationship.

First-year law students also learn that when two people enter into a contract to be performed by one of them to the "satisfaction" of the other, that does not give the person who is supposed to be satisfied the right to be arbitrary. If that person refuses to pay for the performance of the contract, he or she must be able to show that his or her dissatisfaction is both genuine and reasonable. Pugh's argument rested on those generally applicable principles.

But in the employment arena there was a contrary line of authority, which suggested that an employee who claimed an implied or even express agreement for "permanent" employment could get nowhere in court on a suit for wrongful termination without proof that the employee had provided something to the employer by way of "consideration," such as materials or good will, over and above his "mere" labor. Fernando Ferreyra learned that legal "rule" the hard way. He sold his house in Argentina and moved with his family to California after Ernest Gallo told him he would have permanent employment as a foreman on the Gallo ranch, only to be fired after a few weeks. Relying on Gallo's promise and on the ranch manager's testimony that his performance had been satisfactory, Ferreyra sued on the basis of what he thought was his contract of employment, but the trial court would not permit him to present the issue to the jury, and the court of appeal affirmed. The basis for the court's holding was that as a matter of law a promise of permanent employment is not sufficient to limit an employer's absolute discretion to fire at will unless the employee has provided some "consideration" to the employer over and above his services, and that Ferreyra's costs and inconvenience in moving from Argentina to California was not the sort of consideration that would do the trick.

The *Gallo* line of authority seemed to me and my colleagues to be out of step with modern developments in the law, and in *Pugh v. See's Candies* I was assigned to write an opinion saying so. I did that, in an opinion holding that Pugh had made a sufficient showing (a *prima facie* case, we lawyers call it) to get to the jury on the question of whether there existed an implied promise by his employer not to fire him arbitrarily. Consequently, we sent the case back for a full trial.

As it happens, Pugh lost after trial. As far as I know, he deserved to lose. But he had a right to take his case to the jury, and the fact that our opinion said so created a precedent that has turned out to be of considerable significance in the arena of so-called wrongful-termination litigation.

One thing I remember with fondness about Division One was the sense of humor that everyone displayed from time to time, and that helped to lighten the burden of responsibility. None of us could compete, however, with Justice Newsom, whose quick wit and story-telling abilities were worthy of a professional humorist. He is, in addition, very bright. On one occasion a defense attorney was arguing to us that a seizure police had made of certain computer hardware the defendant allegedly had stolen was illegal because though the police had a search warrant, and the stolen hardware was identified in the warrant, the seized hardware had not been adequately identified as the hardware described in the warrant. It seems that the police, who themselves had scant knowledge of computer hardware, took with them a computer expert, who made the identification. Defense counsel argued that the police relied on the expert's identification without insisting that the expert explain how he recognized the hardware; thus they had improperly delegated their responsibility for seeing that the warrant was properly implemented.

In the middle of defense counsel's argument, which was not entirely without merit, Justice Newsom asked, "What about dogs?" Though counsel obviously was well prepared, this was a question he had not expected, and he indicated that he did not entirely understand it. "We allow dogs to sniff packages for marijuana," Justice Newsom explained with a straight face, "and we don't require them to give an explanation when they find it. Aren't computer experts as good as dogs?" The question added some zest to what was beginning to be a boring morning calendar.

3

Presiding Justice

In late 1981 Justice Wakefield Taylor, a highly respected jurist who had been presiding justice in Division Two of District One, announced his retirement, and Byron Georgiou, Governor Brown's new legal affairs secretary (Tony Kline having become a superior court judge), called to ask whether I would be interested in the appointment.

I was at first somewhat skeptical about the idea. I knew the judges in Division Two to be fine people who would make excellent colleagues. There was Allison Rouse, an appointee of Governor Ronald Reagan, who had served on the trial bench and had developed a reputation over the years for both competence and fairness; and John Miller and Jerry Smith, both of them worldly, wise former legislators appointed by Governor Jerry Brown directly from state legislature to the court. I knew all three and was confident that I could work well with them. But I was reluctant to give up the relationships that had developed within Division One during the two years I had served on that court.

Moreover, I knew that being a presiding justice was no great shakes. To the public it means presiding (in effect, chairing the court) at oral argument and signing orders on behalf of the court. Behind the scenes it means a good deal of administrative work to which neither additional compensation nor additional recognition attaches. And contrary to popular impression, the title does not bring with it any added authority in the decision of cases: a presiding justice, like his colleagues, has only one vote, and I have not observed any tendency on the part of associate justices to defer to the views of the presiding justice on how cases should be decided.

So why become a presiding justice in a division that would separate me from colleagues with whom I had an excellent personal and working relationship? That was the question I posed, as usual, to Mat Tobriner. Because, he replied, the governor clearly wanted me to, and if I had any thought of the governor appointing me eventually to the Supreme Court, that was sufficient reason. There would be no guarantee, of course, that such an appointment would be forthcoming, but quite possibly my confirmation and status as a presiding justice would make it easier for that to happen. Georgiou, in a subsequent conversation, implied that the governor had that possibility in mind.

I decided to say yes. Thus far in my life I had never regretted choices that led to new experiences and new options, and even if it turned out that I would remain indefinitely in Division Two as presiding justice, there were surely fates much worse.

Again I went through the process of confirmation by the Judicial Appointments Commission; again I received unanimous approval (including that of Attorney General Deukmejian), and I became "P.J." of Division Two.

One of the responsibilities of a P.J. is to worry about the burgeoning caseload. This is a function, primarily, of the number of trial court judgments per year, which in turn depends on the number of trial court judges. Of course, there are other variables—trial courts may be more or less efficient in trying cases, for example—but trial judges are the intake valves of the system, and mainly it seems that the flow of cases to the appellate courts will vary according to how many trial judges there are. It appears likely that their number will increase in response to increases in population.

There has been a good deal of talk about a "litigation explosion" in our society, and it is fashionable to bemoan a perceived tendency to take all problems to court. But Americans have always been a litigious folk, as Tocqueville observed two hundred years ago. Legal historians point to data that show that, in relation to earlier times, the volume of litigation adjusted by population has actually declined. One study suggests that the rate of filings in Accomack County, Virginia, in the 1860s was more than four times that of any jurisdiction for which we have current data, and another study indicates that in the Missouri Circuit Court in Saint Louis the rate has declined by 50 percent since 1820. A study of Alameda

County, California, by Lawrence M. Friedman and Robert M. Percival shows a fairly small fluctuation in the number of civil filings per thousand people over twenty-year intervals: in 1890 the number was 7.6; by 1910 it had jumped to 13.5; by 1930 it was down again to 10.8; by 1950 down still further to 9.5; and by 1970 up again to 11.0.

The data does reveal a marked increase in civil filings since World War II, but that is understandable. The postwar period has been marked by rapid social change and by the creation of many new legal rights—the right of minority groups not to be discriminated against, the right of consumers to a satisfactory and safe product, the right of workers to a degree of fairness in the work place, the right of the public to a clean environment, and the right of tenants to habitable premises, to name but a few. If people have legal rights, it is not only predictable but also desirable that they assert them—in court if necessary. Of course, there are litigants (and lawyers) who abuse the system by filing lawsuits without substantial merit in the hope of forcing a settlement, but they account for a tiny portion of the litigation, and there are remedies for such abuse, including court-imposed sanctions and countersuits for malicious prosecution.

Talk about a "litigation explosion" tends to detract attention from the main problem, which is how society can fulfill its obligation to provide expeditious, affordable, and just means to resolve disputes. There are many glitches in the present system. *Discovery*, which allows attorneys to ferret out evidence prior to trial, began as a legal reform and has developed into a nightmare of cost and delay. Rules designed to provide flexibility in pleading and procedure are abused by litigants for their self-interest or—even worse— by lawyers for their own self-interest. Procedures are often rigid and inflexible, treating different types of litigation as if they were the same. The expense of civil litigation has placed it beyond the reach of most citizens. The situation, in some areas, is desperate.

The answer is not to discourage access to the courts but to create procedures that provide greater access, with fewer delays and at less expense. Some court systems have moved in that direction, placing more careful controls on the discovery process, providing sanctions against attorneys who abuse the procedures, adjusting procedures to the nature of the litigation, and experimenting with alternative systems of resolving disputes, including mediation and arbitration.

By the time cases reach the appellate level the options are more limited. Apart from assuring the timely filing of briefs, there are only two things that an appellate court can do to expedite the resolution of pending cases: decide them more quickly or promote settlement. In District One we tried both remedies.

Attempting to decide cases more quickly entails the risk that they will be decided less well. There is a danger that the record or the arguments will receive too little attention or that the opinion will not be as carefully crafted. The court can ask the legislature for money to hire more law clerks, but there are limits. A judge can only delegate and supervise so much, and at some point he or she begins to lose effective control over the work product. I was blessed with excellent law clerks throughout my judicial career. Some of them were at least as good at the craft of opinion writing and analysis as I was; indeed, some of them had been at it a good deal longer. But it was I, not they, who had been appointed and confirmed to the job, and the decisions I made, as well as the language in which they were explained, were ultimately my responsibility. My colleagues felt the same way, and a few of them even declined to accept a second law clerk when one became available on the ground that they did not have the time to supervise more than one.

My colleagues and I found room for improvement through flexibility in approach. Instead of treating all cases alike and subjecting them to the same procedure, as was the practice in the past, we identified the cases that looked to be fairly simple and gave them expedited treatment, often dispensing with the usual preargument memorandum and moving directly to a proposed opinion on the basis of a preliminary conference. This procedure left us with more time to spend on the really difficult cases and improved our overall performance.

The court also instituted for all civil cases a mandatory settlement conference prior to the filing of briefs. We took turns acting as settlement judge, and I found I enjoyed that form of mediation. The degree of our success in relation to the allocation of resources to the project, however, was unclear. A number of cases did settle, but then a number of cases always settle before decision on appeal, and the study that was conducted to determine whether our procedures added to that number was simply not definitive.

Our appellate systems often provide a powerful incentive for a judgment debtor (the party who loses a money judgment in the trial court) to appeal even when the chances of winning on appeal are slight or non-existent. If the debtor needs the money less than the judgment creditor (the party who won in the trial court), the debtor can afford to delay and hope that the pressure of time will induce the creditor to settle for less than the full amount. This is particularly so when the amount of interest allowed the judgment creditor by law is less than the market rate of interest. During the 1970s, for example, there was a period when the legal rate of interest in California was 6 percent and the market rate was twice that. Under those circumstances a judgment debtor could actually earn a 6 percent profit (less legal fees and costs on appeal) by holding on to his money and investing it at the higher rate of return. I strongly suspect that some institutional defendants—some insurance companies, for example—make it a practice to do that. The saying is that justice delayed is justice denied, and that is certainly true for the creditor. For the debtor, as one appellate lawyer put it to me, justice delayed is justice. Such a party is not likely to be interested in settlement except on very favorable terms.

Sanctions can be applied for the filing of "frivolous" appeals, but it is not easy to decide that an appeal was filed with no belief in its merit or reasonable hope of success. The law is seldom so fixed and certain that a smart attorney cannot think of a plausible argument. If we are to address the problem of unfairness in appellate delay, apart from attempting to cut down on the delay itself, there are two things state legislatures should do by statute: they should adjust the judgment rate of interest to the market rate, and they should allow for the award of at least a portion of attorney's fees to the prevailing party on appeal in civil cases.

I enjoyed presiding over oral argument, but then I liked oral argument. Not all judges do. Some find it a waste of time. I had one colleague who developed a skillful dual ploy for discouraging what he considered to be excessive argumentation. If the attorney talked about matters contained in the written briefs, my colleague would admonish him, "That's already in your brief, counsel"; but if he raised new arguments outside the brief, my colleague would warn him that oral argument was not the time to raise new issues. If the poor lawyer was able to steer his way between the Scylla of repetition and the Charybdis of originality and thus succeed in continuing to bore my colleague, he would say, finally, "You've made your point very well, counsel," at which moment all but the dumbest of advocates would understand that so far as this judge was concerned, it would be a good time to sit down.

I suppose attitude toward oral argument is a function in part of the way a person thinks. I think best in dialogue with others. To me, reading a brief is boring unless it is written by one of that infinitesimally small number of first-rate brief writers who are capable of making their arguments in a lively way. Besides, briefs often paper over the really difficult issues in a case with obfuscating citations or rhetoric. I found it useful to focus on the critical issues of a case by asking questions of intelligent counsel.

My enthusiasm for oral argument got me into a bit of trouble with my new colleagues in Division Two. After the first round of oral argument over which I presided, I had a visit from Allison Rouse, who was the senior judge of the division. Justice Rouse is a gentle man as well as being a very able and distinguished judge, and he wished to make it clear, he said, that he was not coming to complain—that as presiding justice I could run the division any way I liked—but he thought I would want to know that it had been a tradition in Division Two that the judge to whom the case was assigned for the writing of an opinion would have first opportunity to ask questions of counsel. Apparently, I had violated that tradition in the recent argument session. I thanked him for enlightening me and said I would attempt to abide by the tradition in future sessions, though I must confess in retrospect that I may not have lived up to my promise. The temptation to question, I found, was just too great. Besides, the justice to whom the case was assigned might decide to ask no questions at all.

Sometimes, of course, a judge's mind is pretty well made up before oral argument. In that event the judge will be inclined either not to ask questions or to ask them in a way that is designed to assist the side he or she thinks deserves to win in the hope that a colleague who is on the fence might be persuaded. Sometimes, though, oral argument would persuade me that my tentative views of the case were wrong—on one occasion I told my colleagues I had had a religious experience—and almost always it would sharpen my perception of the issues.

Attorneys sometimes make the mistake of viewing oral argument as a time to make a prepared speech, and they are upset if a judge interrupts them with questions. Instead, they should view it as an opportunity to address each judge face to face, as a human being, and welcome questions as a clue to what is on the judge's mind. It is precisely oral argument that can inject humanity and sensitivity into a process that otherwise threatens to become cold and bureaucratic.

I remember that as a young lawyer I was in awe of judges. I believed that the judges must be so learned in the law that they somehow already knew everything there was to know, and it was my function simply to bring the relevant knowledge to their immediate consciousness, much as one calls up data on a computer. Over time I learned, first through my experience as a lawyer and later as a judge, that the wearing of robes does not impart knowledge and that a good advocate is likely to know quite a bit more than the judges before whom he argues. Certainly, if he has steeped himself in the record as he should, he will know more about the facts and background of the particular case he is arguing. But beyond that, if the lawyer specializes at all in the area of law involved, he is likely to have an edge on the judges, no matter how intelligent and diligent they be, whose time to study the issue is necessarily more limited.

The fact is that judges need help, and they look to the attorneys for guidance. They want to understand the legal principles, and they also want to know the practical implications of the alternatives for decision with which they are presented. They need to decide the particular case, but they need to do so on the basis of principles that will provide a useful and just precedent for the decision of future cases as well. A good advocate is one who understands the judge's perspective and attempts to provide a framework for analysis that will enable the judge to do his work well. I have seen lawyers simply throw arguments at the court, assuming no responsibility for their merit or their coherence. The implicit message is that if the court is stupid enough to accept a silly argument, that is its problem. Such lawyers do not serve their clients well.

My observations apply to briefs as well as oral arguments. I once asked Justice Elkington what I should tell a group of fledgling appellate lawyers about brief writing, and he said, "Tell them to be sure to put the staples in securely so we don't prick our fingers on the points." I think I have equally practical, and possibly more useful, advice. Were I to write a brief, I think what I would do is write an opinion first—the kind of opinion I would like to see the court come up with, taking into account my opponent's argument but ending up with a decision in my client's favor, of course—and then write a brief designed to produce that result. At any rate, that describes the empathy that effective appellate advocacy requires.

One of the things a presiding justice gets to do is supervise the court's consideration of petitions for what are called *writs*. Writs have their origin in very early English law, when persons seeking relief for some wrong would file a petition with the king's judges, who (if they found merit in the petition) would issue a writ in the king's name ordering that things be made right. There were many different kinds of writs, and the petitioner had to ascertain exactly what kind of writ he needed and exactly what he would have to say in his petition for it to be granted. It was good business for lawyers.

In modern times, in appellate courts, writs serve mainly as an alternative to the ordinary appellate process; they fill in gaps that the process does not cover and expedite relief in urgent circumstances. The most famous and most important of the writs is *habeas corpus*. Generally, a habeas corpus proceeding is used to mount an immediate judicial challenge to the detention of a person arrested and held without being charged with a crime or held in prison beyond the legal duration of his or her term. In the appellate system it is used also to bring to the attention of the appellate court in a criminal proceeding something that was not part of the record at trial—newly discovered evidence bearing on the verdict, for example, or evidence that the defendant's counsel was incompetent.

The most common function of appellate writs other than habeas corpus is to review some action by a trial court that occurs before trial or during trial. Appellate courts are reluctant to review trial court actions before judgment, on the theory that if something went wrong it can always be corrected on appeal after the judgment is entered, but sometimes it does not make sense to wait.

For example, it is important to both the prosecution and the defense in advance of a criminal trial to know what evidence is admissible and what evidence will be excluded. If the defendant contends that certain evidence was obtained in violation of his or her constitutional right to be free from unreasonable searches and seizures, he or she may file a motion prior to trial for an order excluding the evidence on that ground, and the trial court will decide the motion so that the parties know where they stand. If the defense or the prosecution is unhappy with that ruling, they may file a petition for a writ with the court of appeal. If that court thinks the trial court was wrong in its ruling, it may issue a writ ordering the trial court to reverse its position rather than allow the trial to proceed on the basis of an erroneous ruling as to the admissibility of what may be critical evidence. Appellate intervention of that type is prophylactic in nature, designed to avoid the time and cost of a trial that may result in a defective judgment. And for the prosecutor, who is not permitted to appeal an acquittal, it is the only avenue of appellate redress.

Sometimes a writ will be sought to prevent what is alleged to be immediate and irreparable harm resulting from a ruling of the trial court before final judgment. In *Simek v. Superior Court* a couple had divorced; custody of their minor children was awarded to the wife, and she was seeking to prevent her former husband from having visitation rights on the ground that he was mentally unstable. In support of that position her lawyers had issued a subpoena for all of the husband's medical records, including diagnoses, reports, test results, and histories prepared by psychologists and psychiatrists the husband had consulted. He resisted the subpoena on the ground that it improperly invaded his privileged communications with therapists, but the trial court ordered the information produced.

Clearly this was not an issue that could be left for appeal. If we denied relief, the husband would have to produce the information, and the purpose underlying the privilege of confidentiality (assuming it applied) would be lost. It was, therefore, an appropriate case for writ relief if we thought the husband was right—and we did. A person's communications with a therapist are ordinarily privileged; and though the California statute creates an exception to that privilege when the person places his own mental state in issue through litigation, it did not seem to us that merely claiming the right of visitation (which presumptively attaches to any parent) was what the legislature had in mind. The wife could seek to establish her husband's unfitness for visitation through other evidence (which in fact she had), and the court had authority to order a mental examination to protect the interests of the children. Accordingly, we issued a writ ordering the trial court to change its ruling.

A presiding justice, in addition to supervising the court, writes opinions as does any other justice. Probably the most significant opinion I wrote while in Division Two was a sequel to *Pugh v. See's Candies*. The case was *Hentzel v. Singer Company*. Mr. Hentzel, a former employee of Singer, alleged that he had been fired because he complained about cigarette smoking by other employees. He believed that cigarette smoke in the work environment was dangerous to his health and had asked that his employer do something about it. As in *Pugh*, the trial court never got to the point of considering the truth of Hentzel's allegation because it ruled that even if it were true, Hentzel had no legal claim; hence it dismissed the case.

Unlike Pugh, Hentzel did not allege facts to support an implied promise of continuing employment. Instead, he relied on the public-policy exception to the at-will principle. But his argument went a bit further than the precedent. Unlike in the *Tameny* case, no one was asking Hentzel to violate any law, nor was Singer violating any law (at the time) by subjecting Hentzel to the smoke of his fellow workers. But California had long maintained a policy protecting the right of employees to voice their dissatisfaction with working conditions. Nearly forty years earlier the California Supreme Court had declared: "The days when a servant was practically the slave of his master have long since passed. In order that the dignity of the employer-employee relation be maintained and that present-day fundamental social concepts be preserved, the employee has the right without breaching his implied obligations to his employer to protest regarding working conditions and rules of his employer and request that they be altered."

In addition, the safety of employees in the workplace had long been a matter of legislative concern in California. Even before passage of the state Occupational Safety and Health Act, the Labor Code required employers to do everything necessary to protect the lives, safety, and health of employees. It appeared to me and my colleagues that achievement of that objective "requires that em-

ployees be free to call their employer's attention to working conditions which they reasonably believe to be a hazard to their own
health or safety, or the health or safety of others . . . so that the
employer can be made aware of their existence, and given opportunity to correct them if correction is needed. The public policy
thus implicated extends beyond the question of fairness to the particular employee; it concerns protection of employees against re-
taliatory dismissal for conduct which, in light of the statutes, deserves to be encouraged, rather than inhibited."

The case was similar, we said, to *Petermann v. Teamsters*, in which
the business agent was fired because he gave testimony before a
state legislative committee that his union-employer did not like. In
that case the court held the termination wrongful because it con-
flicted with the state's policy of encouraging truthful testimony.
For Hentzel to be fired because he reasonably and in good faith
objected to conditions he believed to be dangerous to his health
seemed no less offensive to the policy of the state.

Probably the most controversial case I confronted in Division
Two involved the parole of Archie Fain. Fain was in San Quentin
prison, having served fifteen years of a life sentence for a brutal
murder, kidnapping, and rape, and a subsequent escape attempt.
Under present law Fain would have probably have been committed
to prison without possibility of parole, but under the law as it was
then Fain was entitled to consideration for parole, and the Adult
Authority (as the parole-granting body was then called) had initially granted him a release date of June 18, 1976. His impending
parole drew bitter and vocal opposition, however, from the citizens of Stanislaus County, to which presumably he would be released, and the Adult Authority scheduled a rescission hearing to
determine whether the scheduled parole date was appropriate "in
light of the gravity of the commitment offenses, the inmate's prior
criminal history, and his subsequent conduct while in the custody
of the Department of Corrections." Fain objected to that procedure, contending that he had a right to parole on the date originally fixed absent some intervening conduct by him that might
warrant rescission.

In 1976 Fain's objection to rescission of parole succeeded in
Marin County Superior Court, but the Court of Appeal disagreed,
holding that the Adult Authority had inherent power to reconsider

a grant of parole, and that public outrage, though it "did not in itself command rescission of his parole," nevertheless constituted "new information which indicates that parole should not occur, and which required the authority's consideration of that possibility in compliance with its rules."

Pursuant to the Court of Appeal's decision, in 1977 the Adult Authority rescinded Fain's original parole date and established a new parole date of January 19, 1982. In setting the 1982 date, the authority found that Fain "appears to be a suitable candidate for release on parole, and . . . does not appear to represent an unreasonable risk of danger to society." In so concluding, the panel noted "the consistent, exceptional, laudatory nature" of reports on Fain's prison progress and his "realistic parole release program," which his wife and a minister supported.

As Fain's 1982 release date neared, however, there was renewed public opposition. The Adult Authority received petitions containing 62,500 signatures, resolutions of four city councils and three boards of supervisors, a petition of the attorney general, and a concurrent resolution of the California Senate, all requesting rescission of parole.

This outcry resulted in a hearing by the Adult Authority to determine whether Fain's parole should be rescinded because of "extraordinary public outcry," or whether there existed other grounds for rescission. After a hearing, the authority found that there were no other grounds for rescission, but it nevertheless concluded that the public outcry in and of itself warranted rescission of Fain's parole.

Fain filed a petition for habeas corpus in Marin County Superior Court seeking immediate parole release on the ground that public outcry alone could not be cause for rescinding parole to which a prisoner was otherwise entitled as a matter of law. Judge Breiner of that court agreed. In a courageous and moving opinion, he said: "Unlike the Roman circus, where the roar of the crowd would determine the life or death of the gladiator, our community cannot survive without rules, and whether the object of the justice system is the best of us or the worst, those rules must apply fairly to all."

Judge Breiner's order of immediate release was stayed pending appeal to our court, which was heard by a panel consisting of Justices Rouse and Miller and myself. After oral argument and conference Justice Miller and I agreed (with Justice Rouse dissenting) that the Adult Authority had acted contrary to law in basing its decision to rescind parole on public outcry alone. Justice Miller was of the view that the matter should be returned to the Adult Authority for reconsideration. I believed that to be unnecessary since the authority had already made its position clear and thought we should simply affirm Judge Breiner's decision. To avoid a deadlock, however, I joined in Justice Miller's disposition of the case while expressing my own views in a concurring opinion. The matter went back to the Adult Authority (by then its name had been changed to the Board of Prison Terms), and it ordered Fain's release.

What made the case a difficult one in my eyes was not the legal issue involved. An analysis of the applicable statutes and rules—which focused on the character and conduct of the prisoner, not on the public reaction—persuaded me that the Adult Authority had in fact no authority to do what it had done. If members of the public had brought to the Adult Authority information about the prisoner from which it might be concluded that parole should be rescinded, the outcome could have been different. As Justice Miller wrote in his opinion, "We distinguish—and surely the Legislature meant to distinguish—between emotion and information, between a mere show of hands in opposition to a prisoner's release anywhere, any time, and specific information brought forward by the public relevant to that determination."

Rather, what made the case difficult was awareness of the adverse public reaction that was likely to follow in the wake of the opinion and Fain's release, particularly if Fain should commit further crimes in violation of the terms of his parole (as has since been alleged). Indeed, an adverse reaction was not only predictable but, in light of Fain's egregious criminal conduct, also understandable—perhaps even "correct" in the sense that people who commit the sort of crimes Fain committed perhaps should not be eligible for parole so soon, if at all. But those are decisions the legislature must make. If we are to have a government of laws, as Judge Breiner said, we cannot allow their implementation in a particular case to depend on nothing more than the roar of the crowd. I have no regrets about that judgment.

4

The Supreme Court

By pure coincidence the day in early November, 1982, that we heard oral argument in *People v. Fain* was also the day on which I was told by Governor Brown that he was appointing me to the California Supreme Court. I can't say the appointment was something I always wanted; as a practicing lawyer and a law professor I never even considered that as a goal. But it is certainly something I wanted once I was on the Court of Appeal and began to view it—through the good offices of Mat Tobriner—as a serious possibility.

Mat gave notice of retirement from the court in late 1981, and the governor submitted my name along with several others for consideration by the state bar. But it came as no surprise when in February 1982 he selected Cruz Reynoso to take Mat's seat. Cruz, the former head of California Rural Legal Assistance, a fine lawyer and law professor, would be the first Hispanic ever to serve on the highest court of a state that grew from Hispanic roots. He was a friend; he was well deserving of the appointment, and I felt no resentment. It seemed unlikely, however, that there would be another vacancy before the governor's term expired in January 1983.

Then something entirely unexpected occurred. Frank Newman, former dean of the University of California Law School (Boalt Hall), who had been appointed by Governor Brown to the court only three years earlier, announced his intention to resign and resume teaching. Apparently Newman, whose main interest had been in international human rights, found the work of the court too constraining. I remember discussing Newman's announcement with Mat. "Here we go again," Mat exclaimed.

I knew what Mat meant: he would embark once again on his persistent campaign with the governor to have me appointed. But Mat's health was failing, and he would not live to see Newman's vacancy filled. He died in April 1982. It was, for everyone who knew him and for the state, a terrible loss.

Newman did not actually resign until November, and by then the only prospective nominees to the Supreme Court that had been cleared by the state bar were San Francisco Superior Court judge Tony Kline, San Diego appellate justice Howard Weiner, and myself. It seemed likely that given the limited time remaining in his term, the governor would select from among the three of us, but which one? Janet and I considered going backpacking or on a river trip—to increase the odds—but there was no time.

Weiner, a good personal friend, was and is a superb appellate court justice and would have made a fine appointment. Tony Kline, however, in addition to being highly qualified, had been the governor's roommate at Yale Law School and his legal affairs secretary and closest confidant since the governor was first elected. The Brown administration in its early years had adopted a shake-'em-up attitude toward the legal profession and the judiciary, and Tony, as the point man for that policy, had engendered within the legal community a good deal of skepticism bordering on hostility. But for over a year he had been a superior court judge and had managed during that time to soften much of the negative feeling. He was, it seemed to me, the most likely candidate among the three of us.

To this day I do not know what it is that moved the governor in my direction. I am told that some of the governor's advisers were fearful of adverse political fallout from a Kline appointment, and that may be. Brown had decided not to seek another term as governor, but he was running for the United States Senate, and his advisers may have considered that I was the least controversial among the three candidates. I strongly suspect, however, that the memory of Mat Tobriner had a great deal to do with it. All I know for certain is that it came as a considerable surprise to me.

I was not without notice, of a sort. The Sunday before the appointment my wife and I dined in a local Chinese restaurant, and my fortune cookie turned out to be a doubleheader—two fortunes in one cookie, both of them supremely optimistic. One said that I was about to receive good news; the other, more focused, that I was about to receive a promotion. By Tuesday I had information of a more reliable sort: Connie Kang, a reporter for the *San Francisco Examiner*, called to ask me to confirm that I was about to "move down the hall," as she put it, and professed surprise when I said I had no such information. The truth was that at that point I had talked neither to the governor nor to any of his advisers, but Connie's information (or intuition) proved correct. Perhaps she had her own fortune cookies. That evening Janet and I ate dinner in San Francisco with Justice Racanelli and his wife and then returned home, expecting a call that never came. I learned later that the governor had tried to reach me that evening while I was out. The next morning, after a generally sleepless night, I got to the office early to prepare for the hearing in the *Fain* case, which was scheduled for the afternoon. Shortly after 9 A.M. the phone rang. It was Byron Georgiou; he wanted to know whether I could come to Sacramento right away to meet with the governor. I said that would be extremely difficult because of a hearing we had scheduled. Georgiou then revealed to me what was on the governor's mind—I didn't tell him I already knew on account of the fortune cookies and Connie Kang—and said that because they wanted to make an announcement immediately (the governor's office always seemed in a hurry to make announcements), the governor would call me directly.

More than a nervous hour later I was on the line with the governor. He said, "I guess you've been waiting for this call for quite a while." I didn't know whether he was referring to the last hour, the last few days, or the last year, but since the answer in any event was the same, I said yes. We chatted for a while; I told him how much I appreciated his confidence, and that was that.

My confirmation hearing before the Commission on Judicial Appointments—it would be my third—was scheduled for late December. Chief Justice Bird was still on the commission, of course, and I had little doubt that I would receive her vote. Instead of Justice Caldecott, senior justice of District One, there would be Justice Lester Roth, senior justice of the Court of Appeal statewide, but from everything I knew about him I expected no opposition. The question mark was George Deukmejian, still attorney general but, as a result of the November election, soon to be governor.

In the case of each of the prior three vacancies on the California Supreme Court—those that came to be filled by Justices Otto Kaus,

Allen Broussard, and Reynoso—Attorney General Deukmejian had sent letters to the candidates asking for their views about a variety of matters, including whether they agreed with the holding and rationale in a number of recent decisions of the court concerning criminal law and the death penalty. The candidates, correctly in my opinion, declined to respond to those inquiries on the ground that it would be improper for them to do so since the issues in those cases were likely to arise again for the court's consideration. Justice Kaus, in his response to the attorney general, cited similar positions that had been asserted by Justices Stevens and Frankfurter and Chief Justice Burger in their confirmation hearings to the United States Supreme Court. He offered three reasons in support of his refusal to respond to the attorney general's request: (1) if he were to comment on the issues in those cases, there was a real danger that he would have to recuse himself if those issues came later before the court; (2) by expressing one view or another, he might appear to be currying favor with the commission; and (3) his views, arrived at without the usual study of the record and conference with colleagues, would be misleading rather than helpful. Justices Broussard and Reynoso echoed these thoughts. The chief justice, in a letter to the attorney general, admonished him, in language drawn from a recent opinion by Justice Rehnquist, that for a nominee to the bench "to express any but the most general observation about the law would suggest that, in order to obtain favorable consideration of his nomination, he deliberately was announcing in advance, without benefit of judicial oath, briefs, or argument, how he would decide a particular question that might come before him as a judge."

By the time of my appointment Attorney General Deukmejian apparently had learned his lesson. He sent me a letter asking in general about my views regarding the judicial process, and I was able to oblige.

The commission hearing was in Los Angeles late in December. A number of highly regarded lawyers spoke on my behalf: Jesse Choper, dean of the University of California Law School; Hart Spiegel, who had been general counsel for the Internal Revenue Service during the Nixon administration and was currently president of the San Francisco Bar Association; and Sharp Whitmore, a former president of the state bar of California and a management labor lawyer who had been my adversary in one or two cases when

I was in labor practice. They all spoke glowingly, if a bit embarrassingly, of my qualifications, and things seemed to be going well. Spiegel made reference to the fact that I had been characterized variously as a "liberal," a "moderate liberal," and a "moderate," and the attorney general interrupted to ask whether anyone had called me a "moderate conservative," a question that seemed to break the ice. A state bar representative reported that I had been found to be "exceptionally well qualified" for the job.

The only opposition was from my old friends on the Committee on Law and Order, who trotted out the same material they had presented at the time of my appointment to the Court of Appeal. The attorney general asked me whether the information they had was correct, and the fact of the matter (leaving aside their characterizations and inferences) is that it was, with one exception. They quoted from the Congressional Record some remarks by Senator Eastland of Mississippi on the occasion of the visit I made with other lawyers to his state on behalf of voting rights. He was not enthusiastic about our visit, and he said some things about me— that I had been to the London School of Economics, for example— that to him, apparently, were opprobrious.

One of the things he said, however, was that I was a member of the National Lawyers Guild, and that happened not to be true. But I did not want to be in the position of denying membership in the guild as if that were some terrible misdeed, so instead I made reference to the context in which the allegations appeared and said, "If we believed everything that appears in the Congressional Record, we'd all be in a heap of trouble."

That answer seemed to satisfy the attorney general, and the vote in support of my confirmation was unanimous. After the vote Deukmejian was interviewed by a reporter; he explained that he had studied my opinions on the Court of Appeal—no mean accomplishment for a busy attorney general, I thought—and though we disagreed politically, he considered my work to be both competent and objective. I was grateful for the compliment.

Immediately following my confirmation, Chief Justice Bird administered the oath of office, and I was on my way back to San Francisco to prepare for the January argument calendar in Los Angeles. (The court's headquarters are in San Francisco despite a statute that decrees that the justices "reside at and keep their offices in the City of Sacramento." In the case of *People v. Chessman* Caryl Chessman, sentenced to be executed, argued to the court that the justices were "jurisdictionally foreclosed" from deciding his appeal because of their failure to comply with the statute. The court responded that the statute was an unconstitutional attempt by the legislature to impose qualifications on justices in addition to those required by the state constitution. The legislature has since given up trying to tell the court where to reside, but the court does maintain offices in Sacramento and holds argument there twice a year for several days at a stretch. It also has offices in Los Angeles and travels there four times a year.)

I have tried to recall my feelings during the first few weeks following my appointment, but things happened so quickly that my impressions were a bit blurred, as is my memory of them. I can recall having a sense of awe. I was familiar with some of the court's history, I had studied the fading photographs of bewhiskered former jurists that line its hallways, I was acquainted with all of the current, and some of the earlier, justices, and I had actually served on the court in several cases by assignment of the chief justice to fill temporary absences. But actually becoming a part of this institution was a new impression, and a powerful one.

To say that the California Supreme Court has commanded the respect of the legal world throughout its history would be an exaggeration. Its early history, in fact, was marked more by colorful spectacle than by legal scholarship or creativity. In the 1850s the fourth chief justice, David Terry, made his mark initially by being the first sitting judge to be jailed (by San Francisco vigilantes for stabbing someone in the neck with a dagger) and went on to achieve lasting judicial fame by killing a United States senator in a duel. Senator David C. Broderick had at one time been heard to say that Terry was the only honest justice on the court; it was his retraction of that statement as applicable to Terry that prompted Terry's challenge. Broderick's gun misfired—there were some who said that Terry knew it would—and Terry's shot laid him low. Terry resigned from the court after criminal charges were filed against him, but he managed to obtain an acquittal from a jury when his motion for change of venue was granted to Marin County, across the Golden Gate from San Francisco, and the witnesses for the prosecution, delayed by stormy seas, failed to appear in time for the trial.

Terry's end came in 1889 aboard a train from Los Angeles to San Francisco. Stephen Field, who became chief justice after Terry's resignation, boarded the train at Fresno. Terry, who bore Field a strong grudge, approached Field and slapped him in the face several times. Field's bodyguard ordered Terry to stop, and when he refused, the bodyguard shot him through the heart. Disputes were resolved quickly in those days.

The fastest resolver of disputes by more traditional means in the history of the California Supreme Court, or perhaps any appellate court, was Justice E. B. Crocker. Appointed in 1863 to fill the vacancy created by the resignation of Chief Justice Field, Crocker served only seven months on the court; but he managed during that brief period to issue 237 opinions. Any judge before or since would be pleased to claim credit for a tenth of that number. When it came to quality, however, there was some question. A leading newspaper of the time, upon Crocker's retirement, was rather ungracious: "His name will continue to be uttered, if only in derision. When his opinions are cited, counsel will reply apologetically, 'That's not the Supreme Court, that's only Crocker.' . . . And posterity will point to this sad period in the judicial history of our State, as a convincing illustration of the propositions: that weakness is more pernicious than corruption; that blunders are often worse than crimes; and that speedy injustice is not better than slow justice."

Our chambers were located on the fourth floor of the old state building at the Civic Center in San Francisco, and on the door to my chambers was a metal plaque with the names of all justices who had occupied them since the building was constructed in 1918. One of the first things I did after moving in was to read biographical sketches of my predecessors, and one of them particularly intrigued me. His name was Frank Kerrigan, appointed to the court from District One, Division One of the Court of Appeal in 1921. He was perhaps not a great luminary—his biographer says of him that none of his opinions for the court were noteworthy—but while serving on the Court of Appeal he wrote an opinion that deserves to go down in legal history.

The case arose when a Pomeranian dog owned by the plaintiff died as a result of a fight with the defendant's Airedale. The owner of the Pomeranian sued the owner of the Airedale for negligence, contending that he should have been aware of his dog's aggressive tendencies and kept him under control. The jury agreed, awarding plaintiff five hundred dollars—a quite handsome sum in 1919. (The Pomeranian was a show dog with a remunerative record.) The owner of the Airedale appealed on various grounds, of which the most interesting was that the owner of the Pomeranian should be barred from recovery because his dog did not have a license. It is in response to this argument that Justice Kerrigan had his finest hour.

The lack-of-license argument, Kerrigan opined, "would be well grounded if the plaintiff's omission to comply with the ordinance requiring dogs to be licensed had contributed to the incident resulting in the Pomeranian's untimely end. But for aught that appears the absence of a tag from the collar of plaintiff's dog was unnoticed by the Airedale, and was not the matter that aroused his ire or induced him to make the attack. His was the canine point of view and not that of the license collector." No matter what Justice Kerrigan did after that, so far as I was concerned he had established his place in the annals of jurisprudence, and I was proud to share his chambers.

I think it is fair to say that the great age of the California Supreme Court did not begin until after 1934 when the constitution was amended to substitute retention elections (in which voters choose only to retain or recall a judge) for the previous system of personally contested elections and thus to insulate judges (for a while, at least) from the world of politics. Before that, tenure on the court was quite brief, averaging only a few years. In fact, the dates following one of the names on my doorplate—Justice Nathaniel Conrey—showed him as having served only a few months, from September to December 1927. I thought the poor man died in office, but it turned out he was defeated in the November election.

After 1934 Justice Douglas M. Edmonds occupied my chambers and served a total of twenty years. From a relatively conservative background, Edmonds established a reputation as an independent and courageous judge. He was the lone dissenter in a decision—ultimately reversed by the United States Supreme Court—affirming the conviction of Harry Bridges, volatile leader of the International Longshoremen's and Warehousemen's Union during the 1930s. It was Edmonds who authored the 4–3 opinions supporting the legitimacy of labor activities after Roger Traynor came on the court. And it was Edmonds, as national president of a legal honor society, who interceded on behalf of Allen Broussard, a black, when the national society (which had a caucasians-only clause in its by-laws) threatened to expel the University of California chapter for having admitted Broussard to membership.

In the years that followed, the California Supreme Court began to acquire and retain for substantial periods of tenure judges like Phil Gibson, Roger Traynor, Raymond Peters, Mat Tobriner, and Stanley Mosk—and with them a growing national reputation for taking the lead in developing areas of the law ranging from product liability and consumer protection to the safeguarding of constitutional liberties. In later years, during the Warren era, the United States Supreme Court drew on the intellectual foundations that had been laid by the California court in such areas as due process and self-incrimination rights of criminal defendants.

In recent years the California Supreme Court had come on difficult times. Governor Brown's appointment of Rose Bird as chief justice had been highly controversial, for reasons I intend to explore later, and her confirmation election in 1978 was hotly contested. William Clark, the last appointment of Governor Ronald Reagan to the court, was openly critical of the chief justice, and I understood there were considerable sparks between them on the court as well. Stanley Mosk, who would like to have been chief justice himself, was anything but supportive. The day of the election the *Los Angeles Times* ran an article based on sources within the court suggesting that the decision in a highly controversial criminal case had been deliberately withheld until after the election. The chief justice was confirmed by the narrowest of margins, but afterward the Commission on Judicial Performance conducted a public inquiry into that charge, as well as into the charge that judges or court staff had violated the rules of confidence that surround the actions of the court. The commission found no misconduct, but without doubt the hearings did damage to the court's reputation.

When I came on board in December 1982, however, that episode seemed to be ancient history. William Clark had left to join the Reagan administration in Washington; Stanley Mosk and the chief justice appeared to have established a cordial, if not enthusiastic, relationship; Frank Richardson, an earlier Reagan appointee of generally conservative views, was in every respect a delightful colleague; and as a result of vacancies caused by death or retirement there were several new justices who, like me, had not been on the court during the turbulent hearings and who were in any event on good terms with the chief justice.

Governor Brown's first appointment to the court, along with Rose Bird, had been Wiley Manuel, a trial court judge who had served in the office of the attorney general and who was the first black ever to serve on the court. A beloved figure, Justice Manuel died of cancer after only a few years on the court, and to his seat the governor appointed Otto Kaus. Born in Vienna and educated in England, Kaus had been a practicing lawyer, law professor, trial judge, and Court of Appeal justice before his appointment. He had put in enough years for retirement, and his wife was eager for him to do just that, so Kaus promised her he would serve on the Supreme Court for only three years. Urbane, scholarly, and witty, he was a marvelous judge and a wonderful colleague. The two of us had a special relationship—he lived during the week near me in Berkeley, and the two of us would commute every day to the court in San Francisco along with one or two of the court staff, talking endlessly about pending court matters. He usually found any case before the court stimulating. But there was one exception: once, as I was driving us across the bridge and expostulating profoundly about a case that especially interested me, it occurred to me that Otto was unusually quiet. I turned around and found him sound asleep. I never let him forget it. He resigned from the court in 1986—one year late, according to the promise he had made Peggy, but at a great loss to the court.

To the vacancy created by the resignation of William Clark the governor appointed Allen Broussard, the court's second black justice. Allen and I had been on the debate team together at the University of California at Berkeley. He went on to law school at Boalt Hall, where he was an honor student and an editor of the law review. After several years practicing law he was appointed by Pat Brown to the trial court in Alameda County, where he served with distinction. He is very bright, with a marvelous sense of humor and an extraordinary ability to find his way quickly to the heart of any dispute. Occasionally in oral argument he would capture in a concise metaphor an issue or argument some lawyer was laboriously trying to sketch.

The last appointee prior to me was Cruz Reynoso. Of Mexican heritage and raised in the Imperial Valley in southern California, Reynoso decided after reading books, including a biography of Lincoln, that being a lawyer was the best way to make an impact on the world. After graduating from Boalt Hall with honors, Cruz engaged in a broad range of legal practice, ultimately becoming the head of the then newly established public-interest law firm California Rural Legal Assistance. During his tenure with CRLA the organization was the target of attacks by Governor Ronald Reagan and his point man, Ed Meese—a battle over funding that Cruz and CRLA won with flying colors. He went on to teach law at the University of New Mexico until he was appointed by Governor Brown to the Court of Appeal in Sacramento. An exceedingly able lawyer, Cruz is also one of the most gentle people I have known; with the exception of Ed Meese I never heard him speak ill of anyone—at least not before the election of 1986.

I had known Rose Bird in Sacramento when I went there with the Farm Labor Board in 1975. She was then the head of the Agricultural and Services Agency, the largest department of the state government with a number of agencies under its wing. She had played a key role in the drafting of the Agricultural Labor Relations Act—a formidable enterprise, involving negotiations among Cesar Chavez and his United Farm Workers, the Teamsters union, and various grower organizations. After the legislature adopted the statute, but prior to its effective date, Rose brought to Sacramento a number of consultants from the National Labor Relations Board to put together proposed rules and regulations for the new agency, and it was in that connection that I first met her. My fellow board members and I had a couple of conferences with her on budgetary and related matters, and she seemed to be an efficient and capable administrator. Later there were stories about her being unreasonably adamant in some of her positions, but I was not a party to any such incidents. As the year went by, I had two or three more meetings with her, and in one of these we disagreed over a policy she had instituted of bringing lawyers into the agency as "consultants" to "assist" the general counsel in his prosecution of charges of unfair labor practices. The UFW had been critical of the general counsel and was encouraging more rapid processing of charges, but I thought he was doing a good job and believed that the outside lawyers, who did not have prior experience in labor law, would create an atmosphere of vigilantism. Rose won that argument, but the disagreement was amicable. When she was appointed chief justice and came before the Commission on Judicial Appointments, I testified on her behalf.

Soon after she assumed office, Rose undertook to shake things up within the judicial system. She fired Ralph Kleps as head of the Administrative Office of the Courts, the agency that assists the chief justice in the administration of the entire state judicial system, and appointed a friend of hers, Ralph Gampel, in his place. At the same time she withdrew authority from the head of the AOC that had been in place under prior chief justices and assumed direct responsibility for making or approving decisions concerning judicial administration. In the process she made some useful innovations, such as appointing trial judges to sit temporarily in vacancies on the Court of Appeal and even the Supreme Court, but the judiciary, like any other bureaucracy, tends to be resistant to change. Moreover, the manner in which she brought about changes was not always diplomatic. Presiding judges of superior courts around the state were upset with her because contrary to custom she did not consult with them in the appointment of judges to the appellate division of the superior court. Some of my colleagues on the Court of Appeal were upset with her because she appeared to be unyielding in her opposition to the hiring of permanent law clerks, and some of the permanent law clerks on the Supreme Court staff were upset with her because she appeared to be undermining their status within the court. These were just a few of the burrs that got under people's saddles.

There is no question that Rose was capable of being quite stubborn and that her style of administration was at times hackle-raising. There is also no question that she was absolutely dedicated to the job and on the whole did it well. Mat Tobriner was loyal to her from the outset, and I think he helped her to understand the importance of bending a bit. She modified some of her positions over time, and as the bitterness of the 1978 campaign and the public hearings wore off, she appeared to be more relaxed.

A court like the Supreme Court of California is a unique sort of society. The chief justice has undisputed authority in the assignment of cases for opinions—more extensive than the chief justice of the United States, who has assignment authority only when he is in the majority. But apart from that she has little effective power within the court. Each justice is an autonomous entity, operating his or her own chambers like a separate law firm, hiring and supervising his or her own staff, and making up his or her own mind about what to do in each case and when to do it. The chief justice can urge, suggest, and cajole to develop a consensus, but ultimately has only one vote out of seven.

In that sort of society it would be easy for autonomy to develop into isolation and for disagreements to develop into lingering animosities. While I was on the court, at least, that did not occur. The chief, as she was called by everyone, was somewhat isolated, partly as a result of her administrative burdens, but the atmosphere overall was both congenial and collegial. Our Wednesday conferences took place over bran muffins and trail mix the chief would supply for her male colleagues, and after conference the rest of us would go out to lunch together at a local restaurant where our differences would disappear in talk about everything but cases. Anyone who observed us would not know that we had just been engaged in intense argument.

The diversity within our court gave collegiality a special dimension, and it made me realize that the significance of including women and minorities on a tribunal is much more than symbolic. Bird, Broussard, and Reynoso brought to our discussions perspectives that went beyond my own experience; but even apart from anything they said, their very presence tended to heighten my own sensitivity toward those perspectives, and I believe the same was true for other judges as well.

The Wednesday conference provides the focus for the most important function of the court apart from actually deciding cases, and that is deciding what cases to decide. Except for death penalty cases, in which appeal to the Supreme Court is automatic, the court chooses the cases to place on its calendar. In a sense, as Roger Traynor used to say, it has no one to blame for its problems but itself.

The Wednesday menu is composed mainly of petitions for review by the Supreme Court after decision by the Court of Appeal. Just as the Court of Appeal's caseload grows in proportion to the number of trial court judges, so the size of the Supreme Court's

Wednesday menu enlarges over time as the Court of Appeal is expanded. In 1961 there were 803 such petitions for review, about 66 per month; twenty-five years later the number had increased nearly fivefold to 3,728, or 310 per month. The Supreme Court has time to hear and decide only a small fraction of these cases—5 percent at most. As to the remainder, it has several options: it can simply deny review, letting stand the opinion of the Court of Appeal; it can transfer the case back to the Court of Appeal for reconsideration in light of some applicable authority that that court overlooked or that is more recent than that court's opinion; or if the opinion of the Court of Appeal has been published, it can order the opinion "depublished" so that it can no longer operate as a precedent for the future. Depublication exposes the Supreme Court to the risk of criticism that it is "burying" opinions that it does not like without explaining why, but since the early 1970s the California Supreme Court has found depublication, despite its faults, to be a useful alternative.

Newspaper headlines often suggest that when the court denies hearing in a case, it is approving the opinion of the Court of Appeal. Of course, the court's denial of a hearing carries no such implication; it more frequently means simply that the court does not consider the case one that it is necessary to review at that particular time. There may have been a time when the court could review all cases in which it disagreed with the result in the lower court, but that era has long passed.

How does the court go about deciding which cases to review? The process is easier to describe than the criteria. (Although since I left the court there may have been minor changes in the process of which I am not aware, the following description remains essentially accurate.) Each petition for review is assigned to a staff attorney, usually (but not always) under the supervision of a justice, for the preparation of a "conference memo." This memo describes the case and makes a recommendation as to its disposition. The memos are circulated among all the justices prior to the Wednesday conference, and each justice reviews them, has his staff review them, or both. (My practice was to read the memos myself, then meet with staff on memos that I wanted to discuss.)

To save time, those petitions that seem quite likely to be denied are placed on a "B-list" and are automatically denied unless some justice (it takes only one) indicates a desire to discuss the case in conference. That still leaves plenty of "A-list" cases—usually about fifty—to talk about. The chief justice calls each case at the Wednesday conference, and the discussion moves around the table, each justice stating his or her position. The statement may be simply a vote (to grant or deny review), or it may include an explanation of a vote designed to enlighten or persuade his colleagues. The procedure is similar to that in the United States Supreme Court, but with two differences. That court starts with the junior justice and moves upward in order of seniority—presumably so that the junior justices will not be intimidated by their seniors. In California the custom is the opposite; apparently there is less concern about intimidation. The other difference is more significant: in Washington it takes less than a majority of justices to grant review (four out of nine), whereas in California custom dictates a majority. Justice Mosk has argued for the federal approach, on the theory that if three out of seven justices think the case is important enough to hear, it ought to be heard. My view is that the court has enough cases to hear as it is.

Whether a case merits review by the California Supreme Court may depend on a variety of factors. For the most part the court's attention must be restricted to those cases that pose important issues of law—cases in which there is a conflict of view within the Court of Appeal or in which for other reasons guidance by the highest court of the state is called for. In such cases the court may grant review even though it agrees with the outcome in the Court of Appeal. Occasionally a justice, or even a majority of the justices, will vote to grant review in a case even though it does not pose an important legal issue, simply because he or she, or they, believes that the result is unjust; but the court cannot afford to take too many of those "do-good" cases without jeopardizing its basic function.

Deciding which cases the court should take is a matter of judgment and priorities. Even though a legal issue seems to be important, the justices may decide that it is premature for the Supreme Court to take action, that the opinion should be left standing so that other divisions of the Court of Appeal can have a crack at it first. There may be procedural problems in a case, or in some instances bad lawyering, that render it an inappropriate vehicle for resolution of the issue presented. When I was on the court, I used a

Yiddish phrase, *loch in kopf,* to summarize the reasons for not taking a case. *Loch in kopf* means "hole in the head," as in "we need this case like a *loch in kopf.*" Malcolm Lucas (now chief justice) was particularly fond of the *loch in kopf* principle and invoked it frequently, though with poor pronunciation.

The process of deciding petitions for review consumes a good deal of the court's resources. At first I was spending nearly half of my own time in that process—supervising memoranda by my staff and preparing for the Wednesday conference. The memos from other justices and their staffs would be delivered by Friday. I would read them over the weekend and then spend a good part of Monday and Tuesday reviewing them more intensively. As I gained more experience, I became more efficient and also more confident (some might say opinionated) with respect to my views in certain areas. By my last year on the court I was spending closer to a quarter of my time in the review process. The time spent by staff was considerably greater.

Suggestions are often made as to how the Supreme Court might cut down on the time it takes to determine which cases to hear. Usually, these suggestions take the form of proposals to delegate all or a portion of the discretionary review function to some other tribunal or to additional staff. It is important to consider such suggestions and perhaps to experiment with them, but one must bear in mind that there is a cost associated with any such diversion or delegation of authority. If the proposal actually would save time for the justices of the California Supreme Court, it has to be because someone else would be making the decisions the justices now make; hence it no longer would be their judgment but someone else's that would set the priorities of cases to be heard. That might not be the end of the world, but it would represent a substantial change in the character of the institution.

Once the court has determined to grant review in a case, it can then turn its attention to its principal reason for existence, which is to decide the case and issue an opinion explaining the decision. It is occasionally overlooked that these are two distinct functions. In theory a court can decide a case by issuing a judgment that merely addresses the outcome, such as "judgment affirmed" or "grant defendant a new trial," without giving reasons. In fact, the California Supreme Court used to do precisely that in many cases prior to

1879. Lawyers around the state became upset with that practice because it provided no explanation to them or their clients (much less the public) as to why they won or lost, and because it established no basis for using the case as a precedent. In 1879 the state constitution was amended to require the court to provide a "statement of reasons," now a standard part of appellate decision making in California and in other states.

The process can best be demonstrated by example. (Again, there have been some changes since I left the court, but the fundamentals remain intact.) In 1984 the Court of Appeal decided a case called *Conservatorship of Person of Valerie N.* It was a perplexing case involving a severely retarded twenty-nine-year-old woman with Downs Syndrome. Her parents, who were also her legally appointed conservators, were concerned that her friendly and outgoing disposition, combined with her very low IQ (30), posed a serious risk that she could become pregnant, a situation everyone agreed would be psychologically damaging to Valerie. But the parents believed there were no birth control methods available that would ensure her against pregnancy. Accordingly, as conservators they applied to the trial court for authorization to have Valerie sterilized by tubal ligation.

Application by conservators for authorization to have a medical operation performed on a person under their conservatorship is standard statutory procedure. But the statute that provides for that procedure expressly excludes sterilization as an operation that can be authorized. On that basis the trial court had denied the application, and the Court of Appeal had affirmed. There was, however, a very good dissent in the Court of Appeal by the late justice Richard Sims, an outstanding and highly regarded jurist. Justice Sims agreed that the legislature intended to foreclose authorization for sterilization, but he argued (relying on decisions by other state courts) that it was unconstitutional for the legislature to do so. The constitutional argument stemmed from the fact that sterilization is a procedure available to persons who are capable of consenting to such an operation. Given the relationship that had been held to exist between sterilization and the constitutionally protected right of privacy, to deny to incompetent persons the benefit of sterilization (when it can be said to be a benefit) was, in Justice Sims's view, to deny the equal protection of the laws.

The petition for review was assigned to me through the court clerk's office, and I thought Justice Sims's dissent had merit. I also thought that the issue was of sufficient significance to justify the attention of the court. I approved a staff memo recommending that we grant review, and the recommendation carried the requisite number of votes.

Following what had been the custom of assigning the case to the author of the conference memo responsible for the grant of review, the chief asked me to write the "calendar memo" for *Valerie N.* A calendar memo is designed to provide a basis on which all justices can prepare for oral argument and make up their minds about a case. More exhaustive than a conference memo, it explores the merits through the briefs filed with the court as well as through the independent research of the court's legal staff.

I assigned to one of my staff attorneys the job of preparing a draft of a calendar memo. She read the record and the briefs, as well as prior California decisions and decisions from other states that had bearing on the issues, and she did research on the history of the law relating to sterilization. In the course of that research she formed the opinion that there might be a statutory alternative that could provide a basis for authorizing the sterilization so that the constitutional issue might be avoided. The avoidance of constitutional issues through statutory interpretation is a traditional judicial technique designed to avoid unnecessary confrontation between the branches of government. I encouraged her to proceed in that direction, and we issued a calendar memo that explored both the statutory and constitutional alternatives. We also directed the court's clerk to send a letter to the attorneys asking them to address the statutory issue in their briefs.

At oral argument, however, the statutory alternative won little support from either the lawyers or my colleagues. It seemed to them a bit strained, and I myself was not persuaded. After all the cases for the day had been argued, we met, as was our practice, in the chief's chambers to determine where each justice stood on each case. It was understood that the expressions of opinion at that point might still be tentative, subject to further examination of the record or of arguments yet to be written; but it was important for the court to know in which direction a majority was inclined.

When the *Valerie N.* case came up for discussion, I was called on first to present my views. Since my calendar memo was balanced somewhat between the statutory and constitutional analyses, it was expected that I would state my intentions so that it could be determined whether my views would hold the majority. If not, the chief would assign someone else to write the opinion.

I stated that I did not consider the statutory alternative to be viable and that I would adhere to the constitutional analysis suggested by the dissenting opinion of Justice Sims. At least two of my colleagues expressed skepticism about both alternatives, but there seemed to be a majority for the conclusion and analysis I proposed—to allow sterilization on constitutional grounds—and so I was left to prepare an opinion along those lines.

I then advised the staff attorney of the conference results and asked her to prepare a draft of an opinion on the basis of our constitutional analysis. There were occasions on the Court of Appeal when I would write an opinion from scratch, but I found that on the Supreme Court I simply did not have time to do that. (When I was on the Court of Appeal, I attended an appellate courts conference at which Otto Kaus, then newly appointed to the Supreme Court, said the same thing. I thought he was exaggerating, but unfortunately he was not.) Often, after I received the draft, I would make extensive revisions, and I did so in the *Valerie N.* case even though the staff attorney had done, as usual, a fine job. The degree of my personal participation in the opinion-writing process varied from case to case, but my goal was to make sure that everything in the opinion ultimately reflected my own thoughts, and I believe the other justices tried to do the same.

My proposed opinion then circulated to all justices and their staffs, and this began a process of interaction that is characteristic of collegial opinion writing. Other justices or their staff attorneys would communicate their objections, reservations, or suggestions to the author or his or her staff attorneys through memoranda or conversation, or more formally through a dissenting or concurring opinion. My own practice upon receiving a proposed opinion from another justice was to assign it to one of my staff attorneys to read it and give me his or her thoughts. After my own reading and further discussion I might then instruct a staff attorney to talk with the author's staff attorney about some problem, or I might go talk with the author himself, depending on what I thought would be the most effective approach under the circumstances.

The purpose of this communication would range from pointing out some grammatical error to proposing a substantial modification in the reasoning or the result. Sometimes the latter would be in the form of negotiation: you take out this sentence, or put in this footnote, and I will sign. The author would then have to decide whether he would be willing to accept the modification and whether he would lose any other signatures by doing so. Contrary to what may be the popular impression, such negotiations never go beyond the case in question. I have never had another judge say to me, I will sign your opinion in this case if you sign my opinion in that one. Such an offer would be considered quite unethical.

In *Valerie N.* comments on my opinion focused on two related problems. The first problem was at the heart of the claim by Valerie's conservators that she had a constitutional right to sterilization. The prohibition against sterilization of persons under conservatorship was a legislative reaction to an earlier policy that fostered sterilization of developmentally disabled persons against their will (or without their understanding) as a form of eugenics. The assumption underlying the earlier policy was that mental "defects" were inheritable, and families and societies needed to be protected against their perpetuation. This was the basis for Justice Holmes's famous dictum in *Jacobson v. Massachusetts* (upholding that state's involuntary sterilization law) that "three generations of imbeciles are enough." Our knowledge and our views regarding developmental disability have changed over the years; we no longer regard inheritability as an important consideration, and we accept the fact that developmentally disabled persons can make good and loving parents. The California state legislature was reflecting those changes (and probably also the horrors of involuntary sterilization in Nazi Germany) when it decided to ban sterilization altogether in the absence of knowing consent. Some of my colleagues were reluctant to say that the legislature could not do that.

But the opposite side of that argument is that we have also come to recognize the rights of the developmentally disabled to personal growth and development, and in the case of a woman who is not competent to make choices for herself those rights can only be effectuated through her guardians or conservators. We say that a woman's right to procreative choice lies within the constitutionally protected rights of privacy and liberty; are we to say that a woman who is incapable of making any choice must accept whatever comes along? No one doubted that it would be psychologically damaging to Valerie to become pregnant and bear a child. To prevent that from happening, her parents, as conservators, could make a wide range of choices on her behalf. They could provide her with contraceptives; they could isolate her from members of the opposite sex; they could (with court approval) arrange for an abortion. The ban on sterilization, then, did not protect Valerie's "right" to be a parent; it prohibited her from obtaining the benefit of what might be, for her, the most appropriate means of protecting her right to personal growth and development. The legislature might be justified in viewing sterilization, because of its irreversibility, as calling for special safeguards; but since a fundamental right was involved, the legislature was obligated to use the least restrictive means of effectuating its concern, and a total ban on sterilization did not meet that requirement. Other state courts were supportive of this view. As the New Jersey Supreme Court had put the matter, "We do not pretend that the choice of the [incompetent's] parents, her guardian *ad litem* or a court is her own choice. But it is a genuine choice nevertheless—one designed to further the same interests which she might pursue had she the ability to decide herself. We believe that having the choice made in her behalf produces a more just and compassionate result than leaving [her] with no way of exercising a constitutional right."

Some of my colleagues expressed concern, however, as to the procedures and criteria to be used in deciding whether in a particular case a trial court should authorize sterilization. We all recognized that there could be risk of abuse unless careful restrictions were imposed. Indeed, in Valerie's case the trial court seemed all too willing to authorize sterilization on the basis of a rather flimsy showing. Ultimately, of course, the legislature should prescribe the safeguards, but if what a majority of us were prepared to recognize as a constitutional right was to be given any content pending the adoption of a statute, the court had to be quite clear on that subject.

After some discussion we were able to agree on criteria based on a decision by the Washington Supreme Court. Under that decision sterilization can be ordered only where there is clear and convincing evidence that the individual is and will be incapable of making her own decision; that there is a compelling need for contraception; and that there is no alternative to sterilization. In making that determination, the California court was to insist on independent advice based on a comprehensive medical, psychological, and social evaluation of the woman and, to the greatest extent possible, on her own views.

With these changes I obtained the signatures of four of my colleagues. I was unable to convince Chief Justice Bird and Justice Lucas, who wrote separate dissents.

Not all the issues before the Supreme Court are of such gravity; occasionally a case comes along that is really fun. One such case was called *Spiritual Psychic Science Church v. City of Azusa*. The Spiritual Psychic Science Church and its minister, Fatima Stevens, were wont to engage in the practice of fortune telling and to solicit "contributions" in consideration of that service. The city of Azusa (which is an acronym for "Everything from A to Z in the U.S.A.") regarded that activity as in violation of a city ordinance that prohibited people from engaging for money in a laundry list of activities including astrology, augury, card or tea reading, cartomancy, clairvoyance, crystal gazing, divination, hypnotism, magic, mediumship, necromancy, palmistry, phrenology, prophecy, spiritual reading—and fortune telling. The question was whether the ordinance was valid.

We heard oral argument in the case during a calendar full of depressing criminal cases, and I think we were all feeling a bit mischievous. It seemed quite clear (leaving the "church" issue aside) that principles of free speech were implicated and that the ordinance was overly broad, at best. I remember asking the city attorney, whose job it was to defend that questionable piece of legislation, whether it would prohibit magazines that purported to make stock market predictions. He responded that it would not, because making stock market prediction is a science, whereas fortune telling is a fraud. I asked him whether that was the sort of determination that, in the First Amendment arena, we wanted to leave to city councils. But the best question was the one put to Stevens's attorney by Malcolm Lucas. Surely, Malcolm suggested, his client must have told him how the case was going to come out: would he mind sharing that information with the court? The attorney assured us his client was confident of winning, and in the end her prophecy proved accurate; the court decided in her favor.

I wonder how one goes about giving a court a grade. The national reputation of courts, as of judges individually, is made largely on the cutting edge of the law. A court tends to be perceived as being great or not so great on the basis mainly of its contributions to new developments and new ideas—a standard that favors change. Though the spirit of adherence to precedent is widely lauded, one seldom hears about a court that sits placidly and holds the line.

The California Supreme Court, in years gone by, had a reputation for providing the lead in a number of areas. And, while I was on the court, it continued that tradition, providing new material for the law school casebooks. We decided, for example, that the old notion that strikes by public employees were unlawful under any circumstances, even when no legislature had said so, was no longer viable once the legislature decided that the terms and conditions of employment for public employees could be determined by collective bargaining rather than by the unilateral decision of a civil-service agency. We decided that a criminal defendant (as well as the state) should have the benefit of instructions that give the jury the option of deciding what crime he or she committed. We decided that members of the board of directors of a nonprofit corporation could be held liable for the result of negligence in which they personally and actively participated. We decided that a landlord could, under some circumstances, be strictly liable for damages caused by a defective product that was part of the premises.

But I suppose an overall evaluation would require also looking at what a court does not do—the cases it decides not to hear, the precedents it decides not to upset, the grand movements it decides to forbear in favor of smaller increments—for part of judicial wisdom lies in judging when and how far it is appropriate to push against the constraints of the past. Such an evaluation is not easy to make; it requires looking at the cases in which the court denies review and at the arguments the court decides to reject. My own view while I was on the court was that time was needed for the legal system to digest and consolidate the developments our predecessors were responsible for and that in considering further developments, prudence dictated that we proceed slowly and cautiously. I believe that a majority of my colleagues agreed and that the opinions of the court during the period I served for the most part reflect that consensus. How that ought to affect one's evaluation of the court I served on compared to prior courts I leave for others to decide.

In future years the great problem for the court will be management of its work load. The California Supreme Court is heavily burdened with death penalty cases, which at present come directly to the court after trial, with no intervening opinion by the Court of Appeal. Death penalty cases, because of their complexity and the irrevocable nature of the punishment, tax the court's resources in a manner unlike any other kind of case, and to such an extent that they threaten to absorb the majority of the court's time, making it increasingly difficult for the court to carry out its obligations in other areas. Meanwhile, the number of petitions for review continues to increase. Something will have to be done, or the institution will eventually drown in the flood of demands on its resources.

Adding justices to the court is certainly not the answer; getting even seven justices to agree on anything is difficult enough. And though adding staff can help, it can also hurt. I had marvelous staff attorneys—some of the best lawyers I have ever met—but there is a limit on the extent to which a judge can delegate work to someone else and still claim to be responsible for the analysis and the result. If the only response to the increased work load is additional staff, I am fearful that we will turn our appellate courts from institutions of justice into a bureaucracy of technicians, and the loss to the cause of justice will be great. Something else needs to be done.

There are a number of minor adjustments that can be (and have been) made to improve the efficiency of the court, but I believe that more substantial institutional change is required. Justice Mosk has suggested dividing the Supreme Court into two courts, one civil and one criminal, as is the system in Texas and Oklahoma, but his views have gained little support. I myself am skeptical. Legal issues such as due process of law do not come neatly packaged as criminal or civil; there is a substantial overlap, and some means would have to be provided for deciding those questions that fall on both sides of the fence. Beyond that, I do not like the idea of creating a specialized court, particularly one whose jurisdiction would be confined to that area of the law that is most controversial in the eyes of the public, namely, criminal law. Moreover, the people who would be attracted to serve for an extended period on a court that decided nothing but criminal cases—a substantial portion of them death penalty cases—are not necessarily those I would consider best qualified to decide them. Still, there may be variations on the Mosk proposal, such as creating separate criminal and civil panels within a single court and rotating judges between them, that would minimize these problems.

There are other possibilities. One, as I have mentioned, would be to delegate in some fashion the work of the court in developing its agenda. A second would be to create a mechanism for resolving conflicts of opinion within the intermediate appellate system without those conflicts reaching the level of the Supreme Court. A third would be to channel death penalty cases through the Court of Appeal. Even if the Supreme Court ended up with all such cases on its plate eventually, there would be substantial savings in such a procedure. All these plans have drawbacks, but I am aware of no plan that does not.

These problems are by no means peculiar to the California Supreme Court. The highest courts of nearly every state are suffering from increased demands on their services. If the quality of these institutions is to be preserved, some difficult choices will have to be made.

PART TWO

FUNCTION

5

Common Law

In chapter 2 I talked about a case I had a hand in deciding, *Pugh v. See's Candies*, in which we held that an employer's authority to dismiss an employee could be limited by an implied promise that he would not do so without cause. The basis for that decision did not lie directly in any statute but rather in the law of contracts, which, as any law student can tell you, is at its core a matter of common law.

The law student will also be able to tell you something of the common-law principles that apply to such a contract: there must be something done or given in exchange for a promise ("consideration") before it becomes legally enforceable; a promise need not be express but may be implied from the circumstances; it is not necessary for both parties to a contract to be legally obligated in order to make a promise enforceable; and so forth. Ask where these principles come from and the student may get a bit vague. From my professor, he might answer, or (less deviously), from previous decisions, or, From England. All these responses would be accurate but not very helpful if what you want is knowledge about ultimate origin or about authority.

The fact is that the origin of common-law principles is pretty vague, for the most part. Each of the principles applied in *Pugh*—for example, that a promise enforceable by law need not be express but can be implied from the surrounding circumstances—is traceable to earlier decisions, and those decisions are in turn traceable to still earlier decisions, ultimately by English courts; but at some point the traces become blurred and the genealogy dubious.

73

What we do know is that early common-law principles had their beginnings long before the supremacy of Parliament was established and thus were not dependent on statutory authority. Rather they were thought to represent, or reflect, the common practices of the realm—as seen by the judges, of course.

But the common-law judges did have the authority of the Crown. The Norman rulers who succeeded William the Conqueror found it convenient to establish King's Courts capable of applying uniform legal principles to the myriad of disputes, mainly over land, that beset their subjects. These courts developed a set of forms, or *writs* (the ancestors of today's *extraordinary writs*) through which persons could bring their disputes into the courts for resolution. As time passed, the courts developed new kinds of writs, such as the writs of *trespass*, and *trespass on the case*, which dealt with conflicts over injuries to person or property and eventually grew into the body of law we know as torts. Later still, the courts developed the writ of *assumpsit*, which dealt with obligations arising out of a person's "holding out" to sell certain goods or to perform services to the public, and from that writ evolved the modern law of contracts. Even the definition of crimes was, before the nineteenth century, mainly a matter for the courts. Every lawyer and law student will recognize these four subject areas—property, contract, tort, and crimes—as the mainstays of the contemporary first-year law school curriculum.

Not everyone in England was enamored of the common law. The system of special writs became exceedingly complex, comprehensible only to judges and a handful of elite lawyers. It became exceedingly rigid as well, so rigid that it provoked the development of a rival system, the chancery courts, which applied more flexible principles called *equity*. It was not until the nineteenth century that law and equity became more or less fused into an integrated system.

After the American Revolution there was a move to get rid of the common law, along with the king, and replace it with something like the civil-law system that prevailed in Europe. Under the civil-law system, all laws are (in theory) contained in statutes and thus (in theory) capable of being understood and applied by the common man. But in the end, partly through political choice and partly through inertia (colonial lawyers and judges were deeply entrenched in the existing system), the common law won out and came to be accepted by the states of the new union as the working premise for regulating legal relationships in the absence of statute.

Over time the domain of the common law has shrunk as a result of legislative enactments. The law of crimes was the first to go. Jeremy Bentham, the eighteenth-century English philosopher and reformer, who did not care much for the common law generally, especially denounced the idea that persons should be punished for such conduct as might be declared by a court to constitute a crime. He likened it to the kind of relationship one has with one's dog, in which one punishes the dog first, and then the dog knows what it is not supposed to do. That kind of "dog law" did survive for a period (as late as 1806 a jury in Philadelphia was instructed that it should find workmen who struck for higher wages to be guilty of the crime of "restraint of trade"), but soon was replaced with codes that contain an exclusive listing of the crimes for which a person can be convicted and punished.

Property law, too, came rather quickly under legislative oversight. Old common-law doctrines based on stable relationships between land and families were incapable of accommodating the volatile relationships of the frontier. Land documents needed to be simplified, means of assuring title needed to be devised, security transactions needed to be regularized, and the development of land ultimately had to be regulated by government. For the most part this was accomplished by statute. Some common-law principles of property law survive—in the landlord-tenant relationship, for example—but they are of relatively small scope.

It is in the areas of contracts and torts that the common law is most influential and most dynamic. Here for the most part are to be found the principles that apply to a case like *Pugh* and to some of the other cases discussed in earlier chapters—for example, Dillon's suit for the negligent infliction of emotional distress and Tarasoff's suit against the psychotherapist for failure to warn. Here, too, lies nearly the entire body of law imposing strict liability (that is, liability without regard to fault) on the manufacturers and distributors of defective products.

The modern development of strict product liability principles furnishes a marvelous picture of the common-law process at work. Prior to the industrial revolution of the nineteenth century, the common law did impose something like strict liability through the specialized writs that I have mentioned. Legal obligations were viewed primarily as stemming from the relationship people had to one another—innkeeper to customer, master to servant, and so on. For each relationship there was a set of concepts that governed the rights and duties of the parties—*status* concepts, they are sometimes called. Often these concepts resulted in obligations that were founded neither in consensual agreement nor in fault.

But legal principles based on status were not well suited to the freewheeling marketplace of the industrial revolution. If the market was to operate, then people had to be permitted to determine their relationships through agreement—hence the ascendance of contracts and the legal doctrine that supported them. And if entrepreneurs were to be encouraged to take risks, exposure to liability had to be limited—hence they should be liable only when they acted in a negligent manner. Moreover, even when negligent they were not to be liable for all injury that resulted from their negligence, but only for injury to persons toward whom the courts said they owed a "duty of care."

A well-known decision by an English court in 1842 exemplified these limitations on liability. The case was *Winterbottom v. Wright*. A driver of a mail coach was injured when a coach he was driving to deliver mail broke down. Claiming that the coach was defective, he sued the party who had undertaken, through contract with the postmaster general, to supply the coaches and keep them in good repair. But the court threw his suit out, observing that the *driver* had no contract with the coach supplier, and that to hold the supplier liable to anyone who might be injured as a result of a defect would be "absurd and outrageous."

And so it was that twentieth-century courts inherited a relatively neat package of principles. On the one hand there was the law of contracts, which dealt with obligations arising from consensual agreement; on the other hand there was the law of torts, which dealt with obligations imposed by law. Tort obligations were based mainly on the principle of negligence, so that as a general proposition one could act without fear of liability as long as one kept one's promises and did not act negligently toward those to whom one owed a duty of care as defined by law.

But by the middle of the twentieth century things began to look different. The theoretical model of the contract as the product of negotiation between two freewilling parties had always been strained as applied to certain relationships, such as the employment relationship, but as the changes wrought by industrialization were absorbed into social and political consciousness, the model seemed increasingly out of touch with reality. How could one realistically characterize those pieces of paper that govern our bank deposits, our loans, our insurance, our travel, our residential leases, and our warranties as *consensual* agreement? If they were contracts at all, they were *contracts of adhesion*—contracts prepared by the party with superior bargaining strength and presented to the other party on a take-it-or-leave-it basis. In a way, they represented the imposition of status in the form of a contract.

The limitations on liability that characterized tort law of the nineteenth century also came under stress. As our economy became more interdependent and at the same time more complex, so that people's lives and welfare came to be linked through the chain of production to faceless companies with whom they had no contract, as more sophisticated systems of insurance became available to spread the loss, and perhaps also as social attitudes changed, holding the manufacturer or supplier liable for injuries caused by defective products seemed less absurd and less outrageous.

Contract and tort law played closely related roles in the fascinating judicial drama that developed from these tensions. The first act took place in New York in 1916 at a time when Benjamin Cardozo was a judge of New York's Court of Appeal, its highest court. Donald MacPherson was driving a new Buick he had purchased from a dealer when the car suddenly collapsed, and he was thrown out and injured. One of the wheels on the car, it turned out, was made of defective wood, and its spokes had crumbled into fragments. Buick did not make the wheel, but it was negligent in failing to inspect it carefully before placing it on the car.

The question was whether Buick, which manufactured the car but did not sell it directly to MacPherson, was responsible for his injuries. The lawyers for Buick argued that the company could not be liable in contract because it had no agreement with MacPherson, nor in tort because following *Winterbottom v. Wright* a manufacturer's duty of care runs only to the party that purchases the vehicle from him (in this case the dealer) and not to the ultimate consumer.

Some exceptions to that rule had developed in New York, however. As early as 1852, in *Thomas v. Winchester,* the Court of Appeal held that a woman who purchased a bottle of poison falsely labeled as a mild medicine could sue the chemist who had labeled the bottle and sold it to the druggist. While acknowledging *Winterbottom* as the general rule, the court held there should be an exception for products that were "imminently dangerous to the lives of others." At times the New York court seemed inclined to apply the *Thomas* exception narrowly—holding, for example, that the manufacturer of a machine was not liable for injuries resulting from the explosion of a defective flywheel because a flywheel, unlike poison or gunpowder, is not inherently dangerous. At other times it applied the exception more broadly; a person who constructed a scaffold defectively was held liable when the scaffold broke, injuring a workman, because such a misfortune to third persons was a "natural and necessary consequence of the builder's negligence."

This was the state of the law when *MacPherson v. Buick Motor Company* was argued before Judge Cardozo and his colleagues in 1916. Buick contended that the *Thomas* exception should be confined to products that in their normal operation are instruments of destruction. But Judge Cardozo, in his opinion, noted that the exception had not been so confined, and he drew from the facts and language in the prior opinions a different test. The essence of those opinions, as he read them, was not whether the product is "inherently dangerous" but whether it is likely to be dangerous when negligently made. If it is, and if the manufacturer knows that it will be used by consumers without further inspection by them, then the manufacturer is under a duty to the consumer to make it carefully. In characteristically simple language Cardozo put the principle: "Where danger is to be foreseen, liability will follow."

Act 2: In 1960 Claus Henningsen bought a Plymouth automobile from a dealer in Bloomfield, New Jersey, as a Mother's Day present for his wife Helen. A week later she was driving it at twenty miles per hour on a smooth road when she heard a loud noise by the hood as if something had cracked; the steering wheel spun from her hands, and the car crashed into a brick wall, causing her serious injury. The Henningsens were unable to prove negligence on the part of anyone. The question was whether the manufacturer or the car dealer was liable for breach of warranty.

A warranty is a promise by the seller of a product that the product will meet certain standards. Against the old principle of *caveat emptor* (let the buyer beware) there had developed the principle that every sale carried with it an *implied warranty* that the goods would be "merchantable," that is to say, that they will do what they are supposed to do. On the basis of an implied warranty a purchaser could recover for a defective product even in the absence of negligence.

But for Helen Henningsen there were two problems. First, she was not the person who purchased the car from the retailer, and neither she nor her husband made any purchase directly from Chrysler Corporation (the manufacturer of Plymouth); so how could she claim a contractual relationship, such as warranty constituted, with either of them? Second, even if she could claim rights based on warranty through her husband's purchase, her husband had signed a purchase order form stating he accepted the warranties given on that piece of paper as the only warranties "express or implied," and the document said that the only warranty was a promise to replace defective parts free of charge at the Chrysler factory in Detroit. In the face of that limited *express warranty*, how could any broader warranty be implied?

The New Jersey Supreme Court, in an opinion by Justice John S. Francis, worked its way through this legal maze with astonishing agility. First, it said that under modern marketing conditions when a manufacturer puts a new automobile in the stream of trade and promotes its purchase by the public, the implied warranty must extend to the ultimate consumer. Whereas other courts had attempted to explain this result by a variety of intricate theories, the New Jersey court was content to say that it was required by "the demands of social justice." Second, the court held that Chrysler's attempt to limit its liability by the use of an express warranty was ineffective in such a contract of adhesion. Finally, it held that in the case of an automobile an implied warranty from both manufacturer and dealer extends not only to the individual purchaser but also to the members of the purchaser's family and persons occupying or using the car with the purchaser's consent, so that Mrs. Henningsen could sue after all.

Act 3: In 1963 William Greenman was injured while using a power tool his wife bought him for Christmas. Investigation revealed that the tool was defectively designed—it contained inadequate set screws—and that it was this defect that caused the injury. Greenman sued the manufacturer for breach of warranty, and the case wound its way to the California Supreme Court and the chambers of Justice Roger Traynor.

The *Henningsen* case in New Jersey provided a basis for deciding in favor of Greenman, but it was a shaky one. What the New Jersey court did by holding that the implied warranty of merchantability could not be excluded by an express provision was to transmute an obligation originating in contract into an obligation imposed by law. Justice Traynor had a better idea, one that he had advanced twenty years earlier in a dissent and that had garnered considerable support within the academic community. There are sound policy reasons, he suggested, for holding the manufacturer liable without regard to fault: he is in the best position to anticipate and guard against the occurrence of hazards and to insure against the risk and so distribute its cost among consumers. But if the legal rule is to be tuned to those policies, why talk about warranty at all? Why not just say, as a matter of tort law, that a manufacturer is *strictly* liable (that is, without regard to fault) when he places on the market a product that proves to be defective and causes injury to human beings? Moreover, why not say it also of retailers, who are an integral part of the overall producing and marketing enterprise? That is what Justice Traynor did, and this time his colleagues agreed.

Some form of strict liability came to be accepted by nearly every court in the land, and Traynor's analysis (with some modification) came to be enshrined in the authoritative *Restatement of Torts,* a compendium of tort principles prepared and modified from time to time by a group of judges, lawyers, and professors. Though not a radical approach in terms of outcome—courts had in effect been doing what Traynor said they should do but on different theories—it represented a wholesale modification of the way judges and lawyers think about liability for defective products, a kind of judicial field theory fusing negligence and warranty principles into one comparatively simple and overarching formula.

But there is an epilogue. The drafters of the *Restatement of Torts* worried about the application of principles of strict liability to products, such as pharmaceuticals, that might be extremely beneficial in alleviating pain and suffering or even in maintaining life, but at the same time might be "unavoidably dangerous" because the risk of harmful side effects cannot be avoided through any technology known, or reasonably knowable, at the time they are distributed. If principles of strict liability were to apply to such products, manufacturers might be deterred from placing them on the market, or the cost of insuring against risks might become so great as to price the products outside the reach of people who needed them. Accordingly, the drafters proposed to exclude such products from the reach of strict liability, subjecting the manufacturer to liability only for negligence in the design or manufacture of the product or for failing to warn of risks that the manufacturer either knew or should have known.

Courts in most states have heeded the *Restatement* recommendation in whole or in part, and recently the California Supreme Court followed suit. The court held that persons who claimed to have been injured *in utero* when their mothers took diethylstilbestrol (DES), a drug used to prevent miscarriage, could not rely on a theory of strict liability to establish a defect in the "design" of the drug. To recover against the manufacturer, they would have to prove that the drug had not been properly prepared or that proper warnings had not been given; the Traynor principles did not apply.

Issues such as that posed by the DES case are difficult for courts because ultimately they involve substantial questions of public policy and morality. If it is predictable, and inevitable, that some people will suffer deleterious side effects from a generally beneficial drug, why should not the majority who benefit from the drug help defray the cost of injury to the unlucky few? I am not suggesting that the courts are wrong in the answer they have given so far, only that the answer is not self-evident. And that raises the further question: why do we allow courts such authority? Why do we not insist, on the basis of democratic principles, that the legislature do its job and make laws concerning such areas of public policy? One explanation is historical—that's the way it's always been—but let us put that explanation aside and inquire whether there are any good reasons why we *should* continue to allow courts to do what they are doing.

The classical explanation, and the one I think has the most merit, is that there are certain areas of the law in which development is best left to the judicial process. The legislature, when it does act, necessarily takes wholesale action, making broad rules of general application. Courts, on the other hand, act typically at the "retail" level. Their jurisdiction is invoked not by lobbyists but by litigants in a specific lawsuit. The decision they render can be, and often is, tailored to the facts of the particular case. Of course, the opinion will reflect principles susceptible of broader application, but it may not be necessary, or even possible, to anticipate the precise scope of their application to future cases. The judicial approach is a more empirical, trial-and-error approach than the legislature is capable of, and it is particularly suited to those areas in which the law needs to develop on an experimental basis or in which the varieties of human experience and relationships make it difficult to draw lines.

Some have advanced an additional justification for the continued existence of the common-law process that is more political in nature, and it has to do with legislative inertia. The legislature, so the argument goes, may become so wary of a controversial area, particularly one in which there is likely to be a good deal of lobbying, that it becomes paralyzed, incapable of taking any action even when there are strong arguments to change the existing law. Under such circumstances it may be appropriate for courts to make the first move, not to bypass the legislature, but to put the ball in the legislature's court.

I think there is merit in that argument provided it is not pushed too far. Chief Justice Traynor wrote of the "occupational caution of judges [that] makes them reluctant to take the initiative in overruling a precedent whose unworthiness is concealed in the aura of stare decisis [a legal term meaning to abide by, or adhere to, decided cases]." It takes courage, he said, "to turn a flashlight upon an aura and call out what one has seen, at the risk of violating quiet for the benefit of those who have retired from active thought. It is easier for a court to rationalize that less shock will result if it bides its time, and bides it, and bides it, the while it awaits legislative action to transfer an unfortunate precedent unceremoniously to the dump from the fading glory in which it has been basking." Obviously, Chief Justice Traynor believed that courts should not always wait for legislatures to overturn a precedent that has come to be recognized as a bad one.

Another justification that might be advanced for common law is that although legislatures are expected to give voice to the interests of the people as a whole, they are inclined to listen most carefully to the voices of politically powerful people and groups. As a consequence, they may not hear so clearly, or respond so quickly to, the complaints of those lacking in political power, even when the complaints are supported by strong moral considerations. Such considerations alone do not provide a basis for judicial intervention; but when the complaint finds support in legal principle as well, they may tip the balance in favor of action rather than inaction. The emergence of judicial protection for the job security of unorganized workers, like the earlier development of protection for the rights of workers within unions, can be viewed in that light.

The proper role of courts in the development of principles of common law must be viewed also against the background of ultimate legislative authority. Legislatures could have reacted to any of the developments discussed in this chapter by reversing them or modifying them through legislation. When the California Supreme Court decided on the basis of generally applicable tort principles that a bartender could be liable for injuries resulting from his plying an obviously intoxicated patron with more liquor, the California legislature responded by passing a statute that reversed that holding. (That the legislature may have been subject to heavy lobbying by the liquor industry is beside the point.) But for the most part legislatures have not reacted in that manner to what courts have done in the common-law areas. Rather, they have tended either to ratify judicial decisions or to use them as a basis for more intensive regulation.

Whether the legislature reacts by ratifying, rejecting, or modifying what the court has done, the court's action in such cases can be said to *aid* the democratic process rather than to derogate it. The court, by its opinion, brings a matter to the legislature's attention by saying, This is what we think is right, or at least, This is what we have determined that generally applicable legal principles require.

If in the process it provokes the legislature into dialogue, that is a healthy aspect of our system of separation of powers.

I am not suggesting that it is a primary responsibility of courts to provoke legislatures into social change. If courts took that as their charge, and legislatures were forced to react every time a court decided it had an idea it wanted to try out, the legislative process would probably grind to a halt. Passing legislation is serious, time-consuming business, difficult enough without courts acting as constant provocateurs. What I am suggesting is that the common-law process by which courts, case by case, apply existing principles to different circumstances of fact in changing social contexts is in many instances a useful counterpoint to the legislative process, and awareness of that function helps to account for its continued survival.

I had that thought in mind when I wrote the majority opinion in *Pugh v. See's Candies*. At a doctrinal level *Pugh* represented nothing more than the specific application to the employment context of generally applicable contract principles. But that concept was fairly novel, and precedent as to *how* those principles should apply to a suit for wrongful termination of employment was sparse. I knew that questions regarding their application would likely arise in the *Pugh* case when it got back to the trial court and in future cases as well. The question was how far we should go in attempting to provide guidance in advance. If we gave no guidance at all, we would be insuring maximum confusion in future litigation. On the other hand, we were not a legislature, and we did not want to go too far in anticipating issues that might or might not arise or in trying to answer questions that the lawyers for the parties had not been given adequate opportunity to explore in their briefs.

It was a dilemma that courts constantly confront. Since the case was going back to trial, however, we felt justified in including some observations that otherwise might not have been appropriate but that did double service as guidance for the trial court in the *Pugh* case and for other trial courts in cases to come. We said that See's, which had thus far been silent as to the reasons for Pugh's dismissal, would have to come forward with those reasons and with evidence in support. But we emphasized that Pugh would bear the ultimate burden of demonstrating that his dismissal was wrongful. We discussed the meaning of *good cause* in the absence of a contract for a specified term, and we cautioned against undue interference with the legitimate exercise of managerial discretion, particularly when the employee occupies a sensitive managerial or other confidential position, as did Pugh.

We also left many questions unanswered. To some extent the answers have come, and will come, from subsequent court decisions. Ultimately, I suspect, they will come from the state legislature, for the area is one that is appropriate to regulation through statute. The legislature is able to provide creative solutions that are beyond the powers of a court, such as the resolution of disputes over wrongful termination through arbitration or other remedies. But that is quite different from saying that courts should abdicate their traditional common-law function in the expectation that the legislature will act.

6

Criminal Cases

Reviewing criminal cases is a function that state and federal courts have in common but that consumes much more of the time of the state courts. When I was on the Court of Appeal approximately half of our cases were criminal, and the percentage on the total California Supreme Court docket is about the same. By contrast, criminal cases comprise a small percentage of the federal docket.

It is a function, moreover, that is singularly capable of arousing intense passions. Crime, particularly violent crime, is at or near the top of everyone's list of social concerns. Bringing criminals to justice is a high public priority, and not for reasons of deterrence alone. For victims and their families it is a matter of personal vindication. Even those of us who have not experienced crime directly can empathize with such emotions. Courts are a highly visible part of the criminal justice system, and it seems reasonable to hold them at least partly responsible when that system fails to do its job. This is particularly the case when we observe a trial court dismiss a prosecution or exclude evidence on what appear to be technical grounds, or impose a sentence that appears overly lenient, or when we observe an appellate court overturn a jury's guilty verdict for reasons we do not entirely understand or accept. That "soft on crime" is the most frequent charge leveled against incumbent judges in election campaigns throughout the country should come as no great surprise.

A thoroughgoing evaluation of that charge would require exploration along several different lines. One would need to know the extent of judicial discretion present in the judicial actions criticized. For example, it is hardly appropriate to hold a trial court responsible for dismissing a prosecution when the defendant is not brought to trial within the time limit imposed by statute, for excluding evidence in compliance with the clear mandate of a statute or higher court, or for imposing a sentence that is at the maximum the law allows. To the extent that judicial discretion does exist, particularly in the higher courts, it is by no means an easy matter to evaluate the oft-heard complaint that courts have leaned too heavily in the direction of protecting the rights of criminal defendants at the expense of society's or victims' interests. One needs to look at the legal issues involved and also at the relationship between the determination of those issues and effective law enforcement. For example, whether the Warren Court precedents in the area of criminal justice have hampered law enforcement or resulted in the freeing of guilty persons is a matter susceptible of rational inquiry, but one that requires a good deal of patience and analysis.

I do not intend to embark upon this sort of evaluation here; to do so with any kind of care and thoroughness would consume the entire book. My more modest goal is to focus upon what I perceive to be certain common misunderstandings regarding the role of appellate courts in the review of criminal cases and to set at least these misunderstandings straight. To do this, I need to take the reader inside the process and to provide something of the judicial perspective.

When I went around the state campaigning, for example, I found that many people are under the impression that an appellate court reviews a conviction by reconsidering the evidence (or perhaps even rehearing it) and deciding whether the defendant really is guilty, and if so, whether he or she deserves the particular punishment that was given. I must say—and I did say when I was on the campaign trail—that if I thought that was what appellate courts were supposed to be doing, I would be pretty distressed myself, particularly in cases where the guilt of the defendant seemed to me quite clear and the circumstances seemed to warrant the punishment imposed. I would wonder why we bother to have trial courts and juries, and I would question the sanity of the appellate judges. The fact is, these popular impressions are quite wrong.

In criminal cases it is the defendant who normally appeals because in our system the prosecutor is not permitted to appeal from judgments of acquittal. To subject the defendant to a second trial after he has been acquitted would violate the constitutional prohibition against double jeopardy. The prosecutor does have a limited right to appeal from certain trial court rulings (such as an order dismissing the prosecution for some reason, or a ruling to exclude certain evidence), but such appeals comprise a small portion of the criminal appellate caseload.

When the criminal defendant appeals from a judgment, the appellate court (as in a civil case) reviews the record to determine two things: whether there was substantial evidence to support the verdict, and whether there were errors in the trial of sufficient magnitude to require reversal. If the answer to the first question is yes and the second is no, it is expected to put aside its own views as to guilt or innocence and affirm the conviction. The appellate court will also consider claims that the sentence was not imposed by the proper standards or procedure, but it will not substitute its judgment concerning sentencing for that of the trial court judge (or the jury in a death penalty case).

Reversal of a criminal conviction on appeal is a rare phenomenon; in California it occurs in about 7 percent of the cases. When it does occur, the usual outcome is not that the defendant is set free. Rather, he is returned (typically while remaining in custody) for a new trial. Subjecting him to a second trial on the basis of his own appeal is not considered a violation of the prohibition against double jeopardy except in those exceedingly rare cases in which the appellate court finds there was no substantial evidence to support the verdict. I can recall only two such decisions in which I participated.

The fact that criminal convictions are affirmed in 93 percent of the cases does not mean that there were no errors in those cases. Perfect trials are even rarer than reversals. Affirmation of a conviction means that whatever errors did exist were considered by the court to be *harmless.*

The word *error,* in this context, covers a lot of ground. Usually it refers to something the trial judge did or failed to do, for example, in the process of selecting the jury, instructing the jury, or ruling on the admissibility of evidence. For an appellate court to say that a trial judge committed error in one of these ways does not mean necessarily that the judge was incompetent or that he should go back to judges' school. ("How can so many judges be so dumb?"

someone asked me once, referring to the number of cases in which error was found.) It may mean simply that the trial judge, in making his ruling, failed to anticipate what an appellate court later decides was the "correct" reading of a statute or prior precedent or some constitutional principle. The appellate court gets to do this, of course, on a relatively leisurely basis in comparison to the split-second decision that the trial judge often has to make—a fact of legal life that led someone (no doubt a trial judge) to suggest that appellate judges are like buzzards swooping down after the battle to feast on the remains.

Often what is being argued in a criminal appeal is a defect attributable to the misconduct of persons other than the judge— members of the jury, for example, who disobey their instructions not to discuss the case with anyone, prosecutors who engage in improper argument to the jury, or defense attorneys who fail to provide competent representation. Under the federal Constitution (as well as under most state constitutions) a criminal defendant is entitled to be represented by counsel, at the state's expense if necessary; this entitlement has been construed to embrace the right to competent representation, that is, representation in accordance with the standards of the local legal community. With increasing frequency a defendant's appellate lawyer will argue that the defendant's trial lawyer (usually a different person), by failing to investigate a possible defense or by failing to make a particular argument or objection, acted in a way that was constitutionally inadequate.

While I was on the Court of Appeal, we had a case that defied categorization. A woman testified that while driving home from a party late one evening, she stopped at an intersection, and someone entered the passenger side of her car, threatened her with a knife, ordered her to stop the car in front of a hotel, assaulted her sexually, and stole her mink coat. The description of her assailant that she gave the police fit her husband rather than the defendant (the clothes she described resembled her husband's), and she was unable to identify the defendant in either photographs or a lineup. She did, however, identify a knife in the defendant's possession as the one that was held to her throat. In addition, one witness testified that the defendant had bragged about getting his wife a mink stole for Christmas, and another witness said that the defendant had bragged to him about raping a woman at knifepoint and stealing her mink coat. The jury convicted the defendant of rape, robbery, and kidnapping.

There was no question about the sufficiency of the evidence to support that verdict. In the course of the trial, however, the prosecutor engaged in conduct that representatives of the state charged with responsibility for trying the defendant fairly are not supposed to engage in. During his examination of the rape victim, he asked whether she recalled the "defense attorney's blowing kisses to you at the preliminary hearing," and he adduced testimony from a witness who was present at the preliminary hearing to the effect that both defense counsel and the defendant himself, at that hearing, had made "obscene" gestures and grimaces. Defense counsel made no objection to this evidence at the time though it was utterly irrelevant and undoubtedly inflammatory.

More significantly, when it came time to argue to the jury, the prosecutor made reference to the fact that the defendant himself had not testified. A defendant has a constitutional right not to testify, of course, and it has been held to be a violation of that right for a prosecutor to take advantage of its exercise by inviting the jury to draw an adverse inference, suggesting that because the defendant did not testify, he must be guilty. All prosecutors know that, but this prosecutor tried to be cute. Like Mark Antony telling the Roman audience he was not there to praise Caesar or criticize Brutus ("for Brutus is an honorable man"), he said, "Now you can't stop and think, you can't say because he didn't testify he must be guilty, you can't do that. You can't hold that against him. . . . You can't say, gee, if I were guilty or not guilty I would have testified, I would have done this or that. It's against the law for you to do that." Since the prosecutor knew that the judge would instruct the jury that they should draw no inference from the fact that the defendant did not testify, there seemed little reason for him to mention it unless he wanted to call particular attention to the defendant's silence.

There were other instances of dubious conduct on the part of the prosecutor—attacking the motives of defense counsel, pursuing a line of questioning to which objection had been sustained, asking a witness whether she thought the defendant was guilty (tactics any experienced prosecutor would know are not permitted). But the evidence of guilt being quite substantial, I doubt that we would have reversed the conviction had it not been for the conduct of the defendant's own lawyers. In fact, we said as much in the opinion.

There were two lawyers present at the beginning of the trial, but one of them, the junior lawyer, had no trial experience and was supposed to be there only to take notes and do research. In the middle of the trial the senior lawyer, for unexplained reasons but possibly due to illness, simply did not show up, leaving the trial in the hands of his inexperienced associate. The latter, instead of seeking a new trial or even advising his client that he might be entitled to one, proceeded to do the best he could—which, it turned out, was not very good.

"Things happened in appellant's trial," we wrote, "which simply ought not to happen in a fair proceeding. Whether characterized as prosecutorial misconduct, defense counsel misconduct, judicial error, or a combination of all three, the net result was that the trial was turned into something of a circus, complete with sideshows, disappearing acts, clowning and tricks which could only divert the jury's attention from the serious business of determining guilt or innocence in accordance with proper standards." Accordingly, we reversed.

In chapter 2 I discussed the concept of harmless error in general, but in the context of criminal appeals it deserves some elaboration. The California state constitution provides that a conviction must be affirmed, even with error, unless there has been a "miscarriage of justice." That phrase has been translated by the courts into the general rule that the judgment of conviction should be affirmed unless it appears probable that there would have been a different result absent the error. When, for example, the trial judge allows evidence that should not have been admitted or keeps evidence out that should have been allowed, then, unless the error amounts to a violation of the federal Constitution, the appellate judges are supposed to look at the entire record to determine the likelihood that some member or members of the jury who voted for the verdict might have held out for some other result if a proper ruling had been made. Obviously, that is not a precise science, and the fact that different judges reach different conclusions on the basis of the same verbal formula is not surprising.

When the defect that occurred in the trial court is one of federal constitutional dimension, a different formula applies, and it was a case out of California that established that formula. In a murder trial of the defendant Ruth Chapman, a prosecutor engaged in misconduct by calling the jury's attention to the defendant's failure to testify. The California courts, following the state constitution, affirmed the conviction on the ground that the evidence of the defendant's guilt was "overwhelming," but the United States Supreme Court reversed. That court held that when a defendant has been deprived of a right protected under the federal Constitution, his or her conviction may be affirmed only when the appellate court is able to say that the error was "harmless beyond a reasonable doubt." Emphasizing the egregious nature of the prosecutor's misconduct, the Court held that Chapman was entitled to a new trial.

The *Chapman* test—"harmless beyond a reasonable doubt"—is applicable to a variety of federal constitutional errors. These include the erroneous admission of evidence that must be excluded because it was obtained in violation of the *Miranda* rule that the defendant be advised of his or her constitutional rights prior to questioning, or in violation of his or her right to be free from unreasonable searches and seizures under the Fourth Amendment. Opponents of the exclusionary principle often refer to these sorts of error as technical—meaning, presumably, that the evidence is otherwise reliable and relevant to the question of the defendant's guilt. In the case of admissions obtained in violation of a defendant's *Miranda* rights that is not necessarily true, since the *Miranda* rule is designed in part to protect defendants against the kind of coercion that may lead to unreliable evidence. But it is true that the primary justifications for the exclusionary rules lie elsewhere, namely, in deterring improper police conduct and in protecting the integrity of the judicial process. What is one person's technicality is another person's constitutional right.

Sometimes the defect in a defendant's trial seems so basic, so contrary to fundamental fairness, that no test of harmless error seems appropriate. For example, all of us who saw the event on television know that Jack Ruby was the person who shot Lee Harvey Oswald, the alleged assassin of President John F. Kennedy. But if Ruby had not died in jail, he would have been entitled to trial by jury, and the prosecution would have had the burden of proving him guilty beyond a reasonable doubt. If some overly eager trial court judge had simply pronounced Ruby guilty and sentenced him without benefit of a jury trial, we would not expect our appellate judges to shrug their shoulders and murmur harmless error. Instead, we would expect them to say that the right to a jury trial in our society is so fundamental that the denial of it is tantamount to injustice no matter how certain we are of the eventual verdict.

That sort of miscarriage does not happen, but mistakes short of that do. The United States Supreme Court has held, for example, that in death penalty cases persons who are so opposed to the death penalty that they could not bring themselves to vote for it may be excluded from a jury. The corollary to that principle is that persons may not be excluded who simply express doubt about the death penalty or its propriety. In *Davis v. Georgia* the United States Supreme Court held that the improper exclusion of such a juror impairs the defendant's right to an impartial jury and consequently affects the fairness of the proceeding in such a way as to require reversal *per se*, that is, in itself and without consideration of how weighty the evidence might be of the defendant's guilt.

A similar problem arises when a judge, in instructing a jury, leaves out some part of the definition of a crime. There are those who believe that juries do not understand instructions anyway, so such an omission does not matter. Though there is some evidence of that, there is also evidence to the contrary. People who have served on juries sometimes report that the jury took the instructions very seriously, and in some cases juries have asked very specific questions that reflect a high degree of attention to, and understanding of, the instructions they are read. In any event, we operate on the assumption that juries decide cases in accordance with the legal principles that are explained to them by the judge, and under our system no other assumption is workable. Thus, for example, when a judge omits to tell the jury that penetration is part of the definition of the crime of rape, we have to assume that some jurors who voted to convict the defendant may not have been aware of that requirement. There is language in United States Supreme Court decisions that suggests that when such an omission occurs, it is a denial of due process of law, and the defendant is entitled to a new trial without regard to the evidence—that is, the conviction is reversible *per se*.

This rule of *per se* reversal got the California Supreme Court, when I was on it, into considerable hot water with the public and the press in the death penalty arena. Under California law, as in most states, a defendant may not be sentenced to death unless the jury first determines that whatever murder or murders he or she committed were accompanied by such "special circumstances" as to warrant consideration of the ultimate penalty. These special circumstances are defined by law and include murder for hire, murder by torture, and a murder committed in the course of perpetrating particularly serious felonies such as robbery or rape. This means that a death penalty trial is a three-step procedure: first, the jury decides whether the defendant is guilty as charged; second (if found guilty), whether there were special circumstances; and finally (if so), whether the defendant should be put to death or receive a sentence of life in prison without possibility of parole.

Prior to my appointment the California Supreme Court had decided, in *Carlos v. Superior Court,* that to support a finding of special circumstances in a felony murder, the jury must find that the defendant *intended* to kill the victim—that negligence or reckless disregard of human life was not enough. This holding was based in part on interpretation of the California death penalty statute and in part on United States Supreme Court decisions that seemed to suggest that execution of a person who did not intend to kill would not be permissible under the federal Constitution. After *Carlos* our court was confronted with a very difficult question: what should be done in those felony murder cases tried before *Carlos* in which the trial court failed to anticipate the holding and as a consequence did not instruct the jury that it must find intent to kill in order to find that special circumstances exist?

In *Connecticut v. Johnson* the United States Supreme Court seemed to say that if a jury is not instructed as to all the elements that constitute the crime of which the defendant is accused, then the defendant is automatically entitled to a new trial with a properly instructed jury regardless of how clear the evidence of guilt might be. The reasoning behind that decision was that the constitutional right to trial by jury is not satisfied simply by having a jury determine the defendant's guilt in the abstract; it includes the right to have a jury determine whether the defendant was guilty of each element of the offense.

Strictly speaking, an element of a special-circumstance finding such as intent to kill is not an element of a crime, but it is a condition to someone being executed for a crime, and that is pretty close. Following what we considered to be the mandate of the United States Supreme Court in *Connecticut v. Johnson,* a majority of our court held in *People v. Garcia* that when a jury made a finding of felony murder with special circumstance without benefit of an intent-to-kill instruction, the finding had to be set aside subject to certain narrow exceptions. The state attorney general asked the United States Supreme Court to take the case over, contending that we were wrong in our interpretation of federal precedents, but that court declined to do so. While its refusal did not necessarily mean it agreed with us, it did lend some solidity to our determination.

As a result of doing what we thought the United States Supreme Court required us to do, our court ended up setting aside special-circumstance findings in some gruesome cases in which the defendant's intent to kill seemed quite apparent, and each time we did, most newspaper and television reporters portrayed our decision in terms that must have made the average reader or listener conclude either that we were quite mad or that—as the pro–death penalty group that called itself Crime Victims for Court Reform suggested—we were so unalterably opposed to the death penalty as to seize on absurd reasons for not applying it. Moreover, although the effect of our decisions in these cases was simply to require retrial of the special-circumstance and death penalty phases of the trial—the defendant, still convicted of the underlying crimes, remained in custody—critics of the court made it appear as if we had patted the defendant on the back, returned his weapon, and set him loose.

I and some of my colleagues were uneasy with the situation. The rule of *per se* reversal made sense as a matter of pure logic, but there were cases in which its application seemed highly artificial and unnecessary to the effectuation of justice, and these were the cases in which public respect for the authority of the court seemed especially at risk. The case that disturbed me most was *People v. Billy Ray Hamilton.* Hamilton was convicted of murdering three people in a market and attempting to murder a fourth. He entered the market carrying a list, in his own handwriting, of witnesses who had testified against another murderer, Clarence Ray Allen, whom Hamilton had met in Folsom prison. The first victim, Bryon Schletewitz, was one of those on the list. Hamilton shot him in the middle of the forehead with a sawed-off shotgun from inches away. He then reloaded the shotgun by releasing the lock lever, breaking the gun open, removing the spent shell, and inserting another. He walked to an adjoining room where he shot the second victim in the neck and the third victim in the chest, both at point-blank range. Finally, he tracked the fourth victim into the bathroom, where he was hiding, and shot him in the face from a few feet away. No thanks to Hamilton the fourth victim did not die. After each shot Hamilton had to break open and reload the gun.

The jury found that Hamilton committed these murders, and although it was not asked to find whether Hamilton intended to kill each of the victims, that conclusion seemed inescapable from the circumstances. Our own prior decision in *Garcia* left open the possibility that the court might confirm the special-circumstance finding under such conditions, but only if it could be satisfied that the defendant produced all the evidence bearing on intent to kill that he would have produced if he had known that to be an issue in the case. Theoretically, since neither the prosecution nor the defense regarded intent to kill as an issue, the defendant might have had other evidence, which he did not submit for tactical reasons, that might have created a reasonable doubt in the mind of a juror whether the requisite intent was present. On that basis a majority of my colleagues reversed the special-circumstance finding.

It seemed to me that in such a case the requirements of due process could be met in another way—by allowing the defendant to come forward in a habeas corpus proceeding with any evidence bearing on the issue of intent. (As I mentioned previously, a habeas corpus proceeding allows a convicted defendant to present certain types of evidence that were not presented at the time of the trial.) As a practical matter the only such evidence that seemed at all plausible would be evidence of *diminished capacity*, that the defendant lacked the capacity to form the requisite intent. In light of the evidence of premeditation, that seemed exceedingly unlikely, but it was possible that the defendant had evidence of diminished capacity that he did not present for tactical reasons and that he would have presented had he known it was the only way of avoiding the gas chamber. So, I wrote a dissenting opinion saying that I would have affirmed the finding of special circumstances subject to Hamilton's right to present evidence of diminished capacity or any other evidence of lack of intent in a separate habeas corpus proceeding.

I tell this story merely to illustrate the difficulties that a court may have, especially in a death penalty case, with the question of harmless error. It is possible that my colleagues in the original majority were correct in interpreting United States Supreme Court decisions to require reversal even in a case like *Hamilton*, but we may never know. After Justice Kaus left and Justice Panelli came on the court, there were four votes to rehear *Hamilton*, and it was reheard; but then the 1986 election brought about a further change in the composition of the court, and there was a further rehearing. By that time the newly constituted court had decided (partly on the basis of new United States Supreme Court decisions) to overrule *Carlos*, so that intent to kill was eliminated as an issue. Hamilton's conviction has since been affirmed.

The problem of harmless error is even more acute when it comes to reviewing the penalty phase of a death penalty trial, in which the jury, having decided that the defendant is guilty of a crime that might warrant execution, decides whether in fact the defendant is to be executed.

In California the jury's decision in the penalty phase is limited to two choices: execution, or life in prison without possibility of parole—"LWOP," as it is rather casually called. The death penalty statute makes this sound like a fairly easy, or at least wholly rational, calculation, somewhat like deciding whether to invest in stocks or bonds. It says that the jury is to "weigh" certain "aggravating circumstances" against "mitigating circumstances." If it finds that mitigating circumstances outweigh aggravating circumstances, then LWOP is the verdict; otherwise, the statute says, the jury "shall" impose the death penalty.

In fact, as a matter of federal constitutional law, the task of the jury in the penalty phase is of a more subjective and more responsible nature than the bare language of the California statute would suggest. "What is important," the United States Supreme Court has declared, "is an *individualized* determination on the basis of the character of the individual and the circumstances of the crime." Moreover, the decision is ultimately the responsibility of each juror and no one else. The United States Supreme Court has made clear that "it is constitutionally impermissible to rest a death sentence on a determination made by a sentencer who has been led to believe that the responsibility for determining the appropriateness of the defendant's death rests elsewhere."

On the basis of these federal constitutional considerations our court, in *People v. Brown*, ruled that in a death penalty case the jury should be instructed as to the scope of its ultimate responsibility within the framework of the California statute. We said that the word *weigh* in the statute "is a metaphor for a process which by nature is incapable of precise description. The word connotes a mental balancing process, but certainly not one which calls for a mere mechanical counting of factors on each side of the imaginary 'scale,' or the arbitrary assignment of 'weights' to any of them. Each juror is free to assign whatever moral or sympathetic value he deems appropriate to each and all of the various factors he is permitted to consider." Further, we approved an instruction that omitted the word *shall* from the directions to the jury, leaving it to the jury to determine the appropriate penalty in each case.

It is plain that a jury's determination of the penalty to be imposed is of a quite different nature than its determination that the defendant was guilty of the crimes alleged. In finding the defendant guilty, the jury bases its decision essentially on facts, and if an error is committed in the guilt phase, appellate judges can bring to bear somewhat objective considerations to the question of whether the error was likely to have affected the factual findings. The same is true in the special-circumstance phase of a death penalty trial. But in the penalty phase, where the decision is more moral than factual, objectivity loses ground. Juries have been known to withhold the death penalty from persons whose character and crimes seem far more hideous than those of some defendants who were sentenced to death. Individuals are known to have widely varying views as to the appropriateness of the death penalty generally and in particular cases. How, then, is an appellate judge to go about deciding whether it might have made a difference to some juror if certain information about the defendant had not been improperly withheld, or if the trial judge's instructions had not strayed from legal requirements, or if the prosecutor had not engaged in misconduct by making an improper argument to the jury? Any answer is likely to be highly speculative and ultimately unsatisfying.

Wholly apart from any question of reversible error, the subjectivity and consequent variability of the decision to apply the death penalty is troubling. Of course, there are variables in any litigation, ranging from the personality of the lawyers to the defendant's appearance, that can affect the outcome in a way that may seem arbitrary. But death penalty litigation is unique, and there is an awesomeness and finality to the ultimate sanction that makes the thought of arbitrariness in its application particularly repellent.

Leaving aside the question of whether the death penalty deters crime, which is not likely ever to be resolved to the satisfaction of those who have an opinion one way or the other, and leaving aside also the nagging moral questions posed by the deliberate taking of a human life, there remains the fact—and it is a fact—that imposition of the death penalty among convicted murderers in this country is pretty much a lottery dependent on variables that include the competence of counsel on both sides, the makeup of the particular jury, and characteristics of the defendant that ought to be irrelevant, including his race and social class. Indeed, to the extent that there is predictability, it resides in statistics indicating that murderers of whites are many times more likely to receive the death penalty than murderers of blacks, and if the murderer happens to be black, the odds are even greater.

The United States Supreme Court is aware of this evidence—it formed the basis of a last-ditch stand against the constitutionality of the death penalty in the 1987 case *McCleskey v. Kemp*—but that court has painted itself into a corner. In *Furman v. Georgia* it struck down, under the cruel and unusual punishment clause of the federal Constitution, state death penalty statutes that left imposition of the death penalty entirely to the discretion of the jury on the ground that such a "standardless" scheme was likely to, and in fact did, result in arbitrary and discriminatory executions, particularly of poor blacks. States reacted with death penalty statutes that, like California's, purported to "guide" the discretion of the jury on the basis of neutral criteria, including definition of special circumstances and of penalty phase standards. The United States Supreme Court, in *Gregg v. Georgia*, upheld the constitutionality of such a statute but subsequently insisted, in cases I have referred to earlier, that the discretion of the jury in the penalty phase cannot be constrained. In consequence, the only "guidance" that remains, as a practical matter, is the constraint imposed by the requirement of special circumstances. This constraint serves to limit the pool of murderers who are eligible for the exercise of jury discretion; but that pool remains quite large, and jury discretion, unfettered, still results in the sort of haphazard and discriminatory application of the death penalty that the court condemned in *Furman*. The Supreme Court in *McCleskey* declined to reconsider *Gregg*, and so the tension remains.

There are other problems with administration of the death penalty that are of an institutional nature. Capital cases, because of their complexity and the high stakes, are enormously costly, both at trial and on appeal; indeed, according to some data, it costs the public more to litigate death penalty cases to execution than it would cost to keep the defendant in prison for life. But the costs are not just monetary; there are costs to the system that cannot be measured in dollars alone. Every lawyer and judge familiar with the field knows that issues of criminal law and criminal procedure tend to be decided differently in the context of a death penalty appeal than otherwise. Regardless of one's views about the death penalty, its presence as an issue in a case tends to dominate, and thus to distort, legal analysis.

Moreover, that domination extends to the rest of the court's calendar. Death penalty cases require an enormous amount of judicial attention. The appellate records and the briefs all tend to be exceptionally large, the issues tend to be complex, and once the defendant is executed, mistakes cannot be corrected. Most staff lawyers and judges tend to feel a special sense of responsibility to study the record carefully and to consider issues that may not have been raised by defendant's counsel. It is one thing to talk about the death penalty in the abstract; it is another thing personally to sign your name to a document that results in an execution. Before I did, I wanted to be very sure I was right, and I think that is generally true of other judges as well.

In consequence, death penalty cases consume a disproportionate share of the court's resources of staff and judges alike—I would estimate anywhere from three to ten times the resources expended on the average case. And it is a debilitating loss. The records in these cases depict horrible crimes, replete with torture, decapitation, and other forms of unimaginable cruelty committed by people whose humanity is difficult to discern. Working on them is depressing, and I would be suspicious of any lawyer or judge who did not find it so.

The more capital cases there are, the less likely it is that the court will be able to perform its other duties adequately. Dean Gerald Uelmen of the University of Santa Clara Law School reports that as a result of the volume of pending death penalty cases and the priority assigned to their disposition, the California Supreme Court is granting fewer hearings, filing fewer opinions, and ordering more appellate court opinions depublished than at any time in its recent history. Though some of those statistics are undoubtedly attributable to the turnover in court personnel after the 1986 election, there is no doubt that the problem is a serious one.

I have often asked myself, as others have asked, to what extent my actions as a judge in capital cases were affected by my own lack of enthusiasm for the death penalty. I think it likely that they were affected to some extent. If I had not regarded capital cases as special, I doubt that I would have agonized over them as I did; and if I did not believe that other people might share my reservations, I probably would have brought a looser standard to bear in determining whether error in the penalty phase was harmless.

From what I know of myself, however—and I concede that there are limits to what one may know of oneself—I did not set about to search for ways of overturning death penalty convictions any more than I did with respect to other convictions. The California Supreme Court, in cases decided before I arrived on the bench, had already affirmed three death penalty judgments since the death penalty was restored in 1971. It was inevitable that more would be affirmed and that executions would occur. The public was insistent that the death penalty law be implemented, and there was nothing to be gained by resisting that insistence. Whatever I might think personally about whether the death penalty constitutes cruel and unusual punishment, the California state constitution and the United States Supreme Court said it did not. When I was confirmed, and before I took the oath, I was asked whether I had such reservations about the death penalty as would preclude me from carrying out the law; I replied that I had none. I believed then, and believe now, that this was true, and my signature appears in capital cases to prove it. I also believe, more strongly as a result of my experience on the court, that as a society we would be better off without the death penalty than we are with it.

7

Courts and the
Initiative Process

In 1982 the voters of California overwhelmingly approved an initiative, Proposition 8, called the Victims' Bill of Rights. Sponsored by Crime Victims for Law Reform, and supported by the state association of district attorneys, Proposition 8 was a grab bag of constitutional amendments and statutes affecting various aspects of criminal law and criminal procedure. Its provisions ranged from the definition of insanity to such areas as the admissibility of evidence of prior criminal convictions, the admissibility of illegally obtained evidence, and the discretion of trial courts in sentencing. It did contain some provisions relating to victims directly, such as their right to participate in sentencing proceedings and to receive compensation from the convicted perpetrator. For good measure it declared the right of citizens to "safe schools" though it said nothing about how that right was to be secured. Proposition 8 illustrates a number of special problems the initiative process poses for the judicial branch, and I intend to discuss these after a brief digression into the historical and legal background.

Direct voter participation in the lawmaking process is a product mainly of the Progressive movement, which swept parts of the country, but especially the West, around the turn of the century. It comes in several forms, including provisions that allow the legislature to submit propositions to the people; the referendum, which allows the people to vote on a statute that the legislature has already adopted; the indirect initiative, which requires the legislature to consider a proposal that has received a sufficient number of petition signatures and is subject to a vote of the people if the legislature fails to adopt it; and the direct initiative, whereby measures that garner sufficient support on petitions are submitted to the electorate directly, bypassing the legislature entirely. Twenty-one states presently have the direct initiative; seventeen of these allow its use for amendments to the state constitution as well as for the adoption of statutes. It is the direct initiative that is the focus of this chapter.

The impetus for the initiative process during the Progressive era was a distrust of legislatures and political parties. (In California the legislature was widely, and probably correctly, believed to be in the pocket of the Southern Pacific Railroad Company.) In the past few decades, with a growth in distrust of government generally, the rise of single-issue politics, and the decline of political parties, the initiative has enjoyed renewed popularity—a few more states have moved to adopt it, and its use in states that have it has increased dramatically.

Whether the direct initiative is fulfilling its promise of "power to the people" is debatable. Professor Robert Magleby of Brigham Young University, who has studied the question carefully, presents some troubling findings. Initiatives have become more the instrument of special-interest groups than of the *vox populi*. Obtaining enough signatures to place an initiative on the ballot is expensive unless the proponents have an army of volunteers at their disposal, and an entire industry has grown up around the process. Initiative measures are often too complex for people without special training to understand, and the ballot arguments that accompany them are not much better. Using tests of "readability," which evaluate a text according to vocabulary, sentence length, complexity, and conceptual difficulty, Magleby rates the reading level required by a typical ballot argument at between three years of college and one year of postgraduate work. Not surprisingly, the level of participation in voting on ballot measures tends to be less than in the election of candidates, and the "drop-off" rate is particularly great among people who are less well educated and in lower socioeconomic brackets. "By their own standards," Magleby concludes, "most voters have inadequate knowledge to make their voting choice on ballot propositions"; the result is what he calls a "form of electoral roulette." The people who rule in direct legislation, Magleby says, do not represent the grass roots but rather those who have mastered the process, thus a large number of citizens is effectively excluded from representation.

Initiatives can pose difficult problems for even the most sophisticated voters. In the November 1988 election in California there were a half-dozen measures on the ballot relating to insurance. Trying to understand and evaluate each of them independently was difficult enough, but to add to the problem, some were in conflict with others, and if two conflicting measures passed, the measure that received the most votes would prevail. Voters who preferred measure A to measure B could simply vote yes on A and no on B, but if they preferred measure B to no measure at all, they had a dilemma: if they voted for both measures, they would help assure that one would pass, but they ran the risk that it would be the one they liked least. How to cast an intelligent ballot in such a situation?

I would not want to do away with the initiative process, however, and whether any of the problems I have mentioned are curable by proposed reforms such as regulation of campaign financing or requirements for more simple wording is beyond the scope of my inquiry here. My concern is with the special problems that are posed, for the judicial branch and for the public generally, by the manner in which initiatives are drafted. These problems stem from the fact that initiatives, before they are presented to the public, are not subject to the open consideration, debate, compromise, and potential for amendment that characterize the legislative process. They are drafted by proponents, or more likely by their lawyers, in the privacy of someone's office and then filed with the secretary of state. Once that filing occurs and signatures begin to be obtained, there is no opportunity for modification or clarification, and if the measure qualifies for the ballot it is presented to the public on a take-it-or-leave-it basis.

For the public, the process means being called on to vote yes or no on a number of often complicated and technical ballot measures and having to decide whether the general thrust of each measure is sufficiently attractive to offset whatever portions the voter may disagree with or not understand.

For the courts, charged with responsibility for determining the constitutionality and meaning of measures, these features of the initiative process tend to complicate an already difficult task. Moreover, the measures tend to expose courts to the winds of politics more than they ought to be exposed. Initiatives, because of the unilateral nature of the drafting process and the zeal of the drafters, are much more likely to produce questions of constitutional dimension than legislatively adopted statutes. In addition, the constitutional questions generated by initiatives are much more likely to be political hot potatoes for the judicial branch.

The potatoes are hot because the initiative measure, once adopted, has behind it the political force of the electorate at large. It is one thing for a court to tell a legislature that a statute it has adopted is unconstitutional; to tell that to the people of a state who have indicated their direct support for the measure through the ballot is another. The justices of the California Supreme Court learned that lesson in 1968 when a majority of them declared that an initiative that had been adopted by a two-to-one vote of the people violated the federal Constitution. The measure in question, Proposition 14 on the 1966 ballot, not only struck down existing statutes that prohibited discrimination in housing but would have made it impermissible under the state constitution for the legislature ever to adopt such legislation again. After the California Supreme Court in *Mulkey v. Reitman* held that the measure violated the equal protection clause of the Fourteenth Amendment, there was a wave of protest against the justices responsible for the decision, and court personnel say that Chief Justice Traynor, who was to appear on the coming ballot for confirmation of an additional term on the court, had his bags packed in anticipation of an adverse vote. As it turned out, he and the other justices on the ballot were confirmed, but by far less of the electorate (65 percent rather than 85 percent) than had been typical in prior judicial elections.

Often, before an election at which an initiative is to appear on the ballot, opponents seek an order from the court to keep it off for some legal reason. That process generates a good deal of political heat, particularly if some of the justices are to be on the ballot themselves. One might argue that in a situation like that presented by Proposition 14 it would be better for the court to keep the measure off the ballot in the first place, if it "knew" it was going to hold the measure unconstitutional, rather than expose the institution to the risk of having to decide the constitutional issue in the face of a popular mandate. Indeed, one might argue that in such a situation the public would be better off, as well, to be spared the time and expense of an ultimately futile initiative campaign.

But there are two countervailing arguments. One is political, or institutional, in nature. A court that intervenes to keep a measure off the ballot is perceived as obstructing the expression of the popular will. In addition, if the measure is highly controversial, and particularly if it has partisan overtones, it is inevitable that its supporters will charge the court with acting for "political" reasons. This occurred twice when I was on the court—once when we ordered the secretary of state to omit from the ballot a measure that would have established a new redistricting scheme for elections throughout the state, and a second time when we ordered her to leave off a measure that would have registered voter support for a balanced-budget amendment to the federal Constitution. In support of the charge that our actions were politically motivated, some pointed to the fact that Justice Frank Richardson, the lone Republican appointee to the court at that time, dissented, but presumably those who make that argument would not infer that *his* action was so motivated. I would not make that inference either. I voted as I did because I thought there were sound legal reasons for doing so, and I assume that is true of my colleagues. But there is no question that a court that undertakes to block voting on an initiative runs an institutional risk. Whether that risk is any less if the court waits until after the election and then declares the initiative invalid is another matter; but of course there is the possibility that the initiative will not pass, in which instance the court will not have to decide the issue at all.

The second reason for a court to move cautiously in considering a preelection challenge to an initiative is that the decisional process is likely to be enhanced if evaluation of the challenge is deferred until after the election. Considerations relevant to the constitutional issue may develop in the course of the campaign itself—as they did in the case of the challenge to Proposition 14, in which the court relied in part on campaign arguments to demonstrate the intent underlying the proposition. Moreover, the timing of a preelection challenge seldom leaves room for the studied consideration appropriate to decision of an important legal issue.

Out of these conflicting considerations has developed a distinction that is a bit rough but nevertheless useful. A court will not intervene before an election to decide a constitutional challenge to the *substance* of an initiative measure. As in the case of Proposition 14, it will wait until the measure is adopted even though it may generate greater institutional stress by holding the measure unconstitutional at that time. A court will, however, intervene before an election to consider *procedural* objections to a measure, such as that it is not supported by a petition with the requisite number of signatures. It also will intervene to consider an objection that the *subject matter* of the measure, without regard to its merits, is not appropriate to the initiative process. This was the basis, for example, of the court's decision to keep the redistricting initiative off the ballot. The state constitution provided that there could be but one redistricting per decade, and the initiative (quite apart from its substance) would have violated that prohibition.

Let us return now to Proposition 8, the so-called Victims' Bill of Rights. There was, as I have indicated, an enormous political force behind that initiative. There was also substantial opposition from groups such as the American Civil Liberties Union and the criminal defense bar. Leading San Francisco lawyers undertook *pro bono* to translate that opposition into legal confrontation. Prior to the election of 1982 lawyers filed a petition with the California Supreme Court asking it to keep Proposition 8 off the ballot primarily on the ground that it violated the single-subject rule of the state constitution.

The California constitution contains a provision that reads, "An initiative measure embracing more than one subject may not be submitted to the electors or have any effect." The original version of that provision was itself the product of a constitutional amendment adopted in 1948, apparently in response to a series of colorful initiative measures known as ham-and-egg proposals, which held out to California voters the promise of a bit of something for nearly everyone. According to Professor Lowenstein of the UCLA Law School, the immediate stimulus for the single-subject amendment was a 1948 "bill of rights" measure that was described by the attorney general as follows:

> Establishes 2 percent tax on gross receipts of all kinds. Legalizes, licenses, and taxes bookmaking and other gambling. Abolishes all other State and local taxes and fees. Provides minimum monthly re-

tirement pensions of $100 until July 1952, $130 thereafter, plus increases proportioned to cost-of-living increases since 1944, payable to aged persons, permanently disabled persons, widows, clergymen, teachers. Provides temporary disability and burial benefits. Regulates oleomargarine, certain healing arts, civic centers, public lands, water pollution, surface mining. Reapportions State Senate. Prohibits primary election cross-filing.

The California Supreme Court kept that 1948 measure off the ballot on the ground that it was a constitutional "revision" rather than an "amendment." The single-subject rule came into effect after that decision, but as of October 1982, when the challenge to Proposition 8 reached the court, there had been no case in which the single-subject rule was found to invalidate an initiative measure. There had been challenges under the single-subject rule during that period, but the court in each case had sustained the measure, interpreting the rule to require only that the provisions of the measure be "reasonably germane" to one another.

The court was not unanimous in these cases, however. The "reasonably germane" test was one that the court borrowed from cases applying a similar constitutional requirement that legislative enactments be limited to a single subject, and some of the justices believed that the analogy was inappropriate. Justice Wiley Manuel was the leader in that view. He believed that the opportunity for compromise and modification in the legislative process warranted a more relaxed application of the single-subject requirement, whereas in the initiative process a more stringent application was appropriate to protect voters against undue complexity and against a distortion of the popular will through political logrolling in which a majority of votes is garnered by offering something for everyone. Justice Manuel proposed, and a minority of other justices accepted, a requirement that in order to pass the single-subject test, the various provisions of an initiative be not merely "reasonably germane" to one another but also "functionally related" to one another.

In the case of Proposition 8 a majority of the court declined to rule on the single-subject challenge prior to the election, though a dissenting minority argued (I think correctly) that in light of the purpose of the single-subject rule and its flat declaration that an initiative measure embracing more than a single subject "may not be submitted to the electors," a challenge under that rule is pecu-

liarly appropriate to preelection adjudication. After Proposition 8
passed, the challenge was renewed, and it came initially to Division Two of the Court of Appeal, on which I served as presiding
justice. Opponents were seeking a temporary stay of the measure
pending our determination of its validity, and of course they hoped
that ultimately we would determine that the measure was invalid.

The pendency of a matter of such enormous statewide importance created unusual excitement and tension around my chambers. While we were deciding on the appropriate procedure, I was
frequently visited—every half hour, or so it seemed—by my colleagues and by law clerks with ideas as to what we should do
and how we should go about doing it. Preliminary study suggested
that Proposition 8 would undoubtedly violate the single-subject
rule if Wiley Manuel's functional-relationship test were applied:
there appeared to be no such relationship, for example, between
the proposition's provisions relating to the admissibility of evidence and those relating to the insanity defense. But as an intermediate appellate court we were not free to apply that test unless
and until the California Supreme Court adopted it. Under the more
flexible "reasonably germane" test it seemed a close question. With
the possible exception of the "safe schools" provision, the various
parts of Proposition 8 were undoubtedly "germane" to the general
subject of criminal justice; but the questions were whether a subject
that general could provide the degree of coherence the single-
subject rule requires, and if so, whether the presence of the "safe
schools" provision served to invalidate the measure under that rule.

I am not sure how the issue would have come out if the matter
had stayed in my court. As it happened, the attorney general requested that the Supreme Court assume immediate jurisdiction
over the case, on the theory that a matter of such significance
would inevitably end up in the court's lap sooner or later and that
in light of the uncertainty that was affecting hundreds of cases in
the trial courts, the sooner it did, the better. The Supreme Court
agreed. I cannot say that I was disappointed.

After oral arguments and the consideration of voluminous briefs,
the Supreme Court ultimately adhered to the "reasonably germane" test and (over vigorous dissents) sustained the validity of
Proposition 8 on that basis. I have asked myself how I would have
voted had I been on the court. In principle I am attracted to Justice

Manuel's proposal for the more stringent functional-relationship standard. That standard has the virtue of at least providing some guidance and predictability not only for the courts but also for the drafters of legislation, whereas the "reasonably germane" test is a weak one, almost wholly lacking in principled content. Moreover, I agree with Justice Manuel's argument about the differences between the legislative and initiative processes, and I believe the functional-relationship test best serves the policies underlying the single-subject rule in the initiative arena. This test as applied to Proposition 8 would have required separate initiatives for each portion of the proposition, but on balance I believe it would achieve a better result, one more consistent with the objectives of the single-subject rule, than forcing the voters to accept or reject a package that contains numerous parts linked only by their common relationship to a general subject.

In any event, the Supreme Court decision upholding the validity of Proposition 8 against the single-subject challenge was only the camel's nose. The humps were soon to follow, and they consisted of legal battles over the constitutionality or meaning of nearly every one of the proposition's provisions. These battles continued for at least four years—throughout my tenure on the court—and along with death penalty cases (which also involved an initiative measure) they tended to dominate our agenda. What was much worse, they caused immeasurable confusion and delay in the trial courts, which had to act without definitive appellate guidance. When they acted "wrongly"—that is, when they failed to anticipate the ultimate resolution of the legal issue—the result was often reversal, with the attendant expense and delay.

The sort of problem presented by a complex initiative measure is best illustrated in a case in which I wound up writing the opinion for the court. The case, *People v. Skinner,* involved the test to be used for defining insanity as a defense in a criminal trial. Prior to 1978 California used the so-called *McNaghten* rule, named after an 1843 decision by the English House of Lords in *McNaghten's Case.* Under that rule, it was said that a person was insane, in the sense that he could not be held criminally responsible for his conduct, if as a result of some "disease of the mind" either of two conditions existed: (1) he did not know the "nature and quality of the act he was doing," or (2) he did not know he was doing what was "wrong."

The first prong of the *McNaghten* rule had to do with situations in which the defendant was so deranged as not to be aware, for example, that putting a knife into someone's heart would result in death. The second had to do with situations in which the defendant was incapable of comprehending that it was wrong to kill.

In recent times the *McNaghten* rule has come under a good deal of criticism for its failure to take into account the lessons of modern psychiatry, and courts in a number of states have moved to adopt a new test of insanity recommended by the prestigious American Law Institute (ALI). The new test, generally regarded as more humane, recognizes that a person might know what he is doing, and that what he is doing is wrong, but by reason of mental disease or defect be lacking in substantial capacity to conform his conduct to the requirements of the law.

The California Supreme Court adopted the ALI test in 1978 in *People v. Drew*, but there were those in the law enforcement community who believed that the *McNaghten* rule was better (or at least better for the prosecution), and so they included in the Proposition 8 menu a provision apparently designed to overrule *Drew* and reinstate *McNaghten*. The language they drafted, however, went beyond that. It required a defendant asserting an insanity defense to show that he or she was "incapable of knowing or understanding the nature and quality of his or her act *and* of distinguishing right from wrong at the time of the commission of the offense" [emphasis mine].

By using the conjunctive *and* instead of the disjunctive *or*, Proposition 8, read literally, would modify the *McNaghten* rule by denying the insanity defense to a defendant who was incapable of distinguishing right from wrong even though aware of the nature and quality of his or her act. In fact, that is exactly how the trial judge in *People v. Skinner* construed the language of the proposition. Jesse Skinner was a patient at Camarillo State Hospital suffering from paranoid schizophrenia. A delusional product of his illness was a belief that the words "till death us do part" bestows on a marriage partner a God-given right to kill the other partner if he or she has violated, or was inclined to violate, the marriage vows and that because the vows reflect the direct wishes of God, the killing is with complete moral and criminal impunity. On a day pass from the hospital, he strangled his wife.

Skinner's attorney submitted the insanity defense to a judge without a jury, and the judge agreed that under the second prong of the *McNaghten* rule the defendant was incapable of knowing right from wrong. He also concluded, however, that Skinner was aware of the nature and quality of his act—that is, he knew that he was killing his wife by strangling her—so that under a literal reading of Proposition 8 the insanity defense was not available to him.

In the abstract the question before our court was whether to regard the *and* in Proposition 8 as an intentional modification of the *McNaghten* rule or as a drafting error. But that way of putting the issue tends to cover up a deeper problem. The concept of intent is often pretty spongy in the case of a legislative enactment, but in the case of initiatives it is even spongier. When one is interpreting an initiative measure, there are no committee reports or earlier bills, which often are useful in understanding the background of a statute; there is only the language of the initiative itself and what the voters were told in the ballot pamphlet. One might look to other sources of information, such as speeches, newspaper articles, or television advertisements, but there is no way of knowing how many voters read or saw these, nor is there any principled way of deciding which among the various messages which bombarded voters in the course of an initiative campaign should be regarded as authoritative with respect to the voters' understanding of the measure. For that matter, there is no way of knowing how many voters read the ballot pamphlet, though studies suggest the percentage is very low. Neither is there any reason to believe that all or a majority of persons who voted for a measure did so with the same "intent" as to the meaning of particular provisions.

Proposition 8 as it related to the *Skinner* case illustrates the problem. The fact is that *nothing* in the ballot arguments for or against the proposition made any mention of the provision on the insanity defense, and the attorney general's summary of the proposition simply advised that it contained a provision "regarding . . . proof of insanity." Comments by the legislative analyst included no more than the observation that the provision "could increase the difficulty of proving that a person is not guilty by reason of insanity."

That any significant number of those who voted for the Proposition 8 package were aware of the difference between the *McNaghten* rule and the *Drew* test, much less of the subtle distinction between the two prongs of the *McNaghten* rule, seems on any realistic appraisal to be highly dubious. There were, however, two considerations that led our court—with only the chief justice dissenting—to the conclusion that the insanity provision should not be read literally. One was that if it were the purpose of the provision not only to get rid of *Drew* but also to modify the *McNaghten* rule in such a fundamental way, we would expect that such a purpose would have been made known to the voters in some more instructive fashion. The other was that a literal reading of the provision would pose serious constitutional questions regarding the propriety, under the due process clause, of imposing criminal sanctions on someone incapable of understanding that what he or she is doing is wrong. With that explanation (and with the observation that Proposition 8 contained other obvious drafting errors) we concluded that the insanity provision of Proposition 8 should be construed in accordance with what seemed to be its purpose—to get rid of *Drew* and restore the *McNaghten* rule in all its dubious glory.

Justice Mosk wrote a concurring opinion in *Skinner* that summarized the problem:

> I am convinced that the use of "and" instead of "or" would have been discovered in the traditional legislative process. In an assembly committee, on the floor of the assembly committee, in a senate committee, on the floor of the senate, in the Governor's veto opportunity, such inadvertence would likely have been detected, or if the choice of words was deliberate, such intent would have been clearly declared. In an initiative measure, however, no revision opportunity is possible and no legislative intent is available; the voter has only the choice of an enigmatic all or nothing.

Among the other Proposition 8 cases that came before the court, the one that gave me the greatest concern over its result was *In re Lance W.* Lance, sixteen years old, was accused of possessing marijuana for sale. The prosecution wanted to use certain evidence (a small bag of marijuana) that they had obtained in a search of a pickup truck. The problem was that when the police searched the truck they had insufficient grounds (no "probable cause") for believing that they would find contraband, so that under long-established precedent in federal and state courts the search was unconstitutional. On that basis, the defense lawyers asked that the bag be excluded from evidence.

The general rule in both federal and state courts is that illegally obtained evidence is not admissible. If it were admissible, so the argument goes, then police would be tempted to violate the right of people to be free from unreasonable or warrantless searches, and the criminal justice system would be tainted by a reliance on evidence obtained in a manner that offends constitutional principles. But the United States Supreme Court developed an exception to the general rule: a person who seeks to exclude evidence on the ground that it was obtained illegally may do so only if it was his or her *own* privacy that was invaded by the illegal search. In Lance's case the search of the pickup truck did not violate the defendant's privacy, since he did not own the truck and was not in it at the time. Therefore, under the federal rule Lance had no "standing" to force exclusion of the evidence.

Under California law, however—or at least under California law prior to Proposition 8—Lance did have standing because California courts had interpreted the state constitution to impose independent and more exacting standards than the federal Constitution with respect to the protection of privacy, and because California courts had decided that the constitutional principles could best be served by excluding what the police had obtained through an illegal search, whether the object of that search was the defendant or someone else.

At issue in *In re Lance W.* was the impact on the more generous California exclusionary rule of Proposition 8, and specifically a section of Proposition 8 that declared (with certain stated exceptions) that "relevant evidence shall not be excluded in any criminal proceeding." The provision made exception for traditional evidentiary rules such as those excluding hearsay evidence or evidence subject to some privilege (like the confidentiality of a client's communication with his or her attorney), and it continued to allow trial courts to exclude evidence that was more prejudicial than relevant. But these exceptions aside, the command of the proposition appeared to be quite sweeping.

It seemed fairly clear from the language itself that the drafters of the initiative meant it to do away with the exclusionary rule—at least to the extent that could be done without offending the federal Constitution. Indeed, it was difficult to imagine, and no one suggested to the court, any other meaning for the initiative's language.

Moreover, the legislative analyst, in his analysis of the proposition, which appeared as part of the ballot pamphlet, advised as follows:

> Under current law, certain evidence is not permitted to be presented in a criminal trial or hearing. For example, evidence obtained through unlawful eavesdropping or wiretapping, or through unlawful searches of persons or property, cannot be used in court. This measure generally would allow most relevant evidence to be presented in criminal cases, subject to such exceptions as the Legislature may in the future enact by a two-thirds vote. The measure could not affect federal restrictions on the use of evidence.

The upshot seemed to be that after Proposition 8 evidence could not be excluded in a criminal trial on the ground that it had been obtained illegally unless its exclusion was mandated by the federal Constitution, and since under federal rules Lance had no standing to object to the evidence seized from the truck, that evidence could be used against him. That is what we held, but our opinion stood for a broader principle: after Proposition 8 the state constitutional provisions on privacy, or unreasonable searches and seizures, could no longer be the basis for excluding evidence.

It was not an easy decision, and it is one that still troubles me when I think about it. I believed that it was desirable to allow room for the development and application of a state-based exclusionary rule to give effect to the broader privacy protection that had developed under the state constitution, and that the apparent goal of Proposition 8 to eliminate independent state grounds for the exclusion of such evidence was bad policy. But that was not my decision to make, and I was not persuaded by the argument of my dissenting colleagues that to be accepted as eliminating the state exclusionary rule the initiative measure would have had to refer specifically to the constitutional provisions implicated in that effect. That would have been a novel rule, and for a number of reasons not a very workable one. But I do wonder whether the average voter understood the import of what he or she was voting on. In more general terms, I wonder how well the voter is served by the initiative process in its present form.

A number of California initiative measures have posed similar problems. One assumes that those who voted for Proposition 13 knew that it would bring about a substantial cut in property taxes, but it is questionable whether they were aware of the intricacies of language that were to produce dozens of court opinions before the dust finally settled. And the death penalty initiative of 1978, which superseded a carefully drafted legislative enactment, contained problems (as its drafters have since recognized) that hampered, rather than facilitated, the voters' desire to implement capital punishment.

Some of the problems posed by an initiative like Proposition 8 could be reduced by a stricter application of the single-subject test so that voters would have more of an opportunity to focus on truly independent proposals. That would not, however, solve the sort of drafting problems that Justice Mosk alluded to in his *Skinner* concurrence.

One idea for reform that might have merit would be to require that the proponents of an initiative measure submit the draft (before it is circulated for signatures) to an impartial state agency for a legal opinion, which would point out potential areas of litigation that could be resolved by more precise drafting. In California the Office of Legislative Counsel, which advises the legislature in the drafting of statutes, now has the authority to advise proponents of initiative measures, and this step could be made mandatory. Or, if it is thought that the use of that office might compromise the independence of the initiative process from the legislature, the services of the California Law Revision Commission could be solicited. Time limits would have to be established within which the agency would render an opinion so as not to delay the initiative measure, and it would have to be clear that the views of the agency on the drafting of the measure would not affect the right of its proponents to proceed as they see fit. In other words, it would be up to the proponents to decide what, if anything, to do about the advice they received from the agency. That advice, however, would be made public so that if the drafters chose not to heed it, the opponents could call that fact, and whatever problems the agency might have identified, to the attention of the voters. Such a system would surely not avoid all drafting problems; even carefully drafted legislative enactments often fail to anticipate the kinds of problems that might arise. But it might ameliorate a major flaw in what is otherwise an important and useful part of our democratic tradition.

A more substantial reform would be to require proponents of an initiative to submit it first to the legislature for its consideration and possible action before it is placed on the ballot. The legislature would then have an opportunity to review the proposal carefully and either adopt it as presented, adopt it with modifications, submit a substitute measure to the voters, or of course take no action; but nothing the legislature might do (short of adoption) would preclude the proponents from proceeding with the initiative after a specified period. Such an indirect initiative used to exist in California on an optional basis, but it was eliminated because of nonuse. Its reinstitution on a mandatory basis, subject to safeguards assuring rapid legislative consideration, would be a substantial improvement.

8

State Constitutions

In downtown Monterey, California, within walking distance of Fisherman's Wharf, stands a spacious building of yellow sandstone called Colton Hall. The first floor housed one of California's first public schools. On the second floor is a room, about sixty feet long and twenty-five feet wide, with a railing across the middle and four long tables. It is not a particularly imposing setting, but here, in September 1849, California history was made.

On the first day of that month delegates from various parts of what was soon to become the thirty-ninth state of the Union came together in that room in response to a call for a constitutional convention. It was a tumultuous period in California. People were coming by the thousands in search of fortune, fame, freedom, or whatever it is that inspires adventuresome people to pick up their belongings and try their luck in a new and strange land. There was no generally applicable law, no centralized government, nothing but an accumulation of small and isolated communities stretching from burgeoning San Francisco in the north to the pueblo of Los Angeles in the south, from the coast to the foothills where it was said there was still much gold to be found. Authority, to the extent it existed at all, resided in a de facto military government and in makeshift local arrangements, largely of the vigilante variety. It was apparent to everyone who thought about such things that there needed to be some orderly governance, but the Congress of the United States, anxious about having to confront the slavery issue in a new territory, was sitting on its hands.

It was Brigadier General Bennett Riley, the de facto military governor, who was responsible for the remarkable gathering in Monterey. He had issued the call for a constitutional convention, decreeing that delegates should be chosen at grass-roots meetings in the mining camps and communities throughout the land. To many observers such a convention seemed an unlikely prospect, but almost at the last minute it actually happened. And there they were, arriving by boat, carriage, and horseback, ready to participate in a process that was to provide the legal structure for California's participation in the Union.

They must have been a strange-looking group; they were certainly diverse. Some had lived in California all their lives—these were the "Californios," the Spaniards, with names like Valleo, De la Guerra, Carillo, and Covarrubias. Most of them, however, were newcomers—miners, lawyers, physicians, farmers, businessmen, trackers—who had come to California from the East Coast or, like John Sutter and William Shannon, from places as far away as Switzerland and Ireland. The oldest among them was fifty-three, the youngest twenty-five; the average age was thirty-six.

A historian of the event, Rockwell Hunt, was to observe, "It may be doubted if the members of any previous convention in the United States, with similar purpose, ever came together so totally unacquainted with each other and so entirely wanting in general concert of plans or policies of action." No doubt that is true. But one cannot read the record of their proceedings without being impressed with their dedication and their intelligence. Some delegates had considerable experience with political matters in other states; one delegate, William M. Gwin, had served in Congress and at another state constitutional convention. Most did not have that kind of experience, but all of them took their job seriously, and they put together a document that served the new state quite well for thirty years, when a second constitutional convention was held and substantial changes were made.

One part of the 1849 constitution that was not changed in any significant respect was article 1, called the Declaration of Rights. Article 1 was in fact the first item of business at the Monterey convention after the seating of delegates. It was the product of a drafting committee, and it consists of sixteen sections. Gwin, a spokesman for the committee, reported that half the sections came from the constitution of New York and half from the constitution of Iowa. Copies of the draft were distributed to the delegates. One delegate requested an adjournment for two reasons: first, so that copies of additional state constitutions could be located and brought to the convention room; and second, so that the draft could be translated into Spanish for the benefit of the native Californians (a bit of historical irony, perhaps, in light of the initiative adopted in California in 1986 declaring piously that English is the official language of the state). Gwin explained that translations had already been made, but the convention was nevertheless adjourned until the following day.

After several days of discussion in committee, the delegates as a whole proceeded to consider one by one the sections of the Declaration of Rights. Mr. Botts, an immigrant from Virginia, rose to question some language in section 3 pertaining to freedom of religious practices and worship. The language he objected to was a proviso that "the liberty of conscience hereby secured, shall not be so construed as to excuse acts of licentiousness or justify practices inconsistent with the peace or safety of the state." What is the meaning of that language? Mr. Botts inquired. Would it authorize the legislature to outlaw the Roman Catholic church? Why not, he suggested, use "the most eloquent and beautiful" language on freedom of worship from the constitution of Virginia?

Mr. Sherwood, from New York, rose in reply. The gentleman from Virginia, he opined, was evidently not acquainted with the history of the new religious sects in the state of New York, or he would see the propriety of the restrictions contained in the proposed language. "There have been sects known there to discard all decency," warned the proper Mr. Sherwood, "and admit spiritual wives, where men and women have herded together, without any regard for the established usages of society." The restrictive language was deemed necessary, he concluded, "that society should be protected from the demoralizing influence of fanatical sects, who thought proper to discard all pretensions to decency." The proposed language was adopted over Mr. Botts's objection.

Among the delegates was a Mr. Hastings, a lawyer of sorts who also held himself out as a guide to overland routes. His qualifications in that regard may be suspect—historians of the period say he was more of a promoter, and the fact that his book on emigrant routes was relied on by the ill-fated Donner party is scarcely a recommendation—but he was a thoughtful man nonetheless, and he came forward with what must have seemed a rather startling proposal. He suggested that the committee draft be amended to outlaw capital punishment on the ground that it is as immoral for the state to take a human life as it is for an individual to do so. After what appears to have been some polite, if condescending, discussion, the amendment was defeated. The report of the proceedings does not record the vote.

And so it went. In the end the committee draft was adopted with only minor changes except for one—the addition of a provision prohibiting slavery. Some of the draft provisions received a good deal of discussion, some (at least so far as appears from the report of the proceedings) none at all. Nevertheless, for the reader interested in the relationship between state constitutions and the federal Constitution, the debate vividly illustrates two important lessons.

The first lesson is that the language of article 1 of the California constitution was deliberately drawn from the constitutions of other states, not from the United States Constitution. Despite the frequent use of language similar, and indeed in some cases identical, to that of the federal Bill of Rights, the delegates were not looking to the federal Constitution as their model. The constitution of New York, which formed the basis for roughly half the language of article 1, was adopted before the federal constitutional convention in Philadelphia. The constitution of Iowa, adopted of course after the federal convention, was an equally independent document.

The second lesson is that just as the framers of the California constitution were not looking to the federal Constitution as a model for language, neither were they looking to it as a legal basis for protecting rights and liberties from interference by the new state. At that time the federal Bill of Rights applied only to action by the federal government. It would be another twenty years before the Fourteenth Amendment would be added to the federal Constitution in order to provide protection against certain state action, and another sixty years after that before the United States Supreme Court would recognize the due process guaranty of the Fourteenth Amendment as incorporating most of the protections of the Bill of

Rights and making them applicable to the states. If anything was clear to the delegates in 1849, it was that if there were to be any constitutional protection for the rights and liberties of Californians against action by the state, it would be through the constitution they were drafting in that modest hall in Monterey.

The California constitution is of course not unique in these respects. Every state constitution has its roots in the early state constitutions that preceded the Bill of Rights, and in that historical sense every state constitution is independent of the federal Constitution. A story similar to that of the Monterey convention could be told about the constitution of every state in the Union.

The implication of this independence is of tremendous importance to the law. It means that citizens may have greater rights in some respects under the constitution of their state than under the federal Constitution. Although the federal Bill of Rights (or most of it, at least) applies to the states (through the due process clause of the Fourteenth Amendment), it establishes only a floor of protection. States are free to provide greater protection through their respective constitutions.

This has always been the case, but until the 1970s state constitutional law had been overshadowed by federal constitutional developments. It was the United States Supreme Court that took the lead in developing theories of constitutional protection for such basic rights as freedom of speech, due process of law, and equal protection of the laws. That development began in the 1920s and flourished during the era of the Warren court. Meanwhile state constitutional jurisprudence in the human rights arena was virtually nonexistent. To suggest that state courts should suddenly begin to put flesh on state constitutional skeletons after such weighty pronouncements from the high court seemed like academic chutzpah and in any event would have been of little significance. It seemed a bit artificial, if not redundant, for state courts to speak in terms of their state constitutions when so much was being said from Washington, D.C.

That was my view in 1970 when I took a leave of absence from my law practice to teach at the University of Oregon Law School in Eugene. Among the subjects I undertook to teach was constitutional law, and since I had never taught it before, I consulted an eminent colleague at the school, Hans Linde, who was a constitutional specialist. Hans was then in the process of becoming a leading advocate of the doctrine of "independent state grounds"— the technique of relying on the state constitution instead of the federal constitution—both within academic circles and later, as an associate justice of the Oregon Supreme Court, within the judiciary. He tried his best, in his extremely reasonable and logical way, to convince me of the merits of his position. Not only were state constitutions historically prior to the federal constitution, he argued, they were logically prior as well. Over time it has become accepted that courts will not decide a constitutional issue if they do not have to. When a statute is challenged as being unconstitutional, a court will confront the meaning of the statute first; if the statute can reasonably be interpreted to avoid reaching the constitutional question, that is what a court will do. This procedure is considered to be part of appropriate judicial restraint. Why shouldn't that same restraint operate within the constitutional arena? Linde demanded. If a state statute is under challenge, and there is no room for interpretation that would avoid the constitutional question, why not look first to the *state* constitution since if the statute is unconstitutional under that document, there is no need to look further. This was the essence of Linde's analytical argument.

I must say, though I am not proud of the fact, that I was resistant. It seemed a bit presumptuous, I thought, for a state court to start talking about its state constitutional protection of free speech, for example, when it had deferred for years to the high court's pronouncements on the subject. I patted Hans on the back and assured him that his theory was not without logical charm. He smiled, and waited.

In succeeding years, as the United States Supreme Court pursued a more conservative course and withdrew from some of the Warren court's interpretations of the federal Bill of Rights, the practical significance of independent state grounds became apparent. This retreat made it more attractive to explore the possibility, which had always existed, that people might have rights under the constitutions of their respective states that they did not have under the federal Constitution. In California the implications were made explicit in a constitutional amendment, adopted by voter initiative in 1974, providing as follows: "Rights guaranteed by this Constitution are not dependent on those guaranteed by the United States Constitution."

These developments accelerated the acceptance of state constitutions as independent sources of civil rights and liberties. Concomitantly, however, they laid proponents of state constitutional jurisprudence open to the charge of using state constitutional theory to bypass the United States Supreme Court in order to achieve a particular result. That was not at all Hans Linde's motivation—he was not very fond of Warren court precedents to begin with—but in that atmosphere the logical and historical arguments for the independence of state constitutions tended to get lost.

In my case it was not until I became a judge and began to look at the state constitution in the light of its history and in the context of cases I was called on to decide that I became fully persuaded of Linde's view. The reports of the first California constitutional convention are themselves adequate to convince any skeptic that the framers intended the California Declaration of Rights to stand as an independent document. Moreover, the records of the next convention, in 1878, are replete with discussions that evidence an intent to establish rights that one could argue exceeded the scope of federal protection. I decided that I simply could not be faithful to the oath I took upon becoming a judge without giving full and independent consideration to the constitution of California. I became a convert.

The significance of independent state grounds is nicely illustrated by *Pruneyard Shopping Center v. Robins*. Pruneyard is a privately owned shopping center in Campbell, California. Like most shopping centers it has parking areas, walkways, plazas, restaurants, and shops. At the time of the litigation it also had a very restrictive policy with respect to the circulation of petitions and other such activities: unless it related to the commercial purposes of the center, you could not do it.

A group of high-school students who were opposed to a United Nations resolution against Zionism put that policy to the test. On a Saturday afternoon they set up a card table in a corner of Pruneyard's central courtyard, distributed pamphlets, and asked passersby to sign petitions, which were to be sent to the president and to members of Congress. Their activity was entirely peaceful and orderly, but a security guard informed them that they were in violation of Pruneyard's policy and asked them to leave. They did, but then they filed a lawsuit to enjoin Pruneyard from denying them access.

In 1979, when that lawsuit reached the California Supreme Court, the students' legal situation under the First Amendment to the federal Constitution was extremely weak. The First Amendment says, in effect, there shall be no *law* abridging freedom of speech. In order for the amendment to apply, therefore, some governmental action is required; a private act abridging freedom of speech is not within its reach. At an earlier time, in 1968, the United States Supreme Court had held in *Food Employees v. Logan Valley Plaza* that a shopping center was a sort of town within a town and that even though privately owned, it could not absolutely preclude peaceful political activity on its premises. Four years later, however, in *Lloyd Corporation v. Tanner*, the Supreme Court repudiated that doctrine and held that the First Amendment does not apply to a shopping center; that was the state of the law when *Pruneyard* was argued.

But the students were basing their claim also on the California constitution. Though that document contains language similar to that of the First Amendment, suggesting that state action is required ("A law may not restrain or abridge liberty of speech or press"), it includes other language that does not mention state action: "Every person may freely speak; write and publish his or her sentiments on all subjects, being responsible for the abuse of this right." Partly on the basis of this difference in phrasing and partly on the basis of its finding that in California the shopping center is a particularly significant forum for the exercise of speech and petition rights, the California court, in an opinion by Justice Newman, decided that Pruneyard was in violation of the state constitutional right to free speech.

This story has a sequel. Pruneyard asked the United States Supreme Court to review the state court decision, arguing that California had violated its property rights under the federal Constitution. That court granted review but denied Pruneyard's claim. In an opinion by Justice William Rehnquist, the high court first made clear that its decision holding that a shopping center is not subject to the First Amendment in no way deprived California of the right to adopt in its own constitution "individual liberties more expansive than those conferred by the Federal Constitution." It then went on to consider, and reject, the balance of Pruneyard's claim.

The case is an important precedent in the application of independent state grounds.

Some state constitutions list rights that are not expressly mentioned in the federal Constitution. The right to privacy is the most important example. The United States Supreme Court, in *Griswold v. Connecticut*, held that the federal Constitution contains a right of privacy by *implication*, a holding that "strict constructionists" have criticized both on the ground that it reflects excessive judicial "activism" and on the ground that the right it recognized is too amorphous for principled application. In his testimony before the Senate committee considering his nomination to the Supreme Court, Judge Robert Bork emphasized the vagueness of the concept of a "right to privacy" and suggested that no thoughtful constitutional framer or voter would want to include such an amorphous right in a constitutional listing of protections citizens have against their government.

Judge Bork was apparently unaware of state constitutional developments in that respect. The Washington and Arizona state constitutions contained right-to-privacy provisions as early as 1889 and 1911, respectively. In 1972 the voters of California by initiative amended the California constitution to include privacy among the rights it declares to be "inalienable." The Alaska and Montana constitutions were amended about the same time to add similar language. Louisiana in 1975 and Florida in 1980 followed suit. Apparently, the citizens of these states believed that the word conveyed a meaning the courts could be expected to implement. And in an attempt to clarify that meaning the courts of those states have produced some interesting and important opinions.

The Supreme Court of Alaska, for example, has held that the right-to-privacy provision in that state's constitution is violated by a law prohibiting the possession of marijuana insofar as the law applied to the possession of a small amount in one's home. California courts have relied on the privacy amendment to the California state constitution in holding that public employees may not be required to submit to lie detector (polygraph) tests; that police who believe that someone is growing marijuana in his or her fenced-in backyard must have a warrant before they conduct an aerial search; and that if the state chooses to provide funding for medical procedures for the poor, it cannot withhold funding for abortions. Moreover, the California privacy provision, like the provision on freedom of speech, is phrased in terms that do not refer to action by the state, and California courts have held that its protection (unlike that of the federal Constitution) extends to invasions of privacy by institutions such as a private university. Current litigation will determine whether it may protect employees against overly intrusive methods of testing for drugs.

But even when the language in the state and federal constitutions is the same, there is no compelling reason for a state court to defer to the United States Supreme Court's interpretation of what is, after all, a different document with a different constitutional history. While I was on the California Supreme Court, a case came before us that illustrated that problem in a dramatic way. Police had obtained a defendant's confession after *Miranda* warnings had been given but while an attorney who had been retained by the defendant's friends and family was waiting at the police station to talk with him. The question was whether the police had an obligation to advise the defendant of the attorney's presence and whether their failure to do so rendered the confession inadmissible. Numerous state courts had confronted that question, and their virtually unanimous response was that the confession should not be admitted. But while the case was pending before our court, the United States Supreme Court had an almost identical case on its docket, and they managed to decide theirs first, holding 6–3 that the Fifth and Sixth amendments to the federal Constitution were no bar to admission of the confession.

There were no relevant differences in language between the California and United States constitutions, nor could we point to any distinctive history in support of a different interpretation. But the United States Supreme Court did not rely on history in support of its decision either; rather it was a matter of applying existing principles in the light of fairness and practicality. Our court said that the opinion of the United States Supreme Court in such a case was entitled to "respectful consideration"; but having given it all the consideration we thought it deserved, we found ourselves in agreement with the dissenters in the high court and with the various state courts that had confronted the issue.

The merits of the underlying issue in that case—whether police have a duty to advise a person under questioning that his or her attorney has arrived—are irrelevant to my point; namely, that in such a situation a state court should consider itself free to apply its own view of the matter. Of course, it should consider the views other courts have expressed; but there is no reason to feel constrained by the views of the United States Supreme Court as to the meaning of the federal Constitution, particularly when those views are the subject of deep division within that court itself and when the preponderance of state courts have expressed a different view. There is something to be said in favor of attempting to preserve a consensus about the meaning of core constitutional concepts such as freedom of speech and due process of law, but it is no use pretending that a consensus exists when one does not.

Indeed, a somewhat stronger argument can be made that state courts should defer to the decisions of other state courts on the meaning and application of cognate state constitutional provisions. Historically, such provisions are more likely to share a common ancestry. Moreover, as other commentators have observed, the United States Supreme Court operates within a system that imposes constraints that are either not present or not present to the same degree in state systems. In declaring the content of the Bill of Rights, the United States Supreme Court must take into account that it is providing the constitutional groundwork for fifty states. That court has acknowledged that principles of federalism—sensitivity to the authority of states to adopt their own laws—caution special restraint in that process.

The United States Supreme Court must also take into account the fact that for all practical purposes its constitutional word is final, whereas state constitutions are much more readily subject to amendment. In California, for example, the state constitution can be amended through the initiative process (as in many states), and in recent years it has been amended on several occasions to overrule judicial decisions by constitutional change. This happened after the California Supreme Court ruled in 1972 that the death penalty constituted cruel or unusual punishment within the meaning of the state constitution; it happened again in 1979 in response to rulings that the state constitution required busing to end school segregation even when the federal Constitution did not; and again in 1982 in response to rulings that the state constitution required the exclusion of evidence obtained by searches or seizures even when the evidence would be admissible under federal law. I am certainly not advocating that a state constitution be amended every time it is interpreted to mean something a majority of the voters do not like; stability in our constitutional system and respect for the interests of minorities dictates that constitutional amendment be regarded as an extreme measure. But the potential for such amendment does exist, and in all these respects the various state courts are operating within a similar political environment that is independent of the federal system.

The reliance of state courts on independent state constitutional grounds as a basis for decision has had a checkered history. Few courts are consistent in the manner in which they invoke that doctrine, and this inconsistency tends to detract from the doctrine's integrity. I participated in one case in which the California Supreme Court, before I was appointed to it, had decided that a particular jury instruction offended the federal Constitution without mentioning the state constitution. The decision seemed to be supported by United States Supreme Court precedent; but on review that court held otherwise, and sent the case back to the California Supreme Court. We were then confronted with the task of deciding whether the instruction offended the California constitution, and I joined a majority in holding that it did. In hindsight it seemed clear the court should have decided the case on that ground in the first place so as to avoid the delays inherent in the federal appeal.

In the past, state courts have at times relied on both the federal and the state constitutions as grounds for holding a particular governmental act unconstitutional. This double approach has been criticized—rightly, in my view—as operating unduly to insulate the opinion from both federal review and the political process of the state. This is so because the state court's pronouncement as to the federal Constitution, in addition to transgressing principles of judicial restraint, creates an obstacle to any attempt that might be made to amend the state constitution so as to overrule the court's interpretation. It is not an insurmountable obstacle, to be sure: the amendment could be adopted, and its constitutionality under the federal Constitution could be litigated through the United States Supreme Court. It is a practical obstacle, however, and an unjustifiable one.

I am sympathetic toward state court judges who have participated in such decisions; in fact, were others to undertake a careful
review of my own record in that light—something I have not mus-
tered the enthusiasm to do myself—they might well discover that I
am not blameless. There is an understandable temptation for state
court judges to place the responsibility on the United States Supreme Court for what might be unpopular results, especially in
criminal cases, rather than to assume responsibility themselves by
applying the constitution of their state. I think, however, that both
the public and the institution of the judiciary are best served by
forthrightness in that regard.

Despite occasional vacillations, the doctrine of independent
state grounds is clearly here to stay. Its acceptance within the legal
community is now evidenced, not only by decisions of the United
States Supreme Court, but also by the gradual emergence of law
school programs and casebooks and by academic and professional
conferences. Law students and lawyers are slowly coming to understand that if they have what they regard as a constitutional issue, it
is their responsibility to look first to the state constitution. In this
way a long-lost legacy is being regained.

PART THREE

PERSPECTIVE
AND EVALUATION

9

Do Judges Make Law?

[We want] a judge or justice who would apply the law and
interpret the law, not make the law.

Attorney General Edwin Meese

I take judge-made law as one of the realities of life.

Judge Benjamin Cardozo

The 1987 Senate hearings on the appointment of Judge Robert Bork
to the United States Supreme Court raised to an unusual level of
public consciousness a debate over questions that have inspired
political theorists and legal scholars since the beginning of organized societies. What exactly is the relationship between the judge
and the law? Is it like the relationship of a mathematician to the
principles of geometry, reasoning deductively from established ax-
ioms and postulates to solve an individual problem? Is it like that of
a construction contractor to an architect, faithfully implementing
plans and specifications? Is a judge like a baseball referee, calling
the strikes and balls as he sees them? Or is he more like a great
chef, consulting a recipe for guidance but contributing his own creativity to the final product? Is he like an author in a cooperative
writing project, or perhaps like a painter who works on a portion
of a mural? Is a judge a bureaucrat, a legislator, a village elder?
Does a good judge, a judge who conducts himself as we expect a
judge to do, simply apply rules made by others, or does he somehow have a hand (or a heart or a mind) in the process?

Some legal philosophers will tell us we cannot answer these
questions until we respond to a more fundamental question: what

is law? If, for example, we were to define law as the command of God, we would come up with a quite different model of the judicial role than if we were to define it as a body of rules contained in statutes adopted by a particular legislature, or as a body of principles inherent in the nature of man, or in some other way. But let us finesse that problem for the time being and resign ourselves to a bit of circularity by saying that for our purposes the law is that body of norms (call them rules, principles, policies, or what you will) which in our society and under our constitutions we expect judges to apply in arriving at a decision. This will not satisfy the legal philosophers, but then nothing will.

There is another obstacle that stands in the way of trying to answer broad questions about the judicial role. That obstacle arises from the diversity of functions a judge is called on to perform and the variety of contexts in which that performance occurs. To the extent that there is public debate over "activism" and "restraint" on the part of judges, it is likely to focus in modern times on the function of judicial review in the constitutional arena—the process by which judges are called on to review statutes or other governmental acts and decide whether they pass constitutional muster. Scholars tend toward the same focus; those who write about what courts do are captivated by what has been called the Madisonian dilemma: in a society in which the majority generally decides what is "right," how do we explain an institution that gets to declare the majority "wrong"?

Constitutional review is perhaps the most important duty judges have; but it is not their only duty, and in the state system it represents a relatively small percentage of judicial activity. To use constitutional review as the model for the judicial function, particularly as regards state courts, tends to distort the picture.

Further distortion occurs when legal theorists fail (as they sometimes do) to distinguish among the various levels of the judicial system. Lower courts are obliged by the rules of the system to follow decisions of higher courts, and when it comes to issues involving the federal Constitution, or federal statutes or treaties, state courts are obligated to abide by the rulings of the United States Supreme Court. Judges on a lower court may grumble about a ruling by a higher court, privately or even publicly; as a justice on the Court of Appeal I would occasionally write or join an opinion that suggested—politely, of course—that some Supreme Court decision fell substantially short of legal perfection. But lower-court judges are not allowed to say, We don't like that opinion, and we won't follow it. Any judge who did that would likely be summarily reversed, or worse. There may be, and often is, room for a lower court to maneuver within the precedents, to be sure, but the constraints that operate at the lower echelons of the system are greater than those at the top, and any description of the judicial role must take that factor into account.

A realistic jurisprudence, then, would focus on discrete functions and arenas, exploring diversity as well as unity in the judicial process—an effort, I hasten to add, well beyond the scope of this modest discussion, if not of the author's competence. What this chapter does attempt is a general description of some of the theories that others have advanced, as well as some of my own perspective, in describing the judicial role within each of the three main sources of law in our system: the common law, statutes, and constitutions.

THE COMMON LAW

In chapter 5 I tried to convey something of the dynamic quality of the common-law process—how it produces legal norms that change and grow over time. It seems rather obvious that this product is "judge-made law," not only in the sense that it was originally made by courts rather than by legislatures, but also in the sense that it is continually being remade through a process of evolution.

This dynamic view of the common law, however, is a relatively modern one. During the eighteenth century, in this country as well as in England, the most influential writer on the law was Sir William Blackstone; his *Commentaries on the Laws of England* was in every lawyer's office as well as in the library used by the framers of the United States Constitution. Blackstone came as close as anyone ever has to saying that "the law" has an existence independent of what judges do, so that judges simply find the law and have no hand in making it. The common law consisted in his view of established customs of the realm and of maxims that in turn derive their authority from custom. It is the obligation of judges to know these customs and maxims through study of prior decisions and the application of reason. "[Judges] are the depositary of the laws; the living oracles," Blackstone wrote, and each judge is "sworn to determine, not according to his own private judgment, but according to the known laws and customs of the land; not delegated to pronounce a new law, but to maintain and expound the old one." The conception of the common law that emerged from Blackstone's writings thus tended to be static and at the same time "formalistic"; that is, it viewed law as a closed body of rules and principles that yields answers primarily through the application of logic. It was not a conception likely to survive in a dynamic and pragmatic environment.

One of the first to strike a blow at formalism in this country was a lawyer by the name of Oliver Wendell Holmes, Jr. A veteran of the Civil War, a graduate of, and lecturer at, Harvard Law School poised on the brink of a judicial career that was to make him one of the most famous judges of all time, Holmes in 1880 published *The Common Law*, a book that was to establish his reputation as a great legal scholar. It is one of those books that is seldom read but often quoted. With numerous examples Holmes demonstrated the capacity of the common law for change and growth and emphasized the choices judges must make in that process while taking into account the impact of law on society.

Seventeen years later Holmes, now a justice of the Supreme Judicial Court of Massachusetts, was invited to give a lecture at the ground breaking for Boston University Law School, and he chose the occasion to expand on his earlier theme. That 1897 lecture, published under the title "The Path of the Law," has had profound influence on American thinking about the law and the judicial process.

Holmes first asserted that it was necessary to distinguish, for purposes of analysis, between law and morality—a distinction characteristic of the positivist school of jurisprudence of which Holmes was a leading exponent. In that connection he argued for a definition of the law as nothing more than a *prediction* of how the courts would decide a particular case. He then proceeded to inquire into the forces that determine the content and growth of the law, and his answer to that inquiry put him in direct opposition to the Blackstonian view.

It is a fallacy, Holmes argued, to assert that the only force at work in the development of the law is logic, as if when judges disagree, it is because one of them is not doing his sums right. Holmes did not deny that logic plays a role in judicial thinking and that the language of judicial decision is mainly the language of logic, for "the logical method and form flatter that longing for certainty and for repose which is in every human mind." But the truth, Holmes argued, is that behind the form of logic lies the necessity for value judgments—or, as he put it, for "a judgment as to the relative worth and importance of competing legislative grounds." Courts must make choices between one rule and another, or among differing interpretations of a rule, and such choices must take into account some conception of the public good. "I think that the judges themselves have failed adequately to recognize their duty of weighing considerations of social advantage," Holmes wrote. "The duty is inevitable, and the result of the often proclaimed judicial aversion to deal with such considerations is simply to leave the very ground and foundation of judgments inarticulate, and often unconscious."

Holmes's candor about the judicial role came as a breath of fresh air to American legal scholarship, and his pragmatic emphasis—"the life of the law is not logic, but experience," he said in one of his famous aphorisms—appealed strongly to the American mind. But his writings raised at least as many questions as they answered. Granted that logic alone could not explain all aspects of judging, what were these "considerations of social advantage" that judges were supposed to weigh? Where were judges to find them? And were they the only factor, other than logic, that judges were expected to consider? What Holmes had to say in his "Path of the Law" was of great importance, but what he did not say served as a challenge for those to come.

The challenge was accepted, with characteristic humility, by another great judge, Benjamin Cardozo. He had much in common with Holmes: both were great state court judges, both came to be appointed to the United States Supreme Court, both were interested in the theoretical aspects of the law, and both found in formalism an inadequate explanation of what judges do. But in temperament and perspective they were quite different. Cardozo was introspective, and the view of the law he sought to convey was from the inside rather than from the stance of the dispassionate spectator.

In 1921, while serving on the New York Court of Appeal, Cardozo was invited to give a series of lectures at Yale Law School on the process of appellate judging. Before the lectures began, Cardozo commented that he did not believe anyone would be greatly interested, and apparently Yale was of the same view, for they were scheduled in one of the smaller classrooms. But contrary to expectations the crowds increased until finally the lectures had to be rescheduled in the largest auditorium available. Published under the title "The Nature of the Judicial Process," they represent one of the most remarkable ventures in legal history.

Adherence to precedent is important, Cardozo said, in order to provide stability and predictability in the law and in order that like cases be treated alike. But often precedent is absent or unclear, and sometimes it even has to be changed. Prior decisions may contain useful principles, but judges must decide how they are to be applied—or, to follow Cardozo's dynamic wording, how they are to *develop*, for their application in a particular case establishes a norm that points to the future as well as draws on the past. That judges make law through the interpretation and reinterpretation of precedent, and on occasion by overruling precedent, seemed obvious to Cardozo; one has only to look at his own decision in *MacPherson v. Buick* five years earlier (see chapter 5). The question for him was how and on the basis of what factors judges go about doing that. Cardozo himself put it in more personal terms: "What is it that I do when I decide a case?"

Cardozo identified four ingredients in what he called the "compound which is brewed daily in the caldron of the courts." One was logic, or the method of philosophy—the traditional common-law approach of proceeding by analogy, of pointing to a similar case that has already been decided. But all cases are similar in some respect, and at the same time no two cases are exactly alike. A judge must determine what differences are relevant to the outcome, and that determination cannot be made on the basis of logic alone. Pure logic will not tell us, for example, whether a car is sufficiently similar to poison or explosives such that the same rule of liability should apply. Like Holmes, Cardozo recognized that logic has its limits.

History and custom were two more ingredients in Cardozo's recipe. It is necessary for courts to look to the historical roots of legal doctrines in order to understand them and provide for evolutionary development. And the customs of the community, which for Blackstone constituted the very backbone of the common law, were to be considered as well. These Cardozo referred to as the methods of evolution and tradition.

But the dominant ingredient in Cardozo's view of the judicial process was something he called at times "morals and social welfare" and at other times simply "social justice." What Cardozo meant by these terms was an idea similar to Holmes's "considerations of social advantage," except that Cardozo's conception was broader. Holmes wanted to exclude all talk of morality from the law and speak only in utilitarian terms about what was good for the society as a whole, whereas Cardozo was comfortable with the notion that courts may, even must, take moral considerations ("standards of right conduct") into account in deciding on the evolution of a legal principle.

Cardozo, however, made what was to become a most important distinction in American jurisprudence: what a judge should look to for guidance is not his or her own private morality but the mores of the community. As Cardozo recognized, it is not an easy distinction to maintain; some blurring of the subjective and the objective is inevitable. Judges no more than others can entirely escape "the likes and the dislikes, the predilections and the prejudices, the complex of instincts and emotions and habits and convictions, which make the man." Nonetheless, a judge "would err if he were to impose upon the community as a rule of life his own idiosyncrasies of conduct or belief." Rather, "it is the customary morality of right-minded men and women which he is to enforce by his decree."

While Cardozo's recipe for decision making may have been richer than that of Holmes, they shared the insight that in some sense judges in the common-law system do not simply find the law but help make it, and that insight had a major impact on the development of American jurisprudential thought. In the 1920s and 1930s a generation of legal scholars who came to call themselves Legal Realists entered through the door Holmes and Cardozo had opened, intent on exploring by a variety of techniques the "real"

ground of judicial decision making. Some, like Jerome Frank, invoked psychoanalytic theory to examine the unconscious forces at
work. Others, like Karl Llewelyn, were interested in the role of custom—in his case, custom among merchants. Some, like the great
contract law scholar Arthur Corbin, focused on appellate opinions
to demonstrate that the facts of particular cases were more important than the generalized legal concepts courts used to explain
the outcome. Philosophers like Felix Cohen provided analytical
support.

Yale Law School was the home of the Legal Realists, and when I
attended in the early 1950s their presence and influence, pervasive
and exciting, were still a part of the school's atmosphere. Frank,
Cohen, and Corbin were still there, along with younger professors
whose views tended to the iconoclastic. The study of the law, we
were taught, is not simply the study of legal rules and concepts;
lawyers and judges must also know about society and the way in
which law and society interact. "Public policy" was the magic
phrase. (We used to say that when a Harvard law student did not
know the answer to an exam question, he would talk about "equi-
table estoppel"; a Yalie would invoke "public policy.") Judges as
well as legislators cannot avoid making decisions as to public policy, and therefore it is best that they do so with awareness and
candor.

There was to some extent in Legal Realism a naiveté about the
extent of community agreement on matters of public policy and
about the lessons to be learned from the social sciences. Still, much
debate about the law *is* capable of being channeled into pragmatic
questions about what means are most appropriate to achieve ends
we share, and those responsible for developing the law would certainly be foolish to turn their backs on any information that would
provide useful answers. By bringing that potential into focus, as
well as by ventilating stale notions as to the nature of law and the
judicial process, the Legal Realists made enormous contributions
to our understanding.

The contemporary approach to research and teaching in law
tends to emphasize the relationship between law and other disci-
plines, and this is an outgrowth of the Legal Realist movement.
One finds in the curricula of major law schools courses entitled
Law and Psychiatry, Law and Sociology, Law and Medicine, and of

course Law and Economics. Indeed, over the last two decades it has been the economists who have moved to center stage. Some of them even seem to believe that their discipline is capable of answering the most profound questions of ultimate value through the touchstone of economic "efficiency," as if there were no other ends worthy of societal attention. Other economists, more modest, contend only—and quite properly—that economics can be a powerful and useful tool in the analysis of the sorts of issues that both courts and legislatures have to decide.

Here, however, we come to Grodin's law of ideological dynamics, which says: give any good idea enough time, and it will be carried to absurd extremes. So it was with Legal Realism. That aspect of Legal Realism that focused on the judicial process and insisted quite correctly that there is a lot more to it than pure logic—that there are value judgments to be made and that a judge's own background and experience are likely to play some role in the making of those judgments—came in some quarters to be reduced to the simplistic proposition that judging involves nothing more than the personal predilections, conscious or otherwise, of the individual judge. I call this the ice cream theory of jurisprudence—some judges like chocolate, others vanilla: it is all a matter of taste. Indeed, some of the Legal Realists who surely knew better—Jerome Frank, for example—on occasion wrote and said things that gave impetus to that form of reductionism.

A variation on that reductionist theme came to be elaborated in the 1960s and 1970s by a group of legal scholars centered at Harvard Law School known as the Critical Legal Studies movement. The Crits, as they are called, have made some valuable contributions to the understanding of law in relation to society—they have a utopian, communitarian agenda—but one finds throughout their work a theme of "deconstruction" that bears close resemblance to what the Legal Realists wrote in their more flagrant moods. The law, they say, whether it is "made" in the legislature or in the courts, is nothing but politics, and legal rules and principles are nothing but a rationalization for decisions that are ultimately political, reflecting the values of a capitalist society.

It is important to understand the implications of such a reductionist view. It is one thing to say that the reasons courts give for decisions do not reflect the totality of factors affecting the result—

that the judge, either consciously or unconsciously, is likely to be influenced by considerations that he or she does not (and perhaps cannot) articulate. It is another thing to say that such reasons, usually founded in statutes, precedents, or constitutional principles, have nothing at all to do with the result—that they are pure rationalization, and nothing more. It was this sort of reductionism that Cardozo had in mind when he spoke of those who believe that "law never is, but is always about to be. It is realized only when embodied in a judgment, and in being realized, expires. There are no such things as rules or principles: there are only isolated dooms."

Such a definition of law, Cardozo observed, in effect denies the existence of law. "Analysis is useless," he said, "if it destroys what it is intended to explain. Law and obedience to law are facts confirmed every day to us all in our experience of life. If the result of a definition is to make them seem to be illusions, so much the worse for the definition; we must enlarge it till it is broad enough to answer to realities." I agree.

Certainly the common law is judge-made law, in the sense that we have examined. Courts, in deciding cases, are constantly in the process of creating new norms, but they do so within, and subject to, a framework of existing norms, and we expect them to give those existing norms appropriate deference. Indeed, with rare exceptions we insist that an appellate court write an opinion that justifies the result in reference to existing norms at the same time that it creates a new norm for future application. If the facts of a precedential case cannot reasonably be distinguished, a lower court is bound to follow it; and though the highest court of a jurisdiction is not bound in the same way by its own prior decisions, we expect it to overrule such a decision only for substantial and explicit reasons. It is an evolutionary process tied to the adjudication of particular cases.

If we say that judges make common law, we should add, then, that in the main they do it in a different manner, and subject to greater constraints, than do legislators. There are occasions when a court will undertake a substantial and dramatic change—the replacement of older concepts of contributory negligence with that of comparative negligence is an example—but such occasions are rare and typically supported by demonstrable changes in the legal atmosphere.

The modern legal philosopher Ronald Dworkin has offered an appealing metaphor. He says a judge who decides a case is like an author responsible for writing a chapter in an ongoing novel, the earlier chapters of which have been written by others, and future chapters of which are to be composed by still others yet to come. Such authors would have considerable freedom to use their creative skills, but they would be constrained in two ways—by the obligation to be faithful to the premises and story line of what has already been written, and by the obligation to be concerned about the future development of the novel. In both respects the author would feel a duty to maintain coherence and continuity, as does a judge, even when he or she decides to squeeze the precedents a bit in order to push the law in some new direction. Those inclined to the visual arts may prefer the image of the judge as one who is charged with responsibility for painting a scene in an ongoing mural—free to express his or her artistry, but within the constraints imposed by the context in which he or she paints.

But it is not simply the existence of rules and the principle of continuity that operate as constraints on the judicial process; there is also the distinction Cardozo emphasized between the judge's private morality and the mores of the community. Dworkin's views of the law build on that distinction and stress the principles of ethics and morality imbedded in the institutions of our society— principles a judge is obligated to recognize and apply to the development of the law in lieu of what might be his own idiosyncratic values. Indeed, Dworkin would define law (here we come back to the issue, What is law?) to *include* such principles, along with legal doctrine in the form of rules. This definition enables Dworkin to say that when a judge molds legal doctrine according to principle, he or she is not really making law but is rather applying "law" in the broader sense. There is only one right answer to a legal question, Dworkin asserts, and a judge who is capable of knowing everything there is to know about our society and its political values would know that answer. He calls such a judge "Hercules" in recognition of the fact that the task is beyond the capability of ordinary humans.

Professor Melvin Eisenberg of the University of California at Berkeley published a book in 1988 entitled *The Nature of the Common Law*, in which he builds on Dworkin's theory in a number of ways.

Dworkin believes, for example, that while judges may and should consider matters of principle, it is inappropriate for them to consider matters of policy, by which he means exactly what Holmes thought governed judicial decisions—considerations of social advantage. Such considerations, Dworkin argues, are exclusively the province of the legislative branch. That argument has been subject to considerable criticism by other theorists, and Eisenberg adopts the more catholic view that judges must consider a broad range of "social propositions" that include propositions of "morality, policy, and experience." Judges are not free to pick and choose among these according to their wont; rather, they are bound by what Eisenberg calls "the institutional principles of adjudication" to apply them in a restricted and disciplined way. He says that the common law consists of the "rules that would be generated at the present moment by application of the institutional principles of adjudication." Propositions about the law are of varying degrees of certainty, but in theory (and here Eisenberg agrees with Dworkin) there is a legal answer to every legal question. This Eisenberg calls the "generative conception of the common law." I believe Eisenberg's views come closer to the way judges and lawyers think about the law than Dworkin's. Certainly judges regard themselves as bound to consider the impact on society of the norms they generate through decisions, and they do look to scholarly comment on the law for guidance in the decisional process. I am not so sure, however, what it means to say that there is a legal answer to every legal question, any more than I am sure what it means to say that there is a moral answer to every moral question. What is important here, however, is that both Dworkin and Eisenberg, along with many other modern legal theorists, reject the nihilistic vision of the law as nothing but "isolated dooms" and are searching for ways of accounting for what most of us accept to be the rule of law.

I doubt that most judges, in the process of deciding cases, think in the terms advanced by any of the legal theorists, though of course that does not preclude the possibility that what they do is in fact consistent more with one theory than with another. I have attempted to recall what went through my own mind in the process of deciding *Pugh v. See's Candies*, a case I described in chapters 2 and 5. There is no doubt that I saw the case as an opportunity to "advance" the law in a direction that I thought it ought to go. At the same time, that seemed to be the direction indicated, if not required, by the modern legal doctrine—possibly a happy coincidence. That direction also seemed to be supported by the atmosphere of expectations in the employment community generated in part by developments in such areas as employment discrimination. I remember thinking to myself that unorganized workers did not represent an effective political constituency, so that waiting for the legislature to take some action was impractical as well as unwarranted. The legislature, if it wished, could react to our opinion, or whatever other opinions came down on the subject. I was wary, however, of creating a situation in which every decision by an employer would become potentially a question for a jury, and I was wary of exposing employers to suits for punitive damages or other huge damage awards without principled ground rules. For purposes of that case a contract approach seemed to me both appropriate and adequate, and my colleagues agreed. I am not at all sure what theory of the law that process would support.

STATUTES

When Holmes and Cardozo gave their famous lectures on the nature of law and the judicial process, it was the common law that they had mainly in mind, and for good reason: in their day it was the common law that occupied most of the time and attention of state courts. Statutes were few and far between. Even the Legal Realists, writing in the 1920s and 1930s, relied on the common-law model for their analysis of the judicial function. And today legal philosophers sometimes write as if deciding common-law cases were the primary occupation of judges, or at least as if it made no difference what they were deciding.

That is not true, of course. The domain of the common law has shrunk over the years as legislatures have become more active. I doubt that issues of common law comprise more than 20 percent of the caseload of the modern state court. And that fact does make a difference when it comes to describing the judicial function.

In the "pure" common-law process (that is, where there are no applicable statutes) the highest authority is the courts—unless we say that the principles and policies that courts must look to for guidance constitute a higher authority. A lower court certainly is obliged to follow decisions of higher courts, but the highest court of a jurisdiction is not obliged similarly to follow its own prior decisions. Rather, it is obliged to give them "due weight," which means it should not overrule or modify them without good reason. But it does have the power to overrule and modify, and under some circumstances (as where the premises underlying the prior decision no longer exist or were erroneous to start with) one might argue it has even the obligation to do so.

A court's relationship to a statute is quite different. When the legislature adopts a valid rule, the courts are obliged to apply it; that is a corollary of our system of representative democracy. One notable academic—Guido Calabresi at Yale—has argued for an exception to that principle when the statute is very old and the reasons for its adoption no longer exist; Calabresi says that under such circumstances it is appropriate for a court to refuse to apply the statute unless and until the legislature reenacts it. But no court has adopted that view, and even if we were to accept that courts should do so, the exception is a narrow one.

There is a further difference between a court's relationship to judicial precedent and its relationship to a statute, one that seems to have eluded some of the legal theorists. It is customary to think of a court as an institution existing over time, whose membership changes gradually but which maintains continuity. In referring to a prior decision of its own, a court will typically say in an opinion, In such and such a case *we* held . . . , even though not a single judge who signed the prior opinion remains on the court. This manner of thinking carries over into the legal analysis. If there is ambiguity in the prior opinion, the present court will not say, It is difficult to know what they meant by that. Rather, the court will say, This is what *we* meant.

This use of *we* is more than a manner of speaking: it reflects the way judges look at a prior opinion of the court on which they sit. The prior opinion, from their perspective, is not a command; it does not say to them, "This is what you shall do." It represents simply their own pronouncement on a question of law. They may (and should) feel obliged to accord it substantial weight in making their present decision, and they may (and should) take into account how others have viewed the prior opinion. But if the opinion is ambiguous in some respect, it is not likely that the judges will ask themselves, "Now what did we really mean by that?" and feel obliged to decide in accord with that previous intent. To borrow a phrase of the legal theorists, judges do not regard the prior opinion as "canonical text."

With a statute the situation is quite different. Because of the hierarchical relationship between a legislature and a court in matters of lawmaking, judges feel obliged to follow the directions of the legislature insofar as they can ascertain them. If the directions are unclear, it is the judge's job to make such sense of them as he or she can.

Not that this is an easy job. In some sense language is always unclear. American courts (like those in England) used to rely heavily on the notion that the meaning of certain words and phrases was obvious, in which case no other evidence of legislative intent or purpose was to be considered—the plain-meaning rule, as it was called. A prime example is the decision of the United States Supreme Court in a 1917 case, *Caminetti v. United States,* in which it was called on to construe the White Slave Traffic Act. The language of the statute made it a crime to transport a female across state lines "for the purpose of prostitution or debauchery, or for any other immoral purpose," and the question was whether the defendant could be found guilty of having violated the act by traveling with a woman from Sacramento to Reno for the purpose of making her his mistress. The legislative history of the statute made it rather clear that it was aimed at commercial prostitution, but the court majority doggedly insisted that the plain meaning of the statute covered the defendant's situation.

As the dissenting justices observed, a literal reading of the statute would make it unlawful to travel across state lines with a woman for *any* "immoral purpose," that is, any form of vice; it was scarcely likely that Congress intended the statute to have such a broad sweep. (Suppose the couple had crossed the state line to tell someone in Nevada a lie?) That being the case, some other principled criteria for limiting the scope of the statute had to come into play; plain meaning just would not do the job.

Consider another case the legal theorists are fond of discussing, *Riggs v. Palmer.* A nephew who knows that he is the beneficiary under his uncle's will murders his uncle to expedite the inheritance. There is a statute in New York that says in effect that courts are to enforce "every" will that complies with the statutory requirements—to be in writing, to have witnesses, and so forth. It contains no exceptions for murderous nephews. Nevertheless, said the New York Court of Appeal, the legislature could not have intended such a result, any more than the framers of an ancient edict against drawing blood in the streets of Bologna was meant to apply to a barber. The statute did not supersede the principle that no one shall be permitted to profit by his or her own wrongdoing. The nephew lost the appeal.

Modern courts still talk about plain meaning at times; I can recall having done so on occasion myself. It makes sense at least to start with the assumption that the legislature used words with the intent that they be accorded their "ordinary" meaning, assuming that such a meaning can be ascertained. But modern courts are more likely to talk about the *intent* of the legislature or the *purpose* of the statute, viewing the disputed language not in isolation but in its total context. The problem is that both those concepts—intent and purpose—are rather elusive upon close analysis. Talking about the intent even of a particular individual can be a dubious proposition, let alone of a group of people, particularly when the group is composed of politicians, who seldom agree with one another about anything.

Whose intent are we interested in when we talk about the intent of the legislature? Surely not the intent of those who voted against the statute. But among those who voted for it, do we assume they all intended the same thing? Such an assumption we know to be unrealistic. Statutes are the product of compromise, and different legislators might have different expectations as to how the statute will be interpreted. Paul Brest, dean of Stanford Law School, gives the example (drawing on earlier work by H. L. A. Hart) of a city ordinance that prohibits "vehicles" in a public park. Suppose (to vary his example somewhat) the question is whether the ordinance applies to mopeds as well as to automobiles. Normally courts will not permit individual legislators to be interrogated concerning their intent; but suppose we *could* question each of the council members, and two said they had intended to prohibit mopeds, two said they had not, and the fifth said that the question never crossed her mind. What is a poor judge to do?

Of course, political reality is likely to complicate the situation further. Suppose, for example, we discovered that three of the council members never read the ordinance before they voted for it, or that one council member who would have preferred that there be no ordinance voted for it on the condition that it say nothing about mopeds. Indeed, suppose we discovered that a majority of the members would have preferred to outlaw mopeds explicitly but were deterred from doing so by vigorous opposition at the council meeting from moped owners (or by the promise of hefty contributions from moped makers) and opted for the word *vehicle* in the hope that the courts would give it a broad interpretation. Each of these is a realistic scenario; in each, talk of legislative intent is somewhat fanciful.

The more modern approach is to speak of the *purpose* of the statute rather than the *intent* of the legislature. It would help, for example, if we knew that the ordinance prohibiting vehicles in the park was passed after an automobile ran into a pedestrian and that the discussion surrounding the adoption of the ordinance was directed at preventing future accidents of that sort. Given that information, we would certainly be justified in saying that the ordinance applies to all automobiles, rather than just the particular make and model that inspired the legislation, but that it does not apply to baby carriages since they do not pose the risk at which the ordinance was aimed.

But, as the deconstructionists take pleasure in demonstrating, analysis in terms of purpose also has its limitations. The possibility exists that some legislators voted for the ordinance with motivations they did not disclose. Moreover, even taking the avoidance of accidents as the purpose behind the ordinance does not necessarily resolve the status of mopeds. Though mopeds pose some risk of injury to pedestrians, the risk is not as great as that posed by automobiles, and the riding of mopeds in a park, like the riding of bicycles, has a recreational aspect. A city council that has decided that the danger from allowing automobiles in the park outweighs their utility might not reach the same conclusion about mopeds; knowing the general purpose of the ordinance will not help us resolve that tension between environmental and libertarian values.

In short, there is no such thing as a foolproof method of applying statutes that excludes the necessity for judgment. It is possible to poke holes in any argument, no matter how soundly supported by reference to text or legislative history or legislative purpose, and to demonstrate that the result does not follow as a matter of pure logic. To this extent what Holmes, Cardozo, and the Legal Realists said about the common law has application to the statutory arena. Indeed, the statutory deconstructionists who delight in such hole poking might be thought of as a new breed of Legal Realists—realistic not only about the courts but about the legislative process as well.

It does not follow from all of this, however, that a statute is nothing but the frame for a sandbox in which judges play their favorite games. Certainly that is not the mindset of judges, or at least not of the judges I have known. A judge starts with the premise that a statute represents an authoritative declaration of norms that it is his or her obligation to apply and further in the case at hand. Many judges have served in government, some of them as legislators, and they are not naive about how legislatures work; but that remains their premise, nonetheless. It is a bit like playing softball in the twilight: as the light fades, the batter will find it harder and harder to see the ball, but he acts on the assumption that the ball is there, somewhere, waiting to be hit.

With many statutes it is of course quite clear as a practical matter what the legislature was getting at, so that even a judge who is fully aware of both the indeterminacy of language and the vagaries of the legislative process would nevertheless feel like a damned fool if he or she tried to say that the statute meant something else. Often it is less clear, but it is always a matter of degree of clarity—not, as some of the legal theorists would have it, a matter of "easy cases" and "hard cases," as if those were two separate and distinct categories of legal phenomena.

Even in the less clear cases it is rare that there are not at least some clues as to meaning. If a city council adopts an ordinance prohibiting vehicles in the park, it does not do so in a vacuum. It acts within a context in which it is likely that there are other ordinances that include the term *vehicle* and that cast light on the way the term is typically used. Of course, a skeptic would argue that we cannot assume the city council members were aware of other related ordinances, or if they were, that they necessarily intended *vehicle* to bear the same meaning in each, and there is merit to that argument. But that is a problem with all communications. It is possible that someone you talk to is using words in a unique way, but unless you have some reason to believe that is the case, you will probably assume that he is using the words in a way that he has used them before or (failing evidence of that) in the way that they are usually used within the community in which the communication is occurring.

Moreover, if the person you are talking to is someone you know well and talk to all the time, there is likely to develop between you certain conventions, so that when he uses a particular word or phrase that could carry more than one meaning, he does so with the expectation that you will know what he means. A similar dialogue takes place between a court and the legislature. The legislature may provide the court with a glossary—a set of definitions of terms contained in the statute or somewhere in the codes—but in addition there are likely to be certain conventions that both parties to the dialogue understand and take into account. Those responsible for drafting a statute are likely to be aware, for example, that if a statute tells courts to consider factors A, B, and C in making a particular decision, the courts are likely to view that as a directive that no other factors are to be considered. Hence if the legislature wants to leave the door open to the consideration of other criteria, the drafter would be well advised to use a phrase such as "including but not limited to" in order to make that intent clear.

What, then, is the role of policy in statutory interpretation? Some theorists see a neat division between those cases that a court can resolve on the basis of statutory language, or at least statutory language plus legislative history, and those cases that require a court to bring policy considerations to bear. In the former arena, such theorists are inclined to say, judges are applying the law; in the latter arena they are making law, much as the legislature itself goes about making it.

Based on my own experiences as a judge and my observations of the way other judges apply statutes, such a dichotomy is grossly misleading as a description of what courts actually do. The fact is that as judges work their way into a question of statutory application, they are likely to work at several levels concurrently. They will look at the language in dispute and consider the extent to which it appears to convey a "customary" meaning; they will look at the statutory context and legislative history for clues; and they will consider the consequences for the parties and for society of adopting one view of the statute or another. In their minds, judges will be "testing" alternative interpretations at each of these levels, so that if an interpretation that seems to satisfy the disputed language clashes with other portions of the statute or with legislative history, or appears likely to produce consequences that the legislature would not have wanted, the judge may assign it a low "grade" and go on to consider other interpretations that might produce a better fit.

I recall one case on the California Supreme Court in which I went through this process, finally to be persuaded that my initial premise was wrong. The question was whether the State Board of Equalization (which collects sales taxes) was correct in assessing a tax against the sale by a hospital of its furnishings and equipment. I saw no reason why a hospital should be exempt from tax under those circumstances, either on my reading of the tax statute or as a matter of policy, and I wrote an opinion to that effect. But Justice Frank Richardson wrote a dissenting opinion, arguing forcefully on the basis of legislative history that the transaction fell under an exemption for "occasional sales." I was persuaded, and I withdrew my opinion, signing Richardson's instead. So did everyone else in the end, and the decision was unanimous.

Not only is the process of statutory construction multilevel, as I have described, but the levels are interrelated as well. Legislative history and policy considerations are likely to carry greater weight when the statutory language appears ambiguous than when its meaning appears clear "on its face"; policy considerations are likely to predominate when the result suggested by a literal reading would produce consequences that are seen as particularly egregious; and so forth. It is a bit like deciding what dress to buy for a friend when there is only limited stock and no one dress matches her form or taste perfectly; taking into account a bit too full a cut here and a bit too bright a color there, you will end up with a choice that you think will make her look best overall—the one you think she would have bought if she had been in the store with you.

It is, of course, the legislature's "taste" that the court is obliged to consider. Insofar as there are policy considerations relevant to the outcome of a case, the judge looks first to whatever policies are reflected in the statute, in its background, or in other analogous legislative enactments. These may provide an uncertain degree of guidance, but the fact that such guidance is not explicit does not mean it does not exist.

Compare the position of a football referee charged with responsibility for calling penalties under a rule that prohibits "unnecessary roughness" but does not define it. Logically the language is indeterminate and could encompass a broad variety of judgments. What constitutes "roughness"? Does the rule apply only to physical contact, or would rough language violate the rule? And what does "unnecessary" mean? If a guard is assigned to block a lineman, must he use only such force as is necessary to prevent the lineman from getting to the ballcarrier? Or may he hit him as hard as he can with his body to deter the lineman from charging so fast the next play? Answers to questions such as these are not to be found on the face of the rule, and perhaps not in any commentary to the rule; but does that mean that a referee has discretion to apply any standard he considers appropriate?

Obviously not. The referee is constrained by the kind of game that is being played and by the customs and expectations that have developed surrounding the game. If, for example, he applied to the concept of unnecessary roughness standards derived from basketball, wrestling, or dueling, we would consider him not only to be a poor referee but to have violated his obligations as a referee. The operative constraints in this context, though implicit rather than explicit, are nonetheless very real and, one suspects, very substantial. In fact, so clear are the understandings within what might be called the football community that variation among referees is the exception rather than the rule.

Judges, too, operate within an institutional framework. In resolving policy questions not expressly answered by the legislature, they are expected to bring to bear the standards and values of the community rather than their own idiosyncratic judgment. Of course, that also is a matter of degree. Ours is a diverse society, with many people playing many different games on different fields with different rules, and to speak of community standards and values may be more meaningful in some contexts than in others. Moreover, there is a quite human tendency to justify our own values by projecting them onto a broader screen of universal approbation. I wrote once in an opinion, while in a philosophical mood, that judges may mistake their own policies for those of the society. It is a mistake that conscientious judges, at least, seek to avoid.

The nature of the judicial role vis-à-vis the legislature requires one further observation if the notion of judicial lawmaking through statutory interpretation is to be properly understood and properly limited. That observation flows from the principle of dialogue. The relationship of the courts to the legislature is a dynamic one: when the legislature adopts a statute, it knows that it will be subject to judicial interpretation; when a court interprets a statute, it knows that its interpretation may be reviewed by the legislature and that it may be modified if the legislature decides that the court was "wrong." To the extent that a court engages in lawmaking through interpretation (and some engagement is inevitable), it is through a partnership in which the legislature, as senior partner, has the last word.

CONSTITUTIONS

It is in the constitutional arena that the debate over the role of courts is naturally most intense. When a court decides a constitutional issue, there is usually a good deal more at stake than when only a question of statutory interpretation or common law is implicated. This is so for several reasons. First, constitutional issues typically are more important issues, often touching fundamental questions of governance and rights. Second, a court's decision on a constitutional issue is final in a way that its decision on a common-law or statutory question is not: it remains the law unless and until the court (or a higher court) changes its mind or the constitution is amended. Finally, depending on the nature of the issue and the result, the court's decision may have the effect of frustrating what is perceived to be the popular will.

Whether judges "make law" is a different sort of question in the arena of constitutional adjudication. A constitution bears a certain resemblance to a statute—both are written documents, and both are generally viewed as binding on courts—but there are significant differences. One difference consists in the way constitutions are drafted. There are certain matters that the drafters of a constitution can be quite specific about—the number of legislators, their qualifications, and the manner of their selection, for example. These provisions are similar to statutes and tend to be treated by courts in the same way. But there are other matters—such as freedom of expression or protection against government snooping—concerning which the drafters may consider specificity to be either impossible or (given the anticipated duration of the document and its subject matter) undesirable.

Another difference consists in the more complicated manner in which constitutions are adopted. We have considered the complexity of defining, much less ascertaining, the intent of a single legislative body; in the case of the federal Constitution we have multiple bodies. The main part of the constitution was drafted by a convention (which, incidentally, kept no official minutes of its proceedings) and then ratified by the legislatures of the thirteen colonies. The ten amendments that comprise the Bill of Rights were debated and adopted by Congress and then ratified by the legislatures of various states. The state constitutions, ratified by popular vote, present at least as great a challenge to definition and ascertainment.

The debate over "original intent" must be viewed against the backdrop of these constitutional characteristics. Let us assume, for purposes of analysis, that if we could know precisely what at least a majority of the framers and adopters had in mind when they drafted and accepted such language as "due process of law" and "cruel and unusual punishment" *in the sense of knowing what directions they intended to give to future courts in the interpretation of those terms,* we would expect courts to feel obligated by those directions. But in fact it is extremely difficult to know any such thing. We might, through study of contemporary writings, know what a few of the framers and adopters had in mind when they *thought* about due process of law and cruel and unusual punishment, but that is not the same as knowing what sort of directions they intended to give by such phrasing. They may have intended to allow future courts broad leeway to view the terms of the Constitution in the light of new and changing social conditions and mores rather than be bound by the particular conceptions that prevailed at the time the constitution was adopted. Indeed, one legal historian, Professor H. Jefferson Powell of Iowa Law School, contends that this was the true "original intent."

Some advocates of the original-intent approach accept this expanded view, but somewhat selectively. Judge Bork, for example, indicated he was prepared to accept the result in *Brown v. Board of Education*—that the equal protection clause of the Fourteenth Amendment prohibits racially segregated schools—even though segregated schools were in existence in the District of Columbia at the time that Congress adopted the Fourteenth Amendment and continued to exist until *Brown* was decided. He explained that position on the ground that he found in the equal protection clause a broad *principle* that could not be squared with segregated schools no matter what Congress had in mind specifically on that issue and that the "background assumptions" had changed since the Fourteenth Amendment was adopted.

Judge Bork also expressed the view, however, that prayers in public schools did not violate the First Amendment principle of the separation of church from state because school prayers were a common phenomenon at the time the First Amendment was adopted. But that argument assumes the framers and adopters intended to direct future courts to accept their understanding, in 1791, as to what the separation of church and state required. It is at least plausible to assume (as in the case of the equal protection clause) that the framers and adopters used deliberately broad language to express a *principle* with the intention that it be applied by future courts in a manner consistent with the social patterns and expectations of future generations and not that it be circumscribed by the conditions that existed in the late eighteenth century.

The dilemma is this: if we adopt a theory of original intent that limits us to considering what the framers and adopters would have thought about a particular problem such as school prayer or segregated schools (assuming, of course, that we can know such a thing), we run the risk of becoming captives of an earlier age in a way that the framers and adopters may not have intended and in a way that would make decisions like *Brown v. Board of Education* extremely difficult. On the other hand, if we adopt a theory of original intent that allows us to decide present cases on the basis of broad principles we find in the text of the Constitution, we have the problem of identifying those principles, as well as the level of generality at which they are to be applied, without much in the way of historical guidance.

There is nothing wrong with such an undertaking—it is the kind of adventure on which judges and lawyers embark all the time—

but we should not pretend (as some advocates of the theory of original intent are inclined to do) that it will provide an objective basis for constitutional adjudication. My own view is that we should look to the attitudes and intentions of the framers and adopters as a guide to interpretation but that it is both naive and misleading to expect that we will find some authoritative criterion that will eliminate the necessity for contemporary judgment. Indeed, the right and the obligation to make contemporary judgments may be our most valuable—and burdensome—constitutional legacy.

But how are such contemporary judgments to be made if not on the basis of original intent? Does it boil down, ultimately, to each judge's conception of what is "right" or "good for the country"? The question is a familiar one—we have grappled with it in the contexts of common law and statutory adjudication—but here it has a unique urgency, particularly as concerns the countermajoritarian function of judicial review. If judges are going to rely on the Constitution to strike down a statute that has popular support, we want them to be able to explain why they are doing it, and we are not likely to be satisfied with an explanation that says, in effect, It may have looked O.K. to the legislature, but it didn't look right to us.

Precedent is a source of constraint in the constitutional arena, of course, as it is elsewhere in the law. Indeed, it is possible to view the process of applying the Constitution as very close in methodology to the process of the common law, and the requirement that judges act by majority vote dilutes the significance of aberrant views. Beyond that, modern constitutional scholars have explored a number of areas in search of principled grounds for judicial review. Professor John Hart Ely of Stanford Law School, for example, finds in the federal Constitution and its history support for the proposition that courts are meant to be the guardians of the democratic process, and on that basis he defends heightened judicial scrutiny in certain areas, such as freedom of speech and assembly, the one-person–one-vote principle, and the protection of individuals and minority groups—"discrete and insular minorities," as Justice Harlan Stone called them in a famous footnote to a Supreme Court opinion—that are outside the political mainstream. Others, like Professor Lawrence Tribe of Harvard Law School, insist that a process-oriented approach is too narrow, and that there are values beyond the political process, even beyond the express language of the document, that courts are expected to protect and preserve.

There has been a resurgence of scholarly interest in concepts of natural law—the notion that there exist, independent of any constitutional or legislative enactments or judicial declarations (positive law), some objective and ascertainable values against which positive law should be tested or at least supplemented. Certainly the Declaration of Independence is based in part on such concepts, and there are respectable legal scholars (including my Hastings colleague, Professor Calvin Massey) who are convinced that the Ninth Amendment ("The enumeration in the Constitution, of certain rights, shall not be construed to deny or disparage others retained by the people") was intended to allow for the incorporation of concepts of natural law into the Constitution itself.

I am skeptical of natural-law theories—after all, Aristotle thought it natural for people to have slaves and for men to dominate women —but I do think it is meaningful, at least on some issues, to speak, as some commentators have, of shared community values as something that judges should look to and be guided by, as signposts for constitutional adjudication. By shared community values those commentators mean something different from the public attitude toward a particular problem at a particular time. Most of us now accept, for example, that the internment of Japanese Americans during World War II was offensive to the values of our society though at the time even the Supreme Court rationalized its acceptance. Those who acknowledge and internalize the fundamental importance of free speech to democracy are susceptible of being persuaded that their own values should lead them to reject attempts to limit even highly offensive speech by American Nazis. Such moral dialogue, based on reasoning from accepted value positions, is not the same as natural law in the classic sense, but it is capable at times of producing consensus on moral values.

Consider again the Bork hearings. Granted that the outpouring of opposition to Judge Bork was in part orchestrated, that it was limited to selected issues, and that some consider it to have been misdirected. Still, the opposition was there, and in such intensity that all senators on the Judiciary Committee, including Judge Bork's supporters, tacitly accepted as their premise for questioning and debate that Americans care deeply about their constitutional rights and that if Judge Bork held the constrained views of constitutional protection for individual rights that his opponents said he held, then he was indeed outside the mainstream of both constitutional theory and popular thought.

My reading of the atmosphere surrounding the hearings is that there emerged a perceptible consensus about certain principles that have long divided legal scholars—for example, that the First Amendment should be viewed broadly to protect nonpolitical speech and that the equal protection clause of the Fourteenth Amendment should not be limited in its scope to blacks or ethnic minorities. It also appears that most Americans consider that there exists an area of personal privacy or autonomy that deserves constitutional insulation from government interference, no matter how difficult that area may be to define.

Nonetheless, after all is said and done, I think we must acknowledge that much of constitutional adjudication—when generally phrased statements of rights are involved and when there is no clearly applicable precedent—is ultimately quite subjective, calling for the exercise of greater discretion on the part of the judge than is typical of statutory interpretation. Discretion is not unlimited, however; it is simply very broad.

There is no doubt that in the exercise of such discretion judges cannot entirely escape their own background and experiences. Old-timers around the California Supreme Court tell a story about *People v. Krivda*, in which the court held that police needed a warrant before they could search the contents of a citizen's garbage can. The opinion was written by Justice Louis Burke, who had been appointed to the court by Governor Ronald Reagan and had a reputation for being generally conservative in his constitutional views. The story is that Justice Burke had an aging mother who, for medical reasons, imbibed small quantities of wine on a regular basis. The thought of police rummaging through his mother's garbage cans and finding wine bottles led the justice to conclude that such a search would not be in accord with "reasonable expectations of privacy."

If the story is true—and I believe it is—I find no problem in Justice Burke allowing his decisional process to be influenced by thoughts of his mother's condition. Indeed, if a judge were to maintain that he or she was able to discard all personal experience from judgment, I would be troubled on two grounds: first, because I would doubt the claim, and second, because judgment that is not grounded in experience is not likely to be wise judgment. What we have a right to expect is that judges be aware, as far as possible, of the experiences that influence their thinking and that they balance that experience with what they know or can learn about the experiences of others and the norms of the community.

In discussing the relationship between judges and the law, I have ignored variation among judges, though of course that is part of the picture as well. We speak of some judges as being more "activist" than others, and within limits the label can have some significance. Some judges may be more inclined than others to reconsider precedent, to develop precedent along new lines, and to exercise the function of judicial review. As a general matter, however, it strikes me that the label is not very useful. Judges who play an activist role in some contexts may be more restrained in others, so that to use the label to describe a judge (rather than a particular decision) can be misleading. To use it as a value-laden term connoting either approbation or disapproval is particularly misleading. In some situations it may be the heart of judicial wisdom to act with restraint—say, in deference to the legislature or to a particular precedent; in others it may reflect a lack of good judgment, or even judicial cowardice.

The most misleading use of the activist label is to associate it with a particular political philosophy, liberal or conservative. Activism as such is value-neutral. Adherence to precedent can produce consequences approved by liberals or conservatives depending on what the precedent is. It was equally activist, in terms of directly applicable precedent, for the California Supreme Court to establish principles of strict product liability as it was to decline to apply those principles to prescription drugs. The Warren court may have been activist, but the Rehnquist court is activist insofar as it has refused to follow that court's holdings. Similarly, invalidation of legislative acts on constitutional grounds may produce liberal or conservative results depending on whether the statute is one that restricts freedom of speech or guarantees a minimum wage. The political use of the label "activism" reveals whose ox is being gored.

Someone said that philosophers are generally right in what they affirm of their own vision and generally wrong in what they deny of the vision of others. I find much wisdom in that observation, particularly as applied to philosophizing about the law and the judicial process. Listen carefully, I say, to the insights that the legal philosophers offer, but beware the claim that any particular insight will explain all we need to know. Perhaps some day a legal Einstein will develop a unified field theory that is sufficiently comprehensive to describe all that judges do and at the same time sufficiently specific to be meaningful; but I am not holding my breath. When we start talking about principles and policies, mores and morals, and institutional values, we are toiling in the same vineyards as the value theorists and as moral philosophers since Socrates, and we cannot expect greater objectivity or certainty because the context is law.

My own perspective, and I think the perspective of most judges who ponder such matters, tends to the eclectic. The development of theories of judging is without question a valuable enterprise; it can provide useful insight into the dynamics of the process. But the sad, or perhaps beautiful, truth is that all of the models I have mentioned in this chapter—the judge as geometrist, builder, bureaucrat, chef, referee, artist, village elder, and legislator—have some descriptive, as well as prescriptive, force as applied to some of the things that some judges do some of the time, though none of them serves to capture the entirety of the judicial role. The polarities of finding law and making it, of constraint and discretion, are like the background and foreground of a single painting. Some of what judges do is subject to rather rigid control by rules, some is close to legislation; but most takes place in a middle ground in which the tension between the objective and the subjective is always present, always a matter of degree, and impossible either to quantify or to describe categorically. If those who seek precision in such matters find this an unsatisfying description, I wish them well. As Judge Cardozo said in his last lecture, "If this seems a weak and inconclusive summary, I am not sure that the fault is mine."

10

Elections

A friend asked me, while Judge Robert Bork's nomination to the United States Supreme Court was pending before the Senate Judiciary Committee in 1987, what I would do if I were a member of the committee, and I said I would vote to confirm and pray I would be outvoted. I like to think I was being facetious, and that if I were really in that position, I would act in a more principled fashion, but my answer was faithful to the ambivalence I felt then and continue to feel now.

Many of my liberal friends had no qualms about opposing Bork and did not understand why I should have any; after all, wasn't it Bork's conservative supporters who spearheaded the campaign against me? What's sauce for the goose . . . , my friends said. But then they did not experience the election as I did.

I was skeptical of some of Bork's legal theories and of what seemed to be his tendency to become captive to abstractions, but I felt sympathy for him because I knew what he must have been going through. It is dreadful for a judge to find himself in the midst of a political maelstrom and to see his views exaggerated and mischaracterized by opponents, as Bork's views clearly were at times. When opponents sought to demonstrate his bias by subjecting his opinions to statistical analysis instead of legal analysis, and when they put on television a simplistic and misleading advertisement in opposition to his confirmation, it reminded me of the 1986 California election.

But it was more than sympathy that made me uneasy; it was concern for the integrity of the judicial function and the long-range implications of the kind of campaign that was being waged. Granted that the Senate throughout its history has at times used its constitutional authority to withhold confirmation on what might be called ideological grounds; granted that President Reagan may legitimately be charged with an excess of ideological zeal in some of his appointments to the federal bench; and granted that some of the views that Bork expressed over the years might properly be viewed as extreme, I still was disturbed by the extent to which Bork was questioned (and the extent to which he answered!) as to his views regarding particular precedents and issues as if he were a politician making campaign promises. I was disturbed also by the overall politicization of the appointment. Regardless of the result, it was bad precedent.

Nevertheless, the politicization of the Bork campaign and its portent for the future integrity of the judicial branch were both small-time compared to the nature and potential impact of a full-blown judicial election such as my colleagues and I went through in 1986. The Senate Judiciary Committee and the Senate itself at least provide structured settings for rational inquiry and consideration of the criteria thought to be relevant to a judicial appointment. In fact, the Bork hearings were highly educational; they became for a while a national pastime, and I was astonished to discover how intrigued my nonlawyer friends were with the nuances of constitutional debate. A judicial election—or at least the one I experienced—lacks such a structure and thus tends to degenerate into slogans and thirty-second television spots singularly inappropriate to the evaluation of judicial candidates.

Moreover, the federal confirmation process takes place only once, *before* the candidate has served in the position to which he or she is seeking confirmation. At that juncture there is something to be said for the Senate acting in counterpoint to the president, who after all is free to take, and presumably does take, the candidate's "philosophical" views into account. A judicial election that occurs some time *after* the candidate has served in the position poses a somewhat different problem, for it tends inevitably to become something of a referendum on the content of the candidate's decisions. These characteristics of judicial elections, along with the ugly aspects of campaign fund-raising, pose risks to the integrity of the judicial process that are deserving of far more public attention and scrutiny than they have thus far received. In this chapter I shall try to explain why.

First, a bit of history may be useful. During the American colonial period King George III retained and exercised the power to appoint and remove judges—a circumstance so deeply resented by the colonists that the Declaration of Independence lists among its grievances, "He has made judges depend on his will alone, for the tenure of their offices, and the amount and payment of their salaries." Determined to avoid undue executive influence over the judiciary, eight of the original thirteen states provided in their constitutions for selection of judges by one or both houses of the legislature, and the remaining five states qualified executive appointment by insisting on legislative concurrence. Apparently determined further to protect judicial independence, a majority of the states provided for lifetime appointments, subject to good behavior. At that time popular elections for judges did not exist.

But in the second quarter of the nineteenth century there was something of a revolt among the citizenry. Judges, who had never been very popular as a group, became even less so. Thomas Jefferson, when he was president, had engaged in vehement attacks on Federalist judges whom he regarded as intent on blocking the program of the new Democrats. President Andrew Jackson was the standard-bearer of a new populism that preached voter control over all aspects of government, including the judiciary.

The populist ethos of judicial accountability found common ground with some leaders of the organized bar, who believed that elections would be a means of improving the quality of the bench (mainly because they thought it would give the bar more of a voice in the process) and at the same time of enhancing the authority of the judicial branch by providing it with a base of popular support. The result was a uniquely American phenomenon—the partisan judicial election. From 1849 (when California became a state) through 1913 all newly admitted states adopted the partisan election as a means of filling judicial vacancies upon expiration of a fixed term, and most of the older states amended their constitutions to the same effect.

But then the pendulum swung back. Critics began to charge that elections, and particularly elections based on party politics, were inconsistent with the standards of quality and independence expected of the judicial branch. A search for alternatives began. Around the turn of the century about a dozen states moved to so-called nonpartisan elections, in which party designations were not used on the ballot, but that system also evoked criticism. It was charged that selections were in fact still being made by party leaders, only now the public was being kept in the dark and deprived of cues that would enable them to vote intelligently. Roscoe Pound, famous jurist and dean of Harvard Law School, in 1906 delivered a speech entitled "Causes of Popular Dissatisfaction with the Administration of Justice," in which he asserted that "putting courts into politics, and compelling judges to become politicians in many jurisdictions . . . [had] almost destroyed the traditional respect for the bench."

In 1913 the American Judicature Society, an organization devoted to improving the administration of justice, was formed, and it came to advocate two related changes in the way judges were appointed. First, it advanced what came to be known as the commission plan, or the merit plan, in which a governor in filling a judicial vacancy would be limited in his selection to a list of candidates prepared by some blue-ribbon, and hopefully nonpartisan, commission. Such plans exist presently in about half the states. In the 1960s a commission plan was proposed for California, but the commission it contemplated would have been dominated by the state bar, which was in turn dominated by the large law firms. Former Chief Justice Phil Gibson and many others (including myself) opposed the plan on the ground principally that it would limit the governor's discretion unduly and that several of the great justices of the state (including Gibson himself) would probably not have made it onto the sort of lists that such a commission was likely to produce.

The society's second recommendation was to subject judges initially appointed through the commission plan to a "retention election," in which their names would appear on the ballot without opposition and voters would vote yes or no on the question of whether they should be retained in office. The idea was that the retention election would insulate judges substantially from politics while preserving the right of the people to pass judgment on them.

California was the first state to adopt the retention election system, though without the merit plan component. It did so in 1934 through an initiative amendment to the state constitution. Under that system appellate justices are appointed by the governor to vacancies as they occur, subject to confirmation by the Commission on Judicial Appointments. Once confirmed by the Commission, the justice takes office and begins to serve, but his or her name appears on the ballot at the first gubernatorial election following the appointment, and the justice must receive a majority of the votes cast to continue in office. Appointment is for a twelve-year term, but if the appointee's predecessor left office before the completion of the term, the appointee holds office only for the balance of that term, and then must stand for election a second time. If the appointee receives a majority of the votes cast in that election, he or she does not have to face a retention election for another twelve years. This system applies only to appellate justices; trial court judges, who serve for a shorter term, are subject to being "bumped" from their benches by a challenger in a contested election.

The background of the 1934 constitutional amendment provides a historical perspective and a touch of irony. In that era it was the conservative elements in society that viewed judicial election campaigns as a threat, especially in light of the emerging political strength of labor unions. The Commonwealth Club of San Francisco, then as now a generally conservative Republican organization, had long contended for replacement of judicial elections with lifetime appointments, as in the federal system, but it came to recognize that was not a politically attainable objective. It settled on the retention election model on the theory that it would insulate appellate justices from the political pressures generated by the existing system of electoral challenge. The principal backers of the 1934 initiative—the state Chamber of Commerce and the state Republican party—supported it as a law-and-order measure, necessary to assure that criminals would receive their just deserts instead of the undue leniency unions and other critics of the social order might prefer. And the San Francisco Labor Council was the most vocal opponent of the initiative, arguing that judges should be responsive to the public will. As with the issue of judicial activism, positions seemed to depend primarily on who owns the gored ox.

From 1934 to 1986 no sitting judge had been removed by a retention election in California, but beginning in the 1960s there were portents of such an eventuality. Contrary to the assumption of both the proponents and opponents of the 1934 initiative, however, the challenge came not from the left but from the right.

In chapter 7 I described the sharp decline in affirmative votes for Supreme Court justices in the election of 1966 after the court's decision in *Mulkey v. Reitman* invalidated a popular initiative that had authorized private discrimination in housing. The next substantial challenge occurred in 1978 when Chief Justice Rose Bird was on the ballot for confirmation. There was strong opposition led by ultra-conservative state senator H. L. Richardson and bolstered by a coalition of public officials and agricultural interests. The opposition, contending that the chief justice was lax on crime, focused partly on a concurring opinion she had written in *People v. Caudillo*, in which the majority of the court concluded—quite correctly in my judgment—that in prescribing more serious penalties for crimes involving "great bodily injury," the legislature had not intended to include all rapes in that category. The chief justice agreed with the majority but stuck her neck out to write separately on the issue, and her opponents made it sound as if the first female justice on the Supreme Court did not appreciate the horrors of rape. They pointed also to her reputation for causing friction within Governor Brown's administration and to her lack of prior judicial experience. The latter did not seem to be a major shortcoming in the case of several of her predecessors, including two revered chief justices, Phil Gibson and Roger Traynor (neither of whom had served a day on the bench prior to their appointment); but even some supporters of Governor Brown thought he should have appointed veteran justice Mathew Tobriner or Stanley Mosk to the chief justiceship and made Bird an associate justice, possibly to elevate her at some later time. In addition, the chief had ruffled some feathers within the judicial establishment when she assumed control of the Administrative Office of the Courts and started doing things differently. No one in the opposition ever mentioned the chief's gender, of course, but it would be naive to suppose that it did not play a role in the formation of attitudes toward her chief justiceship. Finally, there was the sensational story that appeared in the *Los Angeles Times* on the day of the election suggesting that the chief had conspired to withhold a controversial decision until after the election (see chapter 4). In the face of all of this opposition Chief Justice Bird was confirmed, but by less than 52 percent of the vote—the lowest percentage in California history.

Some political "experts" decreed that the closeness of the 1978 election was attributable to personal characteristics of the chief justice and was no portent of the future; but the next election, four years later, proved them wrong. In 1982 the chief was not on the ballot, but four associate justices of the Supreme Court were, and three of these (Cruz Reynoso, Allen Broussard, and Otto Kaus) were opposed by conservatives, including the Republican party and future governor (then attorney general) George Deukmejian himself. The three were quite different in background, outlook, and judicial performance. What they had in common was that they were all appointed by the same governor—"Jerry's judges," the opposition called them. But the death penalty issue lurked in the background. Deukmejian, asked by a reporter to explain the apparent inconsistency between his fairly recent vote on the Judicial Appointments Commission in favor of Kaus and his announced opposition, said it was because of Kaus's opinion in a death penalty case. And so the die was cast.

The campaign against the Brown-appointed justices was not strongly financed or well run, but despite that fact the three received the lowest vote percentages for justices in any previous judicial retention election except for the 1978 Rose Bird election. Justice Kaus did the best with 57 percent; Justice Broussard came next with 56.2 percent; Justice Reynoso barely made it with 52.4 percent. The unopposed justice, Frank Richardson, breezed by with 76.2 percent, within the normal range. The impact of the campaign was clear.

My own appointment to the Supreme Court was confirmed by the Commission on Judicial Appointments just seven weeks after that election. I was under no illusions. I knew that I would be on the ballot in 1986 (the next gubernatorial election year) along with Justice Reynoso; I knew that Chief Justice Bird would be on the ballot with us; and I suspected that she, at least, would face organized opposition. But worrying about a retention election was the last thing on my mind at the time; I was far more worried about how I was going to get my work done on the court.

Moreover, from the outset people who seemed to know what they were talking about assured me that I had nothing to worry about. I had an excellent reputation, they said, and Governor Deukmejian, who had voted for me three times as a member of the Commission on Judicial Appointments, had publicly endorsed my competence and fair-mindedness when he voted to confirm my appointment to the Supreme Court.

Then in the latter part of 1984 several groups formed to announce their intended opposition not only to the chief justice but to me and Justice Reynoso, as well, on the grounds that we were too lenient toward criminal defendants in general and too hostile toward the death penalty in particular. (A couple of them threw in Justice Stanley Mosk, also an appointee of a Democratic governor, for good measure.) The groups were for the most part quite right-wing and did not seem to represent a broad spectrum of the electorate; but I met with some close friends, and we decided that I should have the advice of a political consultant just in case a serious threat developed.

It did, and quite soon thereafter. Meeting under the unofficial auspices of the state District Attorneys' Association, a group of deputy district attorneys from throughout California—though again I was assured by "knowledgeable" people that they were only after the chief justice—adopted a resolution opposing the three Brown appointees. Justice Mosk was also scheduled to be on the ballot if he decided to seek an additional term on the court; but though he appeared on the basis of his opinions to be a natural target for the deputy district attorneys, they withheld taking a position on him pending his decision on whether to run.

By the spring of 1985 it was apparent that the opposition campaign was going to be formidable. There were two main organizations. One of them, Crime Victims for Court Reform, was headed by Bill Roberts, former manager of the gubernatorial campaigns of both George Deukmejian and Ronald Reagan. Its publicity featured relatives of victims in a number of murder cases, but it received substantial funding from the Farm Bureau Federation and the Western Growers Association. Additional contributions along the way came from oil and gas interests, insurance interests, and real estate interests.

The other organization, headed by "tax crusaders" Howard Jarvis and Paul Gann (who sponsored Proposition 13 in 1978), was called Californians to Defeat Rose Bird. Despite its name, the organization had identified me, Justice Reynoso, and Justice Mosk as covillains. It relied on extensive direct mailings—a technique developed and perfected by the Jarvis-Gann group—to raise funds for the campaign and, incidentally, for the campaign's organizers. I recall a mailing the group sent out: it invited recipients to identify their own individual targets and contribute a suggested amount for each. I was insulted to discover that the suggested amount for the chief justice was four times the suggested amounts for the rest of us. In early 1986 the two groups joined forces under the banner of the California Coalition for Court Reform and dropped opposition to Justice Mosk.

The question was what sort of campaign, if any, was to be waged on our behalf. One possibility that occurred to me, and that I discussed with my friends, was to do nothing. After all, the early polls showed that I was ahead among people who had an opinion about me, and the fact that this included a relatively small percentage of voters—the remainder either not knowing who I was or having no reaction—seemed to me an advantage rather than a liability. When a friend asked me how it felt to have less name recognition than a baby who had been born the previous week to Farah Fawcett, I said it felt just fine. Moreover, doing nothing and allowing others to come to my defense if necessary—and if they were of a mind to do so—would avoid the unpleasantness and appearances of impropriety that I suspected would attend any vigorous campaign.

Political pros, however, persuaded me that a do-nothing approach was exceedingly dangerous—that low name recognition is evidence of a vacuum that can be filled one way or the other by media advertising, and that if I left it to the opponents to fill that vacuum, I would lose. Though I lost anyway, events proved their analysis was probably correct. My friends persuaded me that trying to remain "pure" by doing nothing was a form of suicide not demanded by legal ethics and certainly not contemplated by the system of elections the state constitution had established.

Justice Reynoso and I both favored encouraging the formation of a single, statewide group, independent and bipartisan, perhaps or-

ganized by leaders of the state bar. Both of us received communications from lawyers and others around the state who were prepared
to move in that direction if we gave the nod. But the chief justice
was adamantly opposed to such a development. On the basis of
her prior experience in the 1978 election she had become wary of
others purporting to act on her behalf, and she insisted on forming
and controlling her own separate committee. In the face of her opposition there seemed little prospect of an independent group
being formed at that time, even one limited to the support of Justice Reynoso and myself. Though there were lawyers and others
who did not like the chief and who did like the two of us, they were
reluctant to go public with that position, and lawyers who were
prepared to support all three of us were reluctant to incur the
chief's wrath. In the end Justice Reynoso and I each formed our
own campaign committees, hired political consultants, and entered the battleground.

Nothing in my prior experience had equipped me for what was
to come. In the late 1960s I ran for the city council in Berkeley (and
lost), but Berkeley politics is hardly a model for the state—I was
the "fascist" candidate in a field that ranged from liberal Democrat
to the far left. In addition, campaigning locally and statewide are
two quite different beasts. I had dabbled in statewide politics, but
mainly advocating issues and not working at the core of any candidate's campaign. Traveling about the state giving speeches and interviews, engaging in intensive political fund-raising, making television spots—all of this was to me a new adventure.

I have to say that there were aspects of the experience that I
enjoyed, or that at least I considered valuable. A candidate is
bound to derive from a campaign a certain amount of ego satisfaction, whatever the nature of the opposition. Besides, I like public
speaking, and I felt a challenge in trying to explain myself and the
courts to audiences in nonlegal communities, such as at Rotary Club
luncheons or union meetings. Speaking to law enforcement groups
(two of which ended up endorsing me) was of course a special
challenge.

Moreover, I learned a great deal in the process, not only about
political campaigns in general and judicial campaigns in particular,
but also about my state and the people in it, and about my self as
well. Appellate justices tend to live rather restricted lives, and the

process of meeting and communicating with people from various parts of the state and various walks of life is mutually instructive. That much, at least, I can say for judicial elections. As a student who came to hear me speak at a state university put it, if it were not for the election, I probably would not have been there.

I would also concede that judicial elections can serve a useful purpose in maintaining public confidence in the judiciary. There was a time in our nation's history when judges were drawn from narrow segments of society and were seen as representing the interests of particular groups or classes. That can happen again. Indeed, perhaps the public in California saw us in that light. The public expression of discontent through the ballot may have a certain regenerative effect.

There is, however, a darker side to a judicial election, which I found myself confronting with increasing intensity as the campaign wore on. I do not mean simply the wear and tear on the candidate—that is a characteristic of any political campaign; and though trying to undertake campaign tasks under the pressure of judicial duties and being attacked publicly as a judge who is callous to the victims of crime are not pleasant experiences, the price is surely one that the public has a right to exact if the process is otherwise worthwhile. It is the peculiar aspects of being a statewide candidate in a *judicial* election that are the subject of my concern.

I did not fully appreciate, when I was appointed to the court, the handicaps that canons and traditions of judicial ethics and decorum impose on a judge in such an election. Unlike most candidates for elective office, I could make no campaign promises. If I knew about opinions yet to be filed that would be pleasing to the voters (as was the case), I could not talk about them. My "platform" was limited to my past.

Moreover, the tradition is that a sitting judge is not supposed to talk publicly about opinions he or she has written or joined in such a way as to provide an interpretation of the decision. Part of the reasoning behind that tradition is that an opinion in which more than one judge joins is a collegial product, and each judge may have a different view as to its meaning. Another part is that a judge should not be in the business of announcing in advance how he or she might rule if a particular issue comes before the court, and public interpretation of a judge's remarks may have that effect.

Whatever their force in the abstract, these considerations are particularly potent when a court has before it cases that bear close resemblance to cases previously decided. This was so, in the 1986 campaign, with respect to death penalty cases. There were about one hundred fifty death penalty judgments awaiting court consideration, and for me to talk publicly about past death penalty cases posed the risk that I would be understood as expressing an opinion about issues in pending cases as well. Death penalty jurisprudence was in a state of flux during this period at the federal level, and there was constant discussion within our court as to what United States Supreme Court precedents required. Anything that I or any other justice said in that sensitive arena was subject to misinterpretation. I decided that it would be improper for me to talk about death penalty cases in more than a very general way.

I also felt constrained about attacking my adversaries in public, and in particular about questioning their motivations. There was good reason to believe that for many of them the death penalty issue was a cover for objections to decisions in other areas or for a simple desire to make room on the court for appointments by a conservative governor whom everyone expected to win reelection in the gubernatorial race. But the fact is that I expected to win also, and I did not want to contribute to an atmosphere of hostility that would continue to hover over the court's deliberations in years to come. After all, the governor, the district attorneys, and the various business interests who were contributing to the opposition campaign were all frequent litigants before the court. So, much to the chagrin of the reporters who constantly lust after direct confrontation, I limited my comments to issues I could discuss in an impersonal way.

The constraints on campaigning were much less troublesome for me than the problem of fund-raising. The opposition started early and was raising big money for an announced media campaign. At first I thought I could get by with a low-level response; but on the advice of persons experienced in politics I decided I had to plan for the worst, and so my committee set out to raise a million dollars on my behalf.

We came close to our target, raising a bit more than nine hundred thousand dollars, but that was peanuts compared to what was raised elsewhere in the campaign. Altogether my committee, those of Chief Justice Bird and Justice Reynoso, and the independent committee formed late in the campaign raised nearly $4.5 million. The opposition raised more than $7 million, and that does not include the amounts spent by political candidates who found it to their advantage to include an anti–Rose Bird message in their own advertising. Twelve million dollars to decide whether three justices of the Supreme Court should remain in office! I could not help thinking how many homeless people could have been housed and fed with all that cash.

The process of raising that money was one of the worst experiences of my life. We had fund-raising events, we sent fund-raising letters, and worst of all we made fund-raising phone calls. At first I resisted personally asking anyone for money, but our canons of judicial ethics in California expressly permit a judge who is opposed in an election to do that, and I was finally persuaded that I had to do it if we were to come anywhere near our fund-raising goal.

Money came from a variety of sources, but a large part of it came from persons and groups—lawyers and labor unions, for example—that had some interest, not to say stake, in the judicial process and in the outcome of cases. The same was true of the opposition: agricultural, insurance, oil and gas, and other business interests contributed large sums. And under California law there was no way I could insulate myself from knowing who had contributed. I had to sign periodic reports to a state agency listing each contribution and its source, and so did the opposition. All of this was not only personally distasteful but also unseemly and, unavoidable as it seemed to be, almost certainly erosive of public confidence in the long run.

The ugliness of fund-raising hit me toward the end of the campaign in a most dramatic way. I was talking to a lawyer in Los Angeles at the bar of a hotel where I was to speak. He informed me that someone had called him to ask for money for both me and Justice Reynoso and had told him that the two of us were keeping tabs on who contributed and who did not and that once we were confirmed, we would keep that in mind when it came to deciding cases. The information made me very upset, and I begged him to tell me the name of the person who had called him so that I could take steps to correct the situation; but he declined to do so. When

I returned to San Francisco, I called my professional fund-raiser (yes, of course, I had several of those) and told him to get the word out that if I learned the identity of anyone who engaged in such tactics, I would personally report him to the state bar. He was surprised at my intensity.

I am confident that any judge worthy of his robes would not be influenced by such considerations. I made clear in my speeches that lawyers and others who supported me could expect nothing more in return than my attempt to do an honest job. But I would think that the appearance of impropriety, especially in the eyes of the general public, is unavoidable. As the Texas Supreme Court met to consider Texaco's appeal from a $10-billion verdict in favor of Pennzoil, the judges (who are elected to their seats in contested elections) heard on both sides from lawyers who had contributed heavily to their campaigns. As it happened, Pennzoil's lawyers had contributed approximately $315,000 to Texaco's mere $72,000. A professor at the University of Texas was quoted in defense of the system as saying, "You use your resources to elect legislators favorable to your position; it's no different than electing judges favorable to your position." I think it is.

Even more disturbing than the fund-raising, however, was the atmosphere generated by the nature and focus of the opponents' attack. Their subtext was in accord with the premise of the Texas professor: confirming judicial appointments through election is no different than choosing among candidates for legislative or executive office; if you like their "voting record," vote for them, and if you do not, vote against them. Many politicians and editorial writers reiterated that view. Early polling showed that the message was well received. Though voters were nominally supportive of an independent judiciary, a poll by Pat Caddell in the spring of 1985 showed that they believed by a margin of 68 percent to 24 percent that they should vote against retention of judges with whose decisions they disagreed.

By *decisions* it is clear that what is meant is not the *opinion* the judge has written or signed, expressing the legal justification for the result, but the result itself, pure and simple. This was the scorecard approach, which achieved its peak in the death penalty arena. Opponents tabulated our votes in death penalty cases so as to show the number of cases in which we had voted to affirm or to reverse, typically without the slightest mention, much less criticism, of the reasons underlying our opinions.

Governor Deukmejian invoked the scorecard approach when in late August of 1986 he finally announced his position regarding Justice Reynoso and myself. He had indicated his opposition to the chief justice back in 1984, and in the spring of 1986 he was challenging his opponent, Mayor Tom Bradley of Los Angeles, to take a position on her retention when a reporter asked him about Reynoso and me. He replied that on the basis of our records to that date he was inclined to vote against us but intended to wait and see how we decided future death penalty cases. Justice (now Chief Justice) Malcolm Lucas, an ex-partner of Deukmejian, told me that he had spoken personally with the governor and recommended that he endorse me. But in August the governor announced his opposition to both of us, relying on the fact that Justice Reynoso had voted to affirm in only one death penalty case, and I in five, to conclude that we were not "objective" in that arena.

The shallowness of that approach is reflected in Governor Deukmejian's comparison of our "voting records" in death penalty cases with that of our colleague, Justice Mosk. He observed that Justice Mosk had voted to affirm in a greater number of cases, the implication being that if another "liberal" judge had found it in his heart to do such a thing, there must be something wrong with our perceptions. The fact is that nearly all of the cases in which Justice Mosk voted to affirm while I voted to reverse fell into one of two categories. Some of them were cases in which the jury had been instructed that it should not consider sympathy for the defendant; Justice Mosk adhered to his dissenting view that such an instruction was permissible, whereas I followed the majority holding in *People v. Easley*, decided prior to my arrival on the court, that such an instruction violated federal constitutional standards. In the other category of cases Justice Mosk and I disagreed on how to apply standards for reversible error established by the United States Supreme Court and our court for situations in which the jury is not instructed that it must find *intent* to kill in order to impose the death penalty. This latter area of the law was in a state of flux, and in one of the pending death penalty cases I wrote a dissenting opinion, which Justice Mosk and Justice Lucas both signed, aimed at arriving at a constitutionally acceptable procedure for dealing with such situations. (I have described the dimensions of that legal and practical dilemma in chapter 6.) My point, of course, is not that I was right and that Justice Mosk was wrong but that there existed between us legitimate legal disagreements that accounted for the difference in the "scores." To concentrate on the results without considering the reasons seems hardly a legitimate means of evaluating judicial performance. Besides, the governor failed to say how many more death penalty judgments I would have to vote to affirm to gain his approval.

The issue is more than that of fairness to the candidate—though I admit I still burn when I think about it. I recognize that politics is often unfair, and that people who choose to enter the political arena (if that is what we want to say judges do when they run for retention) have to take that into account. What concerns me more is the impact on our body politic—on courts and the way we view them—of such a cost-accounting approach to judicial evaluation.

During the campaign I declared that it was my goal to go to bed election night knowing, as best one can know such things, that I had not decided any case differently because of the election. I believe I achieved that goal, but I have to recognize that I may be wrong. At no time while I was on the court did I participate in or overhear any discussion as to how a particular opinion would "play" in the public ear. Any judge who articulated such a concern would have been frowned at by his colleagues. But one would have to be superhuman not to *think* about such things—Justice Kaus said it was like brushing your teeth in the bathroom and trying not to notice the crocodile in the bathtub. And having thought about them, how does a judge make sure that they do not influence his or her opinion one way or the other—by yielding unconsciously to public pressure or bending over backward to avoid it?

After he left the bench, Justice Kaus acknowledged the possibility that a key vote of his during the 1982 campaign when he was on the ballot may have been affected, perhaps subconsciously, by the pendency of that election. There is profound truth, as well as great candor, in that acknowledgment. I would have to acknowledge the same dilemma, particularly with respect to death penalty cases. In any event, whether such a campaign in fact influences how particular judges decide cases, it is likely to give rise to the perception that it does. Indeed, in an election in which the public is told time and again that judges are politicians like anyone else on the ballot, it would be surprising if the public did not believe that.

The point was brought home to me toward the end of the campaign when the court filed an opinion, which I wrote, essentially affirming a death penalty judgment. Justice Reynoso joined in that opinion, and the spokesperson for the crime victims group held a press conference to announce that we had done so only to attract voter support. I could not help reflecting on what the defendant and his attorney must have thought when they read the report of that press conference.

There were people, including some lawyers and law professors, who voiced criticism of Chief Justice Bird on grounds other than her decisions in criminal cases, and to some extent that was true also of criticism of Justice Reynoso and myself. Business interests, particularly, were probably not nearly as concerned with decisions in death penalty cases as they were with decisions they perceived as overly protective of the interests of consumers, workers, and accident victims. A group of lawyers from a Los Angeles firm issued a "white paper" during the campaign in which they identified a number of such decisions and criticized them. I responded by pointing out that I had not participated in most of the cases they criticized and by observing some inaccuracies and distortions in their analysis. I did not consider, however, that I could legitimately ask voter support on the basis that my decisions were favorable to a particular group or class, since I considered that to be a wholly inappropriate criterion for judicial evaluation.

It seems clear, in any event, that the law-and-order issue, and within that primarily the death penalty issue, determined the outcome. My low name recognition and my substantial lead among those who had an opinion remained until the closing weeks of the campaign when the opposition, satisfied that the chief justice was going to lose, went after Justice Reynoso and myself with thirty-second television spots linking the two of us to Rose Bird and the death penalty issue. One of these featured an emotional presentation by a mother complaining that the Supreme Court had set aside the death penalty judgment against the murderer of her child and implying that the murderer was on the loose as a result. The spot did not mention that a second trial had already been conducted and that the murderer had again been convicted and sentenced to death. Another television spot told viewers that if they wanted to keep the death penalty in California, they should vote no on Bird, Reynoso, and Grodin. That spot pictured a hand with a ballot marker coming down on the "no" box opposite each of our prominently featured names. After those television spots began to run, my name recognition increased dramatically, and along with it my negative rating. Polls throughout the campaign showed that it was the perceived leniency of the chief justice and "her" court toward the death penalty and criminal defendants generally that most upset the voters, and exit polls confirmed that it was these issues that did us in.

I had my own television spots. One of them pictured a real superior court judge declaring that I was a "judge's judge" and had written a key opinion applying the Victim's Bill of Rights. A second pictured two police officers walking away from the scene of a nighttime arrest and announcing that both their organizations had endorsed me. A third featured me saying something banal about applying the law. Though professionals thought they were "good spots" (I guess they were), and though they were all truthful, the fact that it seemed necessary to appeal to voters this way was disturbing. The chief justice ran some high-minded ads, whereas Justice Reynoso's ads were similar to mine. An independent group that formed toward the end of the campaign with the participation of former governor Pat Brown attempted to garner public support on the basis of court decisions that "favored" consumers, workers, the environment, and accident victims—roughly the liberal equivalent of the result-oriented campaign of the right. The fact is that nothing we did, or could think of doing, came anywhere near countering the emotional impact that the opponents were able to derive from the opposition's victim-based appeal.

Throughout the campaign I debated—with myself as well as with others—the question of the criteria appropriate to such an election. Editorial writers, politicians, lawyers and legal scholars, and our supporters and opponents all expressed a variety of views. Some of them I found useful, others not. A useful view, it seemed to me, had to begin with some notion of what it means to be a judge and had to combine that with some notion of what it means to have a judicial election. If, for example, one were to view judges as being in the business of making laws in essentially the same manner as legislators, who bring to bear in each case nothing more than their personal policy preferences or the immediate views of their constituency, then it would seem quite appropriate to adopt the criteria implicit (and sometimes explicit) in the opposition to the three of us. In the previous chapter I explained why I think that view of the judicial process is distorted and unfaithful to reality.

I could not in good conscience, however, advocate the polar view—that judges simply apply the law, and nothing more. Such a view would support the proposition that election criteria should be extremely narrow—perhaps limited to impeachable offenses and the like, or possibly extending to some judgment of incompetency based on performance—but it is not a view that comports with my understanding of the judicial process nor, I think, with anyone else's understanding. It requires no legal genius to recognize that Chief Justice Rehnquist and Justice O'Connor of the United States Supreme Court typically reach different conclusions than Justices Brennan and Marshall, nor to understand that the difference must be attributable to something other than their abilities to read the Constitution and prior precedents. Some of our supporters (and perhaps we ourselves on occasion) invoked the model of the umpire to argue for restrictive criteria; but insofar as that model conjures the image of someone simply calling balls and strikes, I cannot say it appealed to me.

In the course of the campaign I attempted to articulate the middle ground I expressed in the preceding chapter—that the judicial function ranges along a continuum from constraint to discretion depending on the area of law involved and the nature of the particular case—but I found it hard going for two reasons. First, the concepts involved in that proposition are not so easy to explain, particularly in a brief interview. Second, the criteria appropriate to the middle ground are not so clear.

There are, I think, several criteria that are in theory appropriate to the middle ground. For example, one might attempt to determine whether a particular judge is in fact faithful to his or her obligation to follow the law in those situations where its meaning seems clear. In those cases in which the judge is called on to bring value judgments to bear, one might attempt to determine whether a particular judge is acting within the historical mainstream of community values, which it is his or her duty to consult. One might ask whether a particular judge is so much the captive of a particular ideology or outlook that he or she cannot perform as a judge is expected to perform.

These are theoretically acceptable criteria; the problem is that they are not particularly useful. Identifying the extent to which a judge's personal outlook may have contributed to a judgment in a particular case is at best a highly esoteric task. Law professors who devote their lives to studying judges and their legal opinions have difficulty making, let alone agreeing on, such judgments. It is extremely difficult in an election campaign for a voter even to obtain information that would support that sort of analysis. Hence what is likely to happen—what in fact did happen during the 1986 election campaign—is that voters will rely on the kinds of judgments with which they are much more familiar and about which the relevant information is far more accessible—namely, whether they agree with the conclusions the judge reached in particular cases or categories of cases. Reliance on that criterion, as I have argued, poses a severe threat to the integrity of the judicial process.

It is possible that I am exaggerating the threat. Some commentators have suggested that the California judicial election of 1986 was a unique phenomenon, the product of a peculiar concatenation of an unpopular chief justice, appointed by a governor who became equally unpopular, and public furor over the death penalty. They may be right, and I hope they are, but I doubt it. Two years earlier a similar law-and-order campaign was waged against my friend Hans Linde of the Oregon Supreme Court, though he managed to prevail. As I write this paragraph I have in front of me an article from the *Wall Street Journal* that describes a similar development in Texas, where for the first time in that state's history a majority of its Supreme Court justices are about to be chosen in a single election. "Fed up with losing court cases that expand the rights of plaintiffs to sue and collect high-dollar damages," the article reports, "the business community has decided to try to eliminate the judges who vote that way—and replace them with judges who think as they do." It says that several important business cases are headed for the state Supreme Court, including one that may determine under what circumstances Texas companies can test employees for drugs; and the business community, through campaign contributions to the justices, political ads, and anticourt editorials in trade publications, are trying to make sure they are decided "correctly." California tends to be a trendsetter, and I suspect its reputation in that respect will endure.

So what to do if I am right, and the California experience turns out to be a model for other states? It is possible, as some political scientists would argue, that even taking into account the drawbacks that exist, we are better off with elections than without them. Elections, they contend, provide a valuable means by which the public may exercise ultimate control over the judicial branch and in the process validate the functions that that branch performs, especially the function of constitutional review. An election may be traumatic to the participants and the institution, and it may result in the removal of some judges who are doing a fine job, but (so the argument goes) public confidence in the judiciary is likely to be enhanced.

I recognize there is some force to that argument, but I am not persuaded. No other country in which courts exercise the function of judicial review depends on elections to validate that function, or indeed any other judicial function. In this country the federal system of lifetime appointments has, on the whole, worked quite well. The quality of federal judges has generally been high—probably higher than in the state courts—and though we have had periods in which the United States Supreme Court was viewed as improperly impeding the public will by declaring legislative acts unconstitutional, we have as a nation resisted the numerous proposals to alter the structure of the court on that account.

Moreover, state courts pose less of an obstacle to the implementation of majoritarian policies than do federal courts. If a state court finds some governmental action invalid under the federal Constitution, its decision is reviewable by the United States Supreme Court. If it finds such an action invalid under the state constitution, its decision is subject to reversal by constitutional amendment far more readily than in the case of the federal Constitution. In fact, there is nothing that state courts do that the public cannot undo—at least for the future—by acting through their elected representatives or directly through the ballot. That concerns about "accountability" should require elections for state court judges but not for federal court judges, though understandable in terms of history, seems illogical.

My first preference, were I given the option, would be the federal model of lifetime appointments, at least for appellate judges. (I concede there may be a better argument for electing trial judges, who come into closer contact with the public and the practicing bar.) I would combine that model, however, with some substantial means of either limiting or passing on the governor's power of appointment so as to enhance public confidence in the selection process. This can be done through a merit system, in which applicants for the bench are screened by a blue-ribbon commission, but for reasons I expressed earlier I think that approach should be viewed with skepticism. I think an expanded procedure for considering the governor's selection would be preferable to a procedure that would limit his or her selection. Expansion could be achieved either through a broad-based commission or through confirmation by a branch of the state legislature. The latter procedure carries a potential for political shenanigans, to be sure, but it is impossible (and in my view undesirable) to exclude politics from the selection process altogether.

Lifetime appointment is not the only alternative to elections. New York has adopted the fixed-term approach for its highest court: gubernatorial appointment, pursuant to a merit plan, to a fourteen-year term of office. That would be my second choice. Whether the judge should be eligible for reappointment under such a system is debatable. If he is not, then the state may be deprived of the services of a great judge in his or her prime. If he is, then we run the risk that the judge may be perceived as currying favor with the incumbent governor through his or her decisions. I am inclined to think that fourteen years is enough.

I realize, however, that neither of these changes is likely in the near future. In the absence of a more persuasive demonstration of the defects inherent in judicial elections, the public is not about to relinquish the right to vote for judges. The immediate question is whether there are things that can be done *within* the system of elections to insulate the judicial process from the types of risk I have described.

One area certainly deserving of attention is the funding of judicial campaigns. Dean Gerald Uelemen of the University of Santa Clara Law School has suggested that judges be required to disqualify themselves in cases in which a party or counsel has contributed in excess of a certain amount to the judge's election or reelection campaign. Such an approach has potential merit at the trial level, where there are other judges who can readily be transferred to hear a case. It would be more awkward at the appellate level, and particularly at the level of the Supreme Court, where there are likely to be hundreds of cases pending at any one time and only a limited number of judges to hear them. There is also the question of the scope of the disqualification principle. To avoid unseemliness, the principle would have to apply not only to cases in which a hearing had been granted but also to those in which a petition for review is pending. And in order to avoid easy evasion, it would have to apply not only to individual lawyers who make contributions but also to the law firms of which they are members. Yet if those had been the ground rules during the 1986 campaign, one or all of the three of us would have been disqualified in a majority of matters pending before the court. Perhaps that is not such a terrible thing in itself, but it certainly would have a chilling effect on contributions by any lawyers who have, or think they may have, a case before the court. That result must be viewed against the fact that the opposition would be operating under no such constraints. Such a system would have to be adjusted to avoid placing the incumbents at a serious disadvantage.

Perhaps a more fruitful approach lies in the direction of public financing, or financing through a lawyers' trust fund, tied to acceptance of limitations on contributions and spending. (Limitations not accepted by the candidate appear to pose serious problems under the United States Supreme Court's decision in *Buckley v. Valeo*, which held that restrictions on the extent of financial support violate the First Amendment.) There have been experiments with all or portions of that approach in various parts of the country, including Cleveland, Monroe County in New York, Dade County in Florida, and the states of Wisconsin and North Carolina. Professor Schotland of Georgetown University Law Center proposes a national project, backed by such organizations as the American Judicature Society, the American Bar Association, and the American Law Institute, to focus attention on the problem and develop solutions.

As regards the more general threat posed by judicial elections—that the substance of the campaign will politicize the judicial process and create the appearance, if not the reality, of judges bowing to public pressure—there are obviously no easy answers. One approach is to bolster confidence in the selection process, perhaps through some form of merit system. The theory is that a public that is satisfied with the manner in which judges are selected will be less likely to be suspicious of them or hostile toward them when they appear on the ballot. My view is that such an approach deserves consideration, but only on the basis of procedures and criteria that assure that the commission assigned to do the screening be truly nonpartisan and broadly based. Avoidance of politics within such a commission is no easy task.

Beyond that, I think we need to work toward a consensus of constraint as to the criteria appropriate to a judicial election. During the 1986 election some politicians and editorial writers made the argument that there was no point in talking about what the criteria should be because the state constitution contained no limits on the sorts of considerations that could be brought to bear by the voters. That argument, of course, is a complete non sequitur. Voters know that they are free to vote on any basis they like; but an intelligent voter considers on what basis, as a good citizen, to cast his or her ballot. There is a consensus in most communities that a recall election demands different criteria than an ordinary election; a similar consensus needs to be developed with respect to judicial elections. All of us have a responsibility to see to that development.

In 1988 in Berkeley a liberal lawyer ran for office against a conservative municipal court judge who had been appointed by Governor Deukmejian. In response to an inquiry from a student at the University of California who knew of my own experience and sought my views concerning the election, I wrote the following:

It is vital to insulate incumbent judges from gross political pressures in the performance of their duties. In order to do that we need to establish a consensus of constraint. As applied to trial judges that means in my view that we should vote to oust an incumbent judge in favor of a challenger not simply because we like the challenger better, nor because we are unhappy with some of the incumbent's decisions, nor because the governor who appointed the judge offends us, but only when it is demonstrated to our satisfaction that the incumbent is deficient as a judge in some important respect. That we may regard a judge as being too "liberal" or "conservative" is not sufficient unless we are convinced that the judge's view of the law and its relationship to society is so extreme that it lies outside the mainstream of legal thought and community values. And we must be very careful in making that judgment, so as to avoid creating an atmosphere in which politics becomes the dominant criterion. If we are unsure, I think we owe the incumbent the benefit of the doubt.

Such a self-imposed restraint, which I would adapt to retention elections for appellate judges as well, is compatible both with our right to vote in judicial elections and with our obligation as citizens to vote with understanding. Moreover, it is essential if we are to avoid damage to the important but fragile principle of an independent judiciary.

Conclusion

If one judges even a single case according to its truth, it is as
if he were a partner with God in the Act of Creation.
                                                    Talmud

We have in this country a tradition that combines an admiration
and respect for our institutions and office holders with a healthy
skepticism bordering on distrust. I, for one, would not have it any
other way. I trust that this book will not be seen as an argument for
exempting courts or judges from public scrutiny, for certainly that
is not its intent. Rather, its intent is to expose to public view the
nature and function of state judicial systems, and particularly of
state appellate courts, so that the public will be better equipped to
engage in intelligent appraisal. For a democratic society, skepticism is healthier the more it is based on understanding.

This book is mainly about courts and judges, but of course they
are only a part of the picture; what I have written has implications
also for the legal profession and the public esteem (or disesteem) in
which that profession is held. Distrust of lawyers by the public has
ancient roots, and no doubt for some lawyers it is well deserved;
but the public's attitudes toward the profession (and for that matter
lawyers' attitudes toward the profession as well) cannot help but be
shape in part by what the public perceives that lawyers do when
they practice law. And since practicing law for most lawyers means
interacting with courts directly or indirectly, the perception of
what lawyers do is inevitably shaped in part by perception of the
judicial function.

I have described and criticized in this book the extreme positions held by those who say on one hand that judges are engaged simply in the application of preexisting rules and on the other that they are engaged simply in the making of new rules. If one were to accept the former position, then the implications for the legal profession would be obvious: lawyers would be doing nothing that a good computer operator could not do better. The implications of the latter position are also quite clear: if judges are nothing but legislators with robes, then lawyers are nothing but lobbyists with law degrees. Neither model is conducive to high public regard or, in the case of the lawyer, to high self-respect.

I have attempted to convey understanding of the sort of principled creativity that I (and many others) believe is the essence of the judicial function—the exercise of judgment in a disciplined way within a framework of democratic procedures and values. If I am correct, then the lawyer's role is neither mechanical nor supplicating; the lawyer and the judge are partners in a creative enterprise. That is the way, I believe, that lawyers should view themselves; and that is the way they (or at least the ones that live up to the role) deserve to be viewed by the public, though in our democratic system the public must ultimately be the senior partner.

Notes

The most famous piece of judicial introspection by a state court judge is the series of lectures in 1921 by then New York Court of Appeal judge Benjamin Cardozo, published under the title *The Nature of the Judicial Process* (New Haven: Yale University Press, 1921). That work is discussed extensively in chapter 9. Law review articles by state court judges about their work include various pieces by Chief Justice Roger Traynor of the California Supreme Court collected in *The Traynor Reader* (Hastings Law Journal 1987) and an article on statutory interpretation by Chief Justice Ellen Peters of the Connecticut Supreme Court, "Common Law Judging in a Statutory World," 43 *University of Pittsburgh Law Review* 759 (1965). An exception to the esoteric tendencies of state judges in their writings is a book by Justice Richard Neely of the West Virginia Supreme Court intended for the general public, *How Courts Govern America* (New Haven: Yale University Press, 1981). His thesis is that to the extent that courts make political decisions (and in his view that is a very considerable extent, indeed), they do a better job of it than legislatures. It is an interesting thesis, with which I agree only in part.

Federal judges have been more forthcoming. In *Courts on Trial* (Princeton: Princeton University Press, 1949) Judge Jerome Frank of the Second Circuit Court of Appeal wrote about his view of trial courts, emphasizing their discretion in the finding of facts. More recently Judge Frank Coffin of the First Circuit Court of Appeal wrote a valuable work on the federal appellate process as seen from the inside, using histories of cases in which he participated, *The Ways of a Judge: Reflections From the Federal Appellate Bench* (Boston: Houghton Mifflin, 1980). A number of former United States Supreme Court justices have written memoirs that reveal the process of that court, including Earl Warren, *The Memoirs of Earl Warren* (Garden City, N.J.: Doubleday, 1977); Felix Frankfurter, *Felix Frankfurter Reminisces* (New

York: Reynal, 1960); and William O. Douglas, *The Court Years 1939–1975: The Autobiography of William O. Douglas* (New York: Random House, 1980). Articles by federal judges abound. A particularly thoughtful piece is Jon O. Newman, "Between Legal Realism and Neutral Principles: The Legitimacy of Institutional Values," 72 *California Law Review* 200 (1984). See also Irving Kaufman, "The Anatomy of Decisionmaking," 53 *Fordham Law Review* 1 (1984); Henry Friendly, "Reactions of a Lawyer–Newly Appointed Judge," 71 *Yale Law Journal* 218 (1961); Patricia Wald, "Thoughts on Decisionmaking," 87 *West Virginia Law Review* 1 (1984); Richard Posner, "The Meaning of Judicial Self-Restraint," 59 *Indiana Law Journal* 1 (1984). *Views From the Bench: The Judiciary and Constitutional Politics*, ed. Mark Cannon and David O'Brien (Chatham, N.J.: Chatham House, 1985) contains a collection of essays by sitting judges (mainly federal) and an excellent bibliography.

Political scientists have written more extensively about state courts than have lawyers. An excellent recent publication is G. Alan Tarr and Mary C. Porter, *State Supreme Courts in Nation and State* (New Haven: Yale University Press, 1988).

1. ON BECOMING A JUDGE

Textual references: Joseph Grodin, *Union Government and the Law* (Los Angeles: Institute of Industrial Relations, University of California, 1961), is my Ph.D. dissertation. The opinions of Justice Tobriner are discussed in a symposium on the Justice published in 29 *Hastings Law Journal* 1–210 (1977). The law review article we coauthored is Matthew Tobriner and Joseph Grodin, "The Individual and the Public Service Enterprise in the New Industrial State," 55 *California Law Review* 1247 (1967). The labor cases pending before the California Supreme Court at the time of Max Radin's abortive appointment are reported in 16 Cal.2d 311, 311–410 (1940).

Bibliographical note: The literature on judicial selection and tenure is voluminous. An excellent bibliography on both state and federal material appears in Nancy Chinn and Larry Berkson, *Literature on Judicial Selection* (Chicago: American Judicature Society, 1980). A standard historical and comparative work is Evan Haynes, *The Selection and Tenure of Judges* (Littleton, Colo.: Rothman, 1981). The varying state procedures are summarized in Larry Berkson, Scott Beller, and Michele Grimaldi, *Judicial Selection in the United States: A Compendium of Provisions* (Chicago: American Judicature Society, 1980). See the bibliographical note to chapter 10 for selected references to works on judicial elections.

2. THE COURT OF APPEAL

Textual references: The probate case in which I wrote the opinion was *Estate of Parsons*, 103 Cal.App.3d 384 (1980). The labor arbitration case in which I dissented was *Service Employees International Union, Local 614 v. County of Napa*, 99 Cal.App.3d 946 (1979).

Bibliographical note: Marlin Osthus, *State Intermediate Appellate Courts*

(Chicago: American Judicature Society, 1980), describes the various models of intermediate appellate systems and contains a state-by-state summary of jurisdictional and procedural provisions.

3. PRESIDING JUSTICE

Textual references: The historical studies of statistics on litigation are George B. Curtis, "The Colonial County Court, Social Forum and Legislative Precedent, Accomack County, Virginia 1633–1639," 85 *Virginia Magazine of History and Biography* 274, 287 (1977); Wayne McIntosh, "Litigation and Private Dispute Settlement in the St. Louis Circuit Court, 1820–1970: A Preliminary Analysis," paper presented at the annual meeting of the American Political Science Association, 1978; and Lawrence Friedman and Robert Percival, *Roots of Justice: Crime and Punishment in Alameda County, California, 1870–1910* (Chapel Hill: University of North Carolina Press, 1981). These studies are summarized and analyzed in Marc Galanter, "Reading the Landscape of Disputes: What We Know and Don't Know (and Think We Know) About Our Allegedly Contentious and Litigious Society," 31 *University of California at Los Angeles Law Review* 4 (1983).

Bibliographical note: Among the many studies of the appellate process and of ways to make it more efficient, see John A. Martin, *Appellate Court Delay* (Williamsburg, Va.: National Center for State Courts, 1981).

4. THE SUPREME COURT

Textual references: The New Jersey Supreme Court decision on the right of incompetent persons to sterilization under restricted circumstances is *In the Matter of Lee Ann Grady*, 85 N.J. 235, 426 A.2d 467 (1981). The Washington Supreme Court decision is *In the Matter of Guardianship of Hayes*, 93 Wn.2d 288, 608 P.2d 635 (1980). The following are names and citations of the California Supreme Court decisions referred to in the text: *County Sanitation District No. 2 v. Los Angeles County Employees Association*, 38 Cal.3d 564, 699 P.2d 835 (1985) gave qualified approval for certain public employees to strike; *People v. Geiger*, 35 Cal.3d 510, 674 P.2d 1303 (1984) required instructions to juries on lesser related offenses; *Frances T. v. Village Green Owners Association*, 42 Cal.2d 490, 723 P.2d 573 (1986) held that directors of a nonprofit corporation could be liable for injuries caused by their negligence; *George Beckman v. I.R.M. Corporation*, 38 Cal.3d 454, 698 P.2d 115 (1985) held that a landlord could be strictly liable for defective products on the premises. Among the cases that might be said to reflect a conservative, or at least cautious, approach on the part of the court were the following: *American Bank and Trust Co. v. Community Hospital*, 36 Cal.3d 359, 683 P.2d 670 (1984), upholding the constitutionality of legislation that limited recovery to plaintiffs in medical malpractice cases; *Coleman v. Gulf Insurance Company*, 41 Cal.3d 782, 718 P.2d 77 (1986), declining to create a new remedy for a plaintiff who contended the insurance company had filed an appeal in bad faith; *Santa Rosa Junior College v. Workers Compensa-*

tion Appeal Board, 40 Cal.3d 345, 708 P.2d 678 (1985), declining to create, in favor of a teacher who worked at home, an exception to the rule barring workers' compensation recovery for injuries incurred while going to or from work; *Halaco Engineering Co. v. South Central Coast Regional Commission*, 42 Cal.3d 52, 720 P.2d 15 (1986), recognizing the vested right of a property owner as against a claim of the Coastal Commission; and various cases decided on narrow grounds, including *Finn v. G. D. Searle*, 35 Cal.3d 691, 677 P.2d 1147 (1984), and *Seaman's Direct Buying Service, Inc. v. Standard Oil of California*, 36 Cal.3d 752, 686 P.2d 1158 (1984).

Bibliographical note: For historical information about individual justices of the California Supreme Court, I have relied mainly on J. Edward Johnson, *History of the Supreme Court Justices of California*, 2 vols. (San Francisco: Bender-Moss, 1963). The story of the 1981 inquiry by the Commission of Judicial Performance into charges of wrongdoing by members of the court is told from quite different perspectives in Preble Stolz, *Judging Judges: The Investigation of Rose Bird and the California Supreme Court* (New York: Free Press, 1981), and Betty Medsger, *Framed: The New Right Attack on Chief Justice Rose Bird and the Courts* (New York: Pilgrim Press, 1983).

5. COMMON LAW

Textual references: The California Supreme Court decision declining to apply strict liability principles to pharmaceutical products is *Brown v. Superior Court*, 44 Cal.3d 1049; 751 P.2d 410 (1988). The court's decision imposing liability on a bartender for serving an intoxicated patron is *Vesely v. Sager*, 5 Cal.3d 153, 486 P.2d 151 (1973). In the subsequent case, *Strang v. Cabrol*, 37 Cal.3d 720, 619 P.2d 1013 (1984), the court acknowledged and applied the supervening legislation. The Traynor quotation is from Roger Traynor, "Reasoning in a Circle of Law," 56 *Virginia Law Review* 739, 745 (1970).

Bibliographical note: The brief historical account of the development of the common law in England is adapted from Martin M. Shapiro, *Courts: A Comparative and Political Analysis* (Chicago: University of Chicago Press, 1981). A standard text is Theodore F. T. Plucknett, *Concise History of the Common Law*, 5th ed. (Boston: Little, Brown, 1956). The story of revolutionary attitudes toward the common law, as well as of the gradual shrinkage in the domain of the common law, is described in highly readable form in Lawrence Friedman, *A History of American Law* (New York: Simon and Schuster, 1973). The article I wrote with Justice Tobriner, noted in the textual references to chapter 1, contains a brief description of the development of the common law from status to contract. The standard text written in 1861 is Henry S. Maine, *Ancient Law* (1861; New York: Dorset Press, 1986), note L, 422. The background of *MacPherson v. Buick* is simply and clearly developed in Edward Levi, *An Introduction to Legal Reasoning* (Chicago: University of Chicago Press, 1949), 1–27.

Notes 193

6. CRIMINAL CASES

Textual references: The rape case that was overturned for a mixture of errors and misconduct is *People v. Rodriguez*, 119 Cal.App.3d 457 (1981). The statistics on the affirmance and reversal rates for criminal cases are based on the annual report of the California Judicial Council for 1985–86 and apply to felony cases that are appealed (almost all of them are). The 7 percent figure is for cases in which the conviction is totally reversed and does not include cases in which the conviction is modified or partly reversed.

The California harmless-error rule is described in *People v. Watson*, 46 Cal.2d 818, 836 (1956); the federal constitutional rule was set forth in *Chapman v. California*, 386 U.S. 18 (1967). *Carlos v. Superior Court*, 35 Cal.3d 131, 672 P.2d 862 (1983), was overruled by *People v. Anderson*, 43 Cal.3d 11014, 742 P.2d 1306 (1987). The quotations from United States Supreme Court opinions on the scope of jury discretion in capital cases are from *Eddings v. Oklahoma*, 455 U.S. 104, 113–115 (1982), and *Lockett v. Ohio*, 438 U.S. 586 (1978). One study that suggests the cost of administering the death penalty is greater than that of maintaining the defendant in prison for life is Margo Garey, "The Cost of Taking a Life: Dollars and Sense of the Death Penalty," 18 *University of California at Davis Law Review* 1221 (1985). Gerald F. Uelmen's work chronicling the impact of death penalty cases on the caseload of the California Supreme Court is *California Death Penalty Laws and the California Supreme Court: A Ten-Year Perspective* (Sacramento: California Legislature Senate Committee on Judiciary, 1986).

Bibliographical note: A thoughtful work on the criminal justice system is Charles Silberman, *Criminal Violence, Criminal Justice* (New York: Random House, 1978). The paradoxes of the harmless-error rule are aptly described in a small book by Justice Roger Traynor, *The Riddle of Harmless Error* (Columbus: Ohio State University Press, 1970). The current state of death penalty law and practice in the United States is described and critiqued in Franklin Zimring and Gordon Hawkins, *Capital Punishment and the American Agenda* (Cambridge and New York: Cambridge University Press, 1987).

7. COURTS AND THE INITIATIVE PROCESS

Textual references: The referenced study of the initiative process is David Magleby, *Direct Legislation: Voting on Ballot Propositions in the United States* (Baltimore: Johns Hopkins University Press, 1984). The redistricting case referred to is *Legislature of the State of California v. George Deukmejian*, 34 Cal.3d 658, 669 P.2d 17 (1983). The balanced-budget case is *American Federation of Labor v. Eu*, 36 Cal.3d 687, 686 P.2d 609 (1984). The older cases are cited and discussed in an article by Daniel Lowenstein, "California Initiatives and the Single-Subject Rule," 30 *University of California at Los Angeles Law Review* 936 (1983). The preelection and postelection Proposition 8 cases are *Brosnahan v. Eu*, 31 Cal.3d 1, 641 P.2d 200 (1982) and *Brosnahan v. Brown*, 32 Cal.3d 236 (1982).

Bibliographical note: David Butler and Austin Ranney, *Referendums: A Comparative Study of Practice and Theory* (Washington: American Enterprise Institution for Public Policy Research, 1978) presents an international perspective of approaches to direct democracy, including a study of the initiative and referendum in California by Professor Eugene C. Lee of the University of California at Berkeley (87–122). League of Women Voters of California published a study expressing dismay over what has happened to direct democracy and discussing possible reforms: *Initiative and Referendum in California: A Legacy Lost?* (Sacramento: The League, 1984).

8. STATE CONSTITUTIONS

Textual references: The quotation is from Rockwell D. Hunt, *The Genesis of California's First Constitution (1846–1849)* (New York: Johnson Reprint, 1973), 37. The New York constitution was adopted in 1777, eleven years before the federal constitutional convention. The Iowa constitution was adopted in 1846.

In *Amalgamated Food Employees Union Local 540 v. Logan Valley Plaza*, 391 U.S. 308 (1968), the United States Supreme Court held that state action was involved in a shopping center's prohibition of speech, but that decision was overruled in *Lloyd Corporation v. Tanner*, 407 U.S. 551 (1972). The holding of the California Supreme Court in *Robins v. Pruneyard Shopping Center*, 23 Cal.3d 899, 592 P.2d 341 (1979), that a shopping center's prohibition of speech violated the state constitution was upheld by the United States Supreme Court against the contention that the holding contravened the federal Constitution. *Pruneyard Shopping Center v. Robins*, 447 U.S. 100 (1980).

The Alaska marijuana case is *Ravin v. State*, 537 P.2d 494 (1975). The California right-to-privacy decisions are *Long Beach City Employees Association v. City of Long Beach*, 41 Cal.3d 937, 719 P.2d 660 (1986), on polygraph tests; *People v. Mayoff*, 42 Cal.3d 1302, 729 P.2d 166 (1986), on marijuana overflights; and *Committee to Defend Reproductive Rights v. Myers*, 29 Cal.3d 252, 625 P.2d 779 (1981), on abortion funding. The California case in which the state Supreme Court failed to consider the state constitution the first time around is *People v. Ramos*, 30 Cal.3d 553, 639 P.2d 908 (1982); but see *California v. Ramos*, 463 U.S. 992 (1983), reversing the judgment, finding no federal constitutional error, and remanding to consider state constitutional issues. On remand in *People v. Ramos*, 37 Cal.3d 136, 689 P.2d 430 (1984), the Supreme Court reaffirmed its original position on the basis of the state constitution. An example of waffling between the federal and state constitutions is *Allen v. Superior Court*, 18 Cal.3d 520, 557 P.2d 65 (1976). The United States Supreme Court put an end to that practice by ruling that it will assume a state court relied on the federal Constitution unless it clearly says otherwise in *Michigan v. Long*, 463 U.S. 1032 (1983).

A law school casebook on state constitutions is Robert Williams, *State Constitutional Law: Cases and Materials* (Washington, D.C.: Advisory Commission on Intergovernmental Relations, 1988). The National Association of State Attorneys General has established a clearinghouse project on state constitutional law.

Bibliographical note: For a general description of the California constitutional convention of 1849, see, in addition to Hunt, Hubert Bancroft, *History of California*, vol. 6 (San Francisco: A. L. Bancroft, 1884), 284–304; Neal Harlow, *California Conquered* (Berkeley and Los Angeles: University of California Press, 1982), 338–53; and Josiah Royce, *California: From the Conquest in 1846 to the Second Vigilance Committee in San Francisco* (New York: Knopf, 1948), 205–13. The debates of the convention were officially recorded in J. Ross Browne, *Report of the Debates in the Convention of California: On the Formation of the State Constitution, in September and October 1849* (Washington, D.C.: J. T. Towers, 1850).

On the development of independent state grounds for deciding constitutional issues, see Hans Linde, "First Things First: Rediscovering the States' Bill of Rights," 9 *University of Baltimore Law Review* 379 (1980); William Brennan, Jr., "State Constitutions and the Protection of Individual Rights," 90 *Harvard Law Review* 489 (1977); Peter Galie, "The Other Supreme Courts: Judicial Activism Among State Supreme Courts," 33 *Syracuse Law Review* 731 (1982); and "Developments in the Law: The Interpretation of State Constitutional Rights," 95 *Harvard Law Review* 1324 (1982). Several law reviews have published collections of articles on the subject. See "The Emergence of State Constitutional Law," a symposium, 63 *Texas Law Review* 959–1375 (1986), and "Symposium on State Constitutional Jurisprudence," 15 *Hastings Constitutional Law Quarterly* 391–478 (1988). For critical comment, see George Deukmejian and Clifford Thompson, "All Sail and No Anchor: Judicial Review Under the California Constitution," 6 *Hastings Constitutional Law Quarterly* 975 (1979), and Earl Maltz, "The Dark Side of State Law Activism," 63 *Texas Law Review* 995 (1985).

9. DO JUDGES MAKE LAW?

Textual references: The Meese quotation is from the *New York Times*, June 29, 1987, A14. The Cardozo quote is from Benjamin Cardozo, *The Nature of the Judicial Process* (New Haven: Yale University Press, 1921). Oliver W. Holmes's "Path of the Law" was published in 10 *Harvard Law Review* 457 (1897). Ronald Dworkin's metaphor of the ongoing novel is from Ronald Dworkin, *Law's Empire* (Cambridge, Mass.: Belknap Press, 1986), 228–32.

The work by Paul Brest discussing the ordinance about vehicles in the park is "The Misconceived Quest for the Original Understanding," 60 *Boston University Law Review* 204 (1980). The original work by H. L. A. Hart that posed the hypothetical ordinance was "Positivism and the Separation of Law and Morals," 71 *Harvard Law Review* 593, 606–15 (1958). The case in which I was persuaded that the majority opinion I had written was wrong was *Ontario Community Foundation, Inc. v. State Board of Equalization*, 35 Cal.3d 811, 678 P.2d 378 (1984). The opinion in which I talked about judges mistaking their own policies for public policy was *Hentzel v. Singer*, 138 Cal.App.3d 290 (1982). The views of Judge Bork with respect to original intent were set forth in an address he gave at University of San Diego Law School on November 18, 1985; the speech was discussed in the *New York Times*, July 2, 1987, A22. Professor Ely's position on constitutional interpretation is explicated in John Ely, *Democracy and Distrust: A Theory of Judicial Review* (Cambridge: Harvard University Press, 1980). The footnote by Justice Stone is from *United States v. Carolene Products*, 304 U.S. 144 (1938). Professor Tribe's views are contained in his comprehensive treatise, Lawrence Tribe, *American Constitutional Law*, 2d ed. (Mineola, N.Y.: Foundation Press, 1988). Professor Calvin Massey has written about the natural-law background of the Ninth Amendment in Calvin Massey, "Federalism and Fundamental Rights: The Ninth Amendment," 38 *Hastings Law Journal* 305 (1987).

Bibliographical note: Writings on legal theory are often complex and technical. Two notable exceptions are Edward Levi, *An Introduction to Legal Reasoning* (Chicago: University of Chicago, 1949), and Richard Wasserstrom, *The Judicial Decision: Toward a Theory of Legal Justification* (Stanford: Stanford University Press, 1961). An excellent synopsis of the history of American legal theory is Grant Gilmore, *The Ages of American Law* (New Haven: Yale University Press, 1977). Dean Roscoe Pound deserves mention as an important precursor of legal realism. See Roscoe Pound, "Mechanical Jurisprudence," 8 *Columbia Law Journal* 603 (1908).

The text does scant justification to Karl Llewelyn, the father of the Uniform Commercial Code and a principal spokesman for the Legal Realists. In 1930 he wrote a sort of manifesto of the movement, Karl Llewelyn, "A Realistic Jurisprudence," 30 *Columbia Law Review* 431 (1930). It is fascinating to compare it with a book he wrote thirty years later, in which he attempted to assure the legal community that there is greater stability in the law than some of the Legal Realists said there was, Karl Llewelyn, *The Common Law Tradition: Deciding Appeals* (Boston: Little, Brown, 1960). A recent history of the Legal Realist movement has been written by Laura Kalman, *Legal Realism at Yale 1927–1960* (Chapel Hill: University of North Carolina Press, 1986). Principal Legal Realist writings, in addition to those by Llewelyn, include Jerome Frank, *Law and the Modern Mind* (New York: Tudor, 1930); Felix Cohen, "Transcendental Nonsense and the Functional Approach," 35 *Columbia Law Review* 809 (1935); and Joseph Hutcheson, "The Judgment Intuitive: The Function of the 'Hunch' in Judicial Decisions," 14 *Cornell Law Quarterly* 274 (1929). For a provocative study of the role of policy in decision making, conducted in the Legal Realist tradition, see John Bell, *Policy Arguments in Judicial Decisions* (Oxford and New York: Oxford University Press, 1983). For a political scientist's empirical perspective, see Glendon Schubert, *Judicial Policy-Making: The Political Role of the Courts* (Chicago: Scott, Foresman, 1965).

Theorists of the Critical Legal Studies movement (the "Crits") are not easy reading. For a helpful attempt at an overview (not fully accepted by some of the Crits), see Mark Kelman, *A Guide to Critical Legal Studies* (Cambridge, Mass.: Harvard University Press, 1987). For perspective and a critique, see a symposium in 36 *Stanford Law Review* 1–673 (1984).

Ronald Dworkin is the most prolific contemporary legal theorist. His major works include *Taking Rights Seriously* (Cambridge, Mass.: Harvard University Press, 1977), *A Matter of Principle* (Cambridge, Mass.: Harvard University Press, 1985), and *Law's Empire* (Cambridge, Mass.: Belknap Press, 1986). For a critique of Dworkin's "one right answer" theory, see Kent Greenawalt, "Discretion and Judicial Decision," 75 *Columbia Law Review* 359 (1975).

A frequently cited piece on statutory interpretation is by Justice Felix Frankfurter, "Some Reflections on the Reading of Statutes," 47 *California Law Review* 527 (1930). Among the more interesting recent literature on statutory interpretation are Kenneth S. Abraham, "Statutory Interpretation and Literary Theory," 32 *Rutgers Law Review* 676 (1980); Michael Moore, "A Natural Law Theory of Interpretation," 58 *Southern California Law Review* 227 (1985); and William Blatt, "The History of Statutory Interpretation: A Study in Form and Substance," 6 *Cardozo Law Review* 799 (1985).

In addition to the works by Professors Ely, Tribe, and Brest referred to in the text, an important book in the area of constitutional theory is Jesse Choper, *Judicial Review and the National Political Process: A Functional Reconsideration of the Supreme Court* (Chicago: University of Chicago Press, 1980).

On the aesthetic component of justice and decision making, see Louis B. Schwarz, "Justice, Expediency and Beauty," 136 *University of Pennsylvania Law Review* 141 (1987); Joseph R. Grodin, "Justice Tobriner: Portrait of the Judge as an Artist," 29 *Hastings Law Journal* 17 (1977).

10. ELECTIONS

Bibliographical note: Susan Carbon and Larry Berkson, *Judicial Retention Elections in the United States* (Chicago: American Judicature Society, 1980), contains a good, brief summary of the history of retention elections and empirical findings on the reasons judges have been opposed in such elections as well as the role of the bar, the public, and the press.

A number of political scientists have studied judicial elections, usually with an eye to the dynamics of the election process and its results. The leading work is Philip Dubois, *From Ballot to Bench* (Austin: University of Texas Press, 1980), in which the author argues on the basis of empirical research that elections are superior to a merit system. His most recent article on the subject, "Accountability, Independence, and the Selection of State Judges: The Role of Popular Judicial Elections," 40 *Southwestern Law Journal* 31 special ed. (1986), cites recent work in the field. Professor Dubois is an advocate not only of elections but of *partisan* elections in which each candidate is identified with a political party. I do not share his enthusiasm. See also William Hall and Larry Aspin, "What Twenty Years of Judicial Retention Elections Have Told Us," 70 *Judicature* 340 (April-May 1987).

Prior to the 1986 election in California, legal scholars advanced differing views on the criteria that should be used by voters. See Robert Thompson, "Judicial Independence, Judicial Accountability, Judicial Elections, and the

California Supreme Court: Defining the Terms of the Debate," 59 *Southern California Law Review* 809 (1986), on the burden on opponents to demonstrate lack of "decisionmaker impartiality" or misuse of administrative authority; Scott Bice, "Four Tests to Judge the Justices," *University of Southern California, Law* 1 (Fall-Winter 1986), setting forth, but not advocating, four models that voters might apply; Larry Simon, "Democracy, Constitutional Law and the Supreme Court's Death Penalty Decisions," *University of Southern California, Law* 28 (Fall-Winter 1986), arguing for a presumption in favor of retention, rebutted if a judge "invents" rather than "interprets" the law; and Erwin Chemerinsky, "Assuring Judicial Independence," *University of California, Law* 44 (Fall-Winter 1986), advocating an impeachment model in which the test is whether the judge acted outside the proper role of a judge. Since the election *Southern California Law Review* has published a symposium on the relationship of adjudicatory theory to election criteria, 61 *Southern California Law Review* 1555–2249 (1988). I have contributed an article to that symposium, expressing essentially the same views I express here; see Joseph Grodin, "Developing a Consensus of Constraint: A Judge's Perspective on Judicial Retention Elections," 61 *Southern California Law Review* 601 (1988).

Reviews (and some Monday-morning quarterbacking) of the California 1986 judicial election appear in the April-May issue of 70 *Judicature:* John Wold and John Cutter, "The Defeat of the California Justices: The Campaign, the Electorate, and the Issue of Judicial Accountability," 348; Joseph Grodin, "Judicial Elections: The California Experience," 365; "After California, What's Next for Judicial Elections," transcript of a panel discussion at the midyear meeting of the American Judicature Society, 356. Dean Gerald F. Uelmen of University of Santa Clara Law School has also published a piece on the election from a historical perspective; see Gerald Uelmen, "Supreme Court Retention Elections in California," 28 *Santa Clara Law Review* 333 (1988).

A thoughtful article on the problems posed by judicial fund-raising and possible solutions is Roy Schotland, "Elective Judges' Campaign Financing: Are State Judges' Robes the Emperor's Clothes of American Democracy?" 2 *The Journal of Law and Politics* 57 (1985). The author's suggestions, aimed primarily at elections for trial court judges, include voluntary spending and contribution limitations—a remedy unsuitable for retention elections; see also Sheila Kaplan, "Justice for Sale," *Common Cause Magazine* 29 (May-June 1987).

Table of Cases
Cited in the Text

Index

Racanelli, John, 17, 24, 48
Radin, Max, 12, 13
Rape, definition of crime of, 93
Ravin v. State, 194
Reagan, Ronald, 33, 54, 56, 159, 163, 169
Reapportionment cases, xiii
"Reasonably germane" test, 108, 109–10
Redistricting initiative, 106, 107
Referenda, xix, 102–4, 105, 112, 115
Rehnquist, William, 49, 125, 160, 180
Religion, California constitution and, 120
Republican party, California, 166, 168
Restatement of Torts, 80–81
Retention elections, 4, 53, 165–86, 198
Reversals: in appellate courts, 88–96, 193; *per se*, 93–96
Reynoso, Cruz, 46, 48–49, 56, 58; in elections, xvii, 168, 169, 170–71, 174, 176, 178, 179
Rhode Island, judge selection in, 3
Richardson, Frank, 54–55, 106, 152, 167, 168
Riggs v. Palmer, 147–48
Riley, Bennett, 119
Roberts, Bill, 169
Robins v. Pruneyard Shopping Center, 194
Roth, Lester, 48
Rouse, Allison, 33, 38, 44–45
Ruby, Jack, 92–93

Sacramento appellate district, 16
"Safe schools" provision, of Proposition 8, 109
Saint Louis, rate of filings in Missouri Circuit Court of, 34
San Bernardino appellate district, 16
San Diego appellate district, 16
San Francisco appellate district, 16
San Francisco Labor Council, 166
San Jose appellate district, 16
Santa Rosa Junior College v. Workers Compensation Appeal Board, 191–92
Schletewitz, Bryon, 95–96
Schotland, Roy, 184–85
Scorecard approach, in election, 175–76
See's Candies, 27–28, 30, 84–85
Segregated schools, 128, 156
Senate, U.S., 163
Senate Judiciary Committee, xviii, 158–59, 162, 163
Separation of church and state, 156
Settlement conferences, in Court of Appeal, 36–37

Shannon, William, 119
Shopping centers, free speech in, 125–26, 194
Simek v. Superior Court, 41
Sims, Richard, 64
Single-subject rule, of California constitution, 107–8, 109, 110, 116
Sixth Amendment, 127
Skinner, Jesse, 111–12
Skinner case, 110–13, 116
Slavery, California constitution and, 121
Small-claims department, 15
Smith, Jerry, 33
Social justice, and common law, 139
South Carolina, judge selection in, 3
Southern Pacific Railroad Company, 103
"Special circumstances," warranting death penalty, 94–96, 98
Specialized knowledge, generalist tradition and, 21–24
Speech, freedom of, 125, 159, 194
Spiegel, Hart, 49–50
Spiritual Psychic Science Church v. City of Azusa, 67
Stanford Law School, 8
Stare decisis, 82
State Board of Equalization, 152
State constitutions, xii, xiii–xiv, xix, 118–30, 155, 182; Alaska, 126; Arizona, 126; Florida, 126; Iowa, 120, 121, 194; judge selection in, 3, 164; Louisiana, 126; Montana, 126; New York, 120, 121, 194; Washington, 126. *See also* California constitution
State courts, xi–xii, xiv–xv, xviii–xix, 3, 15, 182–83. *See also* Appellate courts; Trial courts
State powers, xii, xiii–xiv, 123–30
Status concepts, 76
Statutes, 83, 145–55, 157; purpose of, 148, 149
Sterilization law, 65–67
Stevens, Fatima, 67
Stevens, John Paul, 49
Stone, Harlan, 157
Strang v. Cabrol, 192
Substantial evidence, 20
Sullivan, Raymond, 16
Superior court, 15
Supreme Courts: Alaska, 126; New Jersey, 66, 79–80, 191; Oklahoma, 69; Oregon, 181; Texas, 69, 175, 181–82; Washington, 66. *See also* California Supreme Court; United States Supreme Court
Sutter, John, 119

DP: 69, 99, 100

Compositor: G&S Typesetters, Inc
Text: 10/13 Palatino
Display: Palatino
Printer: Bookcrafters
Binder: Bookcrafters